Against the Tides

Against the Tides

A Memoir

MARGARET MEANEY HENDRICK

ISBN: 1537648306
ISBN 13: 9781537648309
Library of Congress Control Number: 2016915280
CreateSpace Independent Publishing Platform
North Charleston, South Carolina

To
Jed

Preface

I wrote this memoir after hearing for many years that some thought my life was a story worth telling. I will let the reader decide whether that is true. What has interested many about my life is that it includes the experience of being adopted as a child.

There are so many preconceived notions about what being adopted means. Being adopted doesn't mean a life is immediately terrible or terrific. What an adoptee gains is often countered by what is lost.

Adoptive lives are lived like all others, but are different. Many want to assert that isn't true, but I have concluded after many years that a common thread does run between all our adopted lives, which binds adoptees together in spirit.

My memoir is a true story, helped by a long memory, which simply needed to be put on paper. It is about mothers and daughters, fathers, needs, desires, pain, disappointments, exhilaration, love, friends and family.

I have changed the names of some people in this book, but I often use the known name of those who are deceased.

I hope the reader will come away with a new sense of what it is like to be adopted, not the fantasy, but a real life with all its complexities, controlled by other people's decisions.

To all those who turn to the next page,

All my Best.

In all of us there is a hunger, marrow deep, to know our heritage—to know who we are and where we came from. Without this enriching knowledge, there is a hollow yearning. No matter what our attainments in life, there is still a vacuum, an emptiness, and the most disquieting loneliness.

—Alex Haley

Contents

Chapter 1

The Dress

The unexamined life is not worth living

—Socrates

But how do you examine a life with so many parts unknown?

Leaves and paper blew about my ankles as the Red Line train thundered into the tunnel, screeching to a halt at my feet. The doors sprang open. Riders poured onto the Washington Street platform, while patient passengers rushed to fill the vacant seats. I followed subway protocol and led with my shoulder through the blockade of standing-room only. The conductor called for everyone to step back, but not a foot moved. I grabbed for a strap and stumbled backward, as the train lurched forward.

It was early afternoon and I was on my way home. That morning, I had gone into Boston to look at prom dresses. Even though the trip was a yearly event, I had never actually bought one. If I found a dress I liked, I'd go over to Jordan Marsh and buy a pattern and fabric to make one just like it. But this morning, I found the perfect dress. I loved it. It was a *Lanz* dress, and I knew I couldn't make it myself.

As the subway rumbled along toward home, I became nervous thinking how I could convince my mother to let me buy a dress. Mum had always encouraged me to make my dance dresses. But my sewing projects didn't always work out. I'd be in my parent's bedroom stitching on the old sewing machine, yelling and stomping my feet, when I couldn't fit a sleeve into a bodice or stitch a smooth seam. Mum would look at me as if I had lost my mind. And I usually had.

Making dresses was one of the routines at the heart of my family. What was repeated every day, every year was expected. The past was prologue. And in some way I found that comforting. Staying close to home, right here in the Boston area, was what my parents did—the same house, the same friends, the same jobs, while holding onto the same ideas. And with all that sameness, they were completely satisfied. Even when my parents began their family, they only moved one town away.

At Ashmont Station I stepped off the subway platform and skipped over to the family car. I opened the Chevy door and threw my pocketbook across the front seat. Then I slid in and turned on the ignition. Visions of the dotted Swiss, *Lanz* dress with its subtle hue of blue, filled my mind as I pulled onto the Southeast Expressway. I took Braintree's Washington Street exit. At the top of Edgemont Road, I turned into our narrow driveway next to the gray bungalow. I hurried up the back stairs. Mum wasn't in the kitchen, but I heard her voice coming from the living room. I squeezed between the dining room table and the china hutch before I saw her sitting at the end of the sofa. I rushed into the room filled with excitement.

"Mum, I found the perfect dress… it's just what I've always wanted. Can I please buy it? Oh, please, can I?"

My mother straightened up, looking a bit startled and said, "You did? I thought you went to Boston to look for fabric. Aren't you making your dress?"

"Well, I thought I was going to, but I went to Filene's and found the perfect dress. Oh, Mum, I really love it. It's a *Lanz* dress. I've always wanted a *Lanz* dress, and it isn't even that expensive."

"Well, why don't you make it?" she said.

My heart sank. She didn't get it. But I wasn't going to let her discourage me…not this time.

"Mum, I can't make it. It has too many details. I'd never be able to find the special trim or ribbon."

While I tried to contain my disappointment, I wasn't sure she was even listening. Mum was not an intense person, and she didn't like when I was. She hated my loud, passionate pleadings, particularly when my voice rose to what she called my "high G." In many of our disagreements, I tried talking over her, hoping to hold off that moment when my idea would be squashed. I didn't understand her though. I thought, as a student of English literature, she would appreciate my Jane Eyre style of confident confrontation, but actually Jane's stepmother chastised her for that.

In the middle of my last plea, Mum stood up and strolled over to the living room windows. I took that as my cue to leave. I had probably pushed her too far. I didn't mean to. I just really wanted that dress. Unexpectedly, she turned back.

"You are just like your mother!" she said in an intense voice.

Mother? What mother? My mother was standing right in front of me. Oh, oh… she must be talking about the woman who gave birth to me. But why was she bringing her up now? I thought we were discussing dresses. And why was she calling her "your mother"? I never thought of that woman as my mother.

My mind raced to reorient from the dress discussion to my adoption by the Meaney family. But that topic had run its course years ago. All I knew was I came from an "agency" because "your mother couldn't take care of you." The discussion wasn't off limits, but it was like the sex talk—you had to wait until your parents exhaled before everyone relaxed again.

My mother and I had never spoken specifically about the woman who gave birth to me until last fall when a college application required an autobiography. I used the essay as an excuse to bring up the topic. I really didn't expect to hear anything new. But then I did.

"Your parents weren't married," my mother said.

Really? I should have guessed that, but it had never occurred to me. Hearing something new was exciting. Then it hit me…if my parents weren't married, I must have been born a bastard. I had never thought of "bastard" outside of its pejorative meaning, but now being a bastard appeared to be an integral part of my identity. Some might not think it was a great part, but to me it was singularly better than having no identity at all.

So my college autobiographical essay began, "I was born a bastard." It was direct and descriptive, just like my English teachers had taught me, but apparently it didn't go over so well, because I wasn't accepted to that college.

I looked over at my mother. She was standing her ground in the middle of the living room, as if defending her declaration about the woman I didn't think she knew anything about. I suddenly feared she might have regretted raising the topic. My muscles tightened. I didn't want to lose this chance. Her revelation was like a little bird in my hand. If I squeezed it, I might kill it, but if I loosened my grip, it might fly away.

"Really?" I finally said, with enough intensity to let her know I was curious, but softly so she wouldn't think I was too interested. The words came out of me in an unusually measured, calm voice.

"Tell me about her."

There, now she knew. I couldn't hide it any longer. Until that moment, I had no idea how much I wanted to know about that woman. My reaction surprised both of us. I feared Mum was going to pull back and go silent.

"We were told your mother refused to go to school because she didn't have nice enough clothes to wear."

Oh…I drank in that information like T. E. Lawrence did the well water after crossing the Nefud Desert. But what was her point? I never refused to go to school. I waited another moment, hoping the topic wouldn't close up like a handled clam.

"What did she want to wear?" I asked.

"I don't know. I just assumed she was being unreasonable."

I tried to ignore Mum's less-than-sympathetic tone and asked, "What else do you know?"

"That's all. I think she was in high school at the time." Mum shared this as if she were telling me the lady next door had planted petunias instead of pansies.

Still bursting with curiosity, I asked, "Can you think of anything else?"

My mother paused, as if giving herself time to consider whether she wanted to answer another question. Then I heard, "Your mother"—long pause—"was from Boston." Another moment went by. "Your father was an engineering student at a college in Boston. But he wasn't from here."

My mind felt lighter than air. I had always wanted to know more about myself, but I didn't think anyone knew anything.

My mother settled back down on the sofa, as if spent from my questions. That was usually my cue to move along. This time I didn't care if I had been dismissed, as I walked toward my bedroom. This time I *needed* to go. Hiding my excitement in front of her would have been difficult. Her comment that the woman who gave birth to me liked nice clothes, was stubborn, and stood up for things she considered important, reverberated through every fiber of my being. Everything my mother had said about my birth mother resonated with me.

I closed the door to my bedroom and reveled in the news my mother had just shared. Even from the little she told me, I understood my birth mother was nothing like my adoptive parents. That wasn't necessarily bad, but it might explain why I seldom did things the way they did. I seldom did things their way.

I laid back on my bed and reached for my teddy bear. This new information was giving me permission to be different, something more than Midge and Dave Meaney's adopted daughter. I was no longer just the refrain to my parents' song. Like other daughters, I now had a reference point to gain a better understanding of myself. I realized for the first time I was more complicated than I had been led to believe—maybe for better, maybe for worse. Either way, the beginnings of a new identity seemed to be developing deep inside.

Chapter 2

BLANK SLATE

The next morning, I rushed out the door and ran through the back yard. I stepped gingerly over the beaten-down fence before I cut through to the next street. From the top of the hill, I could see the kids waiting at the bus stop below. I slipped on the leftover winter sand and salt as I made my way down the steep slope of Cedarcliff Road. At the bottom I scooted onto the bus and fell back into my seat as we pulled away from the curb.

Gathering books and instrument in my lap, I watched the neighborhood houses blur in the bus window. I couldn't stop thinking about the adoption discussion the day before. I didn't understand why Mum had kept to herself what she knew about my birth mother. Was she was afraid I might want to meet the woman? She didn't have to worry about that. I had no interest in meeting her. I was just excited to hear about my life before I was adopted. And anyway, my mother told me years ago my records were sealed, and I'd never have a chance of finding that woman. Maybe Mum held back the information because she didn't want me to obsess over it… just as I was doing now.

But Mum knew I loved hearing stories about my early years, so why didn't she share that one? She told me once about seeing my godfather,

John Hofferty, at the supermarket. Mum was pushing me in the grocery cart, when he stopped to chat. He put his head close to mine and asked, "And what is your name?"

My mother said I didn't answer him.

"Is it Margaret?" he asked.

"No," I answered.

"Well, is it Mary?"

"No," I responded.

My mother said he tried a few more names, but I was not answering to any of them.

Then he said, "Is it John?" whereupon I surprised them both by saying, "Yes."

"Is it John Adams?" he asked, trying to be funny, as we were only a mile away from the former president's birthplace.

"Yes," I said emphatically, surprising both of them.

And from then on, according to my perplexed mother, anyone who asked my name received the answer: John Adams.

I liked stories. I liked the story about my parents adopting my brother, Robbie. My parents visited him and his nice foster mother before they finally took him home to their apartment. A year after Robbie's adoption, they were ready for their girl. The agency offered them an infant girl, but they couldn't take her. My mother said they were too busy caring for her dying mother. But a couple of months later my parents received another call. This time the agency offered them a different girl… it was me.

On my "delivery day," my mother's sister Dot came over to their apartment and took care of Robbie, while my new parents drove into Boston to pick me up at the adoption agency. But before the social worker could even put me in their arms, I was screaming. My mother said I never stopped crying until I cried myself out long after they got home.

My new parents were Midge and Dave Meaney from Quincy, Massachusetts. They had met when they were both teaching school. Midge began teaching right out of college. Dave's first job after college was digging ditches for the City of Quincy. Eventually, he began substitute teaching and found himself in Midge's school. It was love at first sight.

Just before World War II, they became husband and wife in the rectory of Dave's Catholic Church. They couldn't get married in the big cathedral-style church because Midge was not Catholic and she wasn't interested in converting. They had a nice reception in Midge's parents' backyard with family and friends. The newlyweds wanted to enjoy their new married life together so they held off starting a family.

A year later Pearl Harbor was bombed, and Dave tried to enlist. Neither the Army nor the Navy would take him due to his poor eyesight. He told me Mr. Magoo and he had a lot in common, because without glasses, neither could see beyond the hand in front of his face. But even with bad eyes, Dave wanted to join the war effort and was delighted when the Navy finally enlisted him. He became a pharmacist's mate on a ship in the Pacific, and Midge with her artistic background, became a draftsman at Fore River Shipyard.

At the end of the war, Dave came home, as did Midge's sister, Dot, who had been a battleground nurse in the African Campaign. When she arrived in Rome during its liberation, her doctor told her she had a serious heart condition and having babies might kill her. So about the time Dot found out she shouldn't have children, Midge and Dave found out they couldn't.

Using Dot's connections in the Boston medical community, Midge and Dave visited a fertility doctor. Tests revealed that no matter how hard they tried to get pregnant, they were never going to conceive a child of their own. The doctor thought the problem came from a severe sunstroke that Dave had suffered after playing two hatless rounds of golf in the hot sun.

The doctor recommended that my parents contact an adoption agency. Adoption was becoming more common, he told them, although none of my parents' childless friends had adopted anyone. Many people thought it was strange to raise "someone else's child." But Dave understood that adoption was the only way he would ever have a family, and Midge always wanted to make Dave happy.

The fertility doctor allayed any fears Midge and Dave had about adopting.

"I have never known an adopted child who had difficulties in life or turned out badly. They are blank slates," he said. "Whatever you impart to them, they will grow that way. You should have no worries."

After my arrival in the Meaney household, one of the first things my new parents did was change my name. They first considered names on my father's Irish side of the family. He liked Kathleen, but if he sang his favorite song, "I'll Take You Home Again, Kathleen," it could have been awkward. So they settled on Margaret, the name of my mother's best friend. My middle name was the same as my mother's, so our initials would be the same. For a brief time, my mother insisted on everyone calling me Margaret Helen, but like most names, mine morphed into a nickname, Margy, pronounced with the silent Boston *R*, and a hard *G*—"Maahgee."

My actual adoption day took place six months later. I was just over a year old when my parents took me to the Norfolk County Courthouse. The social worker met us in the hallway, and we followed her into the courtroom. We all settled on a crowded wooden bench.

When the judge walked in, dressed in his black robes, everyone stood up and then they sat down. All that time I was in my mother's arms trying to squirm out.

The business of the court began, and the judge became preoccupied with lawyers conferring at his bench. The social worker thought it best to spend as little time as possible in a crowded courtroom, so she turned to my mother and said, "Pinch her."

My mother was surprised and looked back quizzically at the social worker.

The social worker repeated her directions. "Pinch her. We need to get the judge's attention."

My mother quickly reached down to my bare leg, took a bit of flesh between her thumb and forefinger, and squeezed. At first, I didn't react.

But the social worker was determined to get the judge's attention and said, "Pinch her again," so my mother gave me a second, more intense pinch, which provoked from me a loud screech.

The judge turned to see who was disturbing his courtroom. He saw a small, blond, hazel-eyed, one year-old girl, all dressed up, turning red with pain and anger. He immediately halted the business in which he was engaged, consulted with his clerk, and then attended to my case. Whatever needed to be done was done. When we walked out of the courtroom, I was no longer whoever I had been. I was now Margaret Helen Meaney.

My birth certificate was rewritten with my new name and my adoptive parents were listed as my parents, looking as if they had given birth to me in a town they had never visited. With that courtroom procedure, I had a new family. I had two cousins, two aunts, and an uncle. I received no new grandparents because they were all dead. My biological family no longer existed, as far as the court was concerned. Anyone who had ever known me or known about me before the adoption would never be allowed to know anything about me again. And I was never to know anything about them. Whether I liked it or not, I had entered into a little person's form of witness protection.

Chapter 3

TALK RADIO

*T*he very last days of my senior year of high school had arrived. I stepped down off the school bus and trudged back up the steep hill. I caught my breath in the driveway just before I ran in the back door. Thoughts of my birth mother had been pushed far to the back of my mind. The prom and graduation were now prominently at the front.

As I entered the back hall, I heard my mother straight ahead in her bedroom. She was working on the old sewing machine and finishing up the formal coat we were making to go with the *Lanz* dress she let me buy. I had never heard of formal coats, but my friend Kathy was making one, and hers looked lovely. Kathy and her mother were always ahead in fashion.

"How's the coat coming?" I asked.

"Good. We can hem it tonight. How was school today?"

"Fine. They're collecting our books, so there isn't much to do."

"Guess what they're talking about on Paul Benzaquin's show today?"

"I don't know, what?"

"Adoption. The topic is adoption," Mum said.

I was surprised, but not because there was anything wrong with adoption. People just didn't talk about it.

"What were they saying?" I asked.

"A woman called the show. She had adopted a little girl. She told Mr. Benzaquin that she wasn't going to tell her daughter she's adopted. What do you think about that? Don't you think she should tell her?"

"Well, yes, of course, she should tell her," I said without hesitation.

I felt strongly about the issue, although I hadn't put much thought into it. I pretty much repeated what my parents said, whether it was about adoption or anything else. Robbie and I had been told we were adopted when we were too young to even remember.

"Weren't you always glad you knew you were adopted?" Mum asked.

"Yeah," I said. I probably said a lot more, because keeping quiet was not a strong personal trait of mine.

"Why don't you call the show and tell them how you feel about it?" she encouraged. "They should be happy to hear from someone who's been adopted."

"Really?" I was surprised to hear my mother say that, because she usually argued against my opinions.

I picked up the phone and nervously dialed the number. A woman's voice came on the line. She asked my opinion on the topic and then put me on hold. In another moment the talk show host himself greeted me.

"Hello, Margaret. How are you today?"

"I'm fine, thank you," I said, trying to control the shaking in my voice.

"I understand you want to say something about adoption? Are you adopted?"

"Yes, yes, I am," I answered with a little more confidence. But talking to an audience on the radio was much more difficult than I imagined. The man sounded nice, but I was afraid I might say something to upset him or someone who was listening.

"Can you tell us what you think about adoption?" he asked.

"My mother told me a woman called you earlier, and she had adopted a little girl, but the mother wasn't planning to tell her daughter she's adopted. I think she should tell her. I always knew I was adopted."

"That's very interesting," Mr. Benzaquin said. "So you think she should tell her daughter because you were told and everything worked out for you?"

"Yes," I said.

"Margaret, this mother was afraid that her daughter might someday hold it against her if she knew she was adopted. When the daughter is a teenager, she might get angry and say, 'You're not my real mother.'"

I was surprised to hear him say that. I had only heard biological kids say things like that. I had never heard adopted kids say those things.

"Has knowing you were adopted ever made you want to tell your mother she isn't your real mother?"

"No," I answered. I couldn't imagine saying something that sounded so cruel. And although I never would have admitted it, it was too close to some kind of truth.

Mr. Benzaquin and I chatted on a bit. I told him that my adoptive parents were my "real" parents, and he became even more pleasant. Some people liked to hear me say that. But I believed it, too. My adoptive parents were the only parents I knew, and I didn't want my life complicated by any competing parents.

When I affirmed my adoptive parents were my real parents, people like Paul Benzaquin seemed to relax. Perhaps he was worried I was one of those unhappy adoptees people talked about. But he didn't have to worry about me. Whenever I reassured people that my adoptive parents were my real parents, I could sense a significant, societal sigh of relief.

Mr. Benzaquin told me how grateful he was that I had called his show and it had been a pleasure talking to me. "You sound like such a nice girl. What grade are you in?"

"I'm a senior."

"Oh, so you must be graduating soon?"

"Yes, in a couple of weeks."

"What are you doing after graduation?"

"I'm going to the University of Maine."

"Oh, so you're going to college?"

"Yes," I said, ignoring his surprised tone.

"Is there a senior prom?" he inquired.

"Yes, next weekend."

"Well, if you don't have a date, I'll be happy to take you."

"Oh, no, thank you. I'm going with my boyfriend," I said.

"Well, I just wanted to make sure you were going to your prom. You sound like such a nice girl. I'd hate to think you weren't going."

"Thank you," I said. It was a kind offer, but I didn't understand why he thought I needed a date.

We exchanged goodbyes. I was glad it was over. I hoped I hadn't upset anyone. My mother came around the corner from the kitchen. She had been listening on her radio. I could see moisture in her eyes, but she looked happy. She seemed to have needed to hear that I considered her my real mother. Her reaction reaffirmed what I already understood. If I ever told her she was not my real mother, it would devastate her. I protected her, and in the process, I protected me.

Chapter 4

CAPE COD

*P*rom night arrived and my *Lanz* dress fit perfectly. It was more tailored than most of the other gowns, but I loved it. Our dinner-dance was held at a hall named The King Philip, after a Native American who went to war against a good part of Massachusetts in 1675. All must have been forgiven because even our Braintree High School's mascot was named after his tribe.

Graduation was held a couple of weeks later on our school's football field, on a lovely June Sunday afternoon under the hot sun. After the last diploma was handed out for the class of 1967, we threw our mortarboards in the air, commemorating the beginning of our new lives.

The next morning my mother helped me pack a family car with everything I needed to begin my summer waitressing job on Cape Cod. Going to the Cape without my parents felt strange, but I knew they'd be coming along soon. My father had two more weeks of teaching English and Latin before his summer break. Mum and I filled up the car with the extra family linens, towels, and other necessaries. As I backed out the driveway, I rolled down the window and waved goodbye.

My family had been going to Cape Cod every summer since my parents fell in love with the sandy beaches and salty air on their honeymoon. Even before purchasing a house of their own, they bought a small cottage on Longell Road in Dennisport. Today's trip to Cape Cod was one of many I'd made over the years. The first time I went to Cape Cod, I was the newly adopted addition to the Meaney family. In those early years, before highways had been built, we ambled along for hours on two-lane roads, past cranberry bogs and through old colonial villages, before we arrived at the cottage.

To break up the trip, we always stopped at Howard Johnson's in Kingston for hot dogs and mocha frappes. As we approached the Cape Cod Canal in Bourne, my father would point out how the Sagamore Bridge appeared and disappeared as we followed the warp of the road. When the bridge crept into our sight, Dad would sing, "Up, up, up," in a rising crescendo. Then as the road descended and we watched the bridge disappear, he'd say, "Down, down, down," his voice matching the direction of the bridge. We all laughed and sang along with him. Then after we drove over the bridge, Cape Cod welcomed us with the sweet smell of pine trees mixed with the salty ocean air.

My earliest memory of Cape Cod was arriving in Dennisport after dark and pulling up in front of the Longell Road cottage. It was exciting and mysterious. When the car stopped, Robbie and I opened the car door and jumped down from the running board. Pine needles crunched under the rubber soles of our sneakers. A cool breeze blew up from the ocean, mixed with a bit of damp fog. The chill made us run up on our father's heels as he fumbled with the key at the front door. Robbie and I followed him into the living room, which became warmly lit by the lamp Dad found in the pitch-dark. The aged yellow-pine walls reflected a soft candlelight effect. Their sweet woody smell made you want to breathe it all in like you did the leather of your new Buster Browns.

The next day after breakfast, Robbie and I hurried to get our bathing suits on. My mother would line us up to apply sun lotion. Daddy always covered his bald head with an old Navy cap, because all he had left was a monk's ring of black hair around the sides and back. But every morning, he meticulously brushed and parted the remaining hairs on his head, even if it were only one stray.

Then we'd gather up our blankets, towels, pails and shovels, and walk down the short, sandy road to the ocean. The waves of Nantucket Sound were usually small, and that day they broke gently on the shore. As soon as I stepped onto the clouds of white sand, I let go of my father's hand and ran to the water's edge. Before anyone could catch me, I had fallen face-first in the wet sand left behind by a retreating wave. My father gathered me up, set me straight, and later took me into the ocean for bouncing and dipping in the waves.

Our family stayed all day at the beach, soaking up the sun and salt. When the cool afternoon fog rolled in, my mother wrapped us up in warm, fuzzy sweatshirts. Then we'd gather everything we brought down, along with our newly collected seashells, and stroll back to the cottage. That night, clean from a tin tub bath and dressed in our cozy pajamas, Robbie and I would listen to our father read a Dr. Seuss book in front of the crackling fireplace. My brother and I received the complete attention of our parents on these early Cape Cod visits. The cottage, the beach, those pine trees, the soft sand—it all came together and created an adoptive womb for me. Cape Cod was where I fell in love with my new family.

We enjoyed that cottage on Longell Road for a few more years, but when I was three my parents sold it so they could buy their first real home. They bought a six-room bungalow in East Braintree, off Quincy Avenue where we still lived. My brother had the larger bedroom next to the bathroom where I wanted to be. My bedroom was off the dining room where I had to walk past scary shadows to get to the bathroom at night.

My mother said Robbie should have the better bedroom because he was older and a boy. That was the same reason she used when Dot bought us our dog Teddy. It was Robbie's dog because, "Every boy should have a dog." My mother's family was from England, and in England, she told me, boys and older children had more privileges. Boys could be made kings, but only when there were no boys could a girl become a queen. That was why we had Queen Elizabeth. She liked Queen Elizabeth, but she had liked King George better.

Every workday my father dressed in a Harris Tweed sports jacket and bow tie and went off to teach at North Quincy High School. My brother would grab his lunch box and join the other neighborhood kids and go off to kindergarten. My mother washed the breakfast dishes and made the beds before she got dressed for the day. Mum didn't wear flowered housedresses with aprons like the other mothers on the street. Her outfits—mostly of gray wool with slacks or skirts—were an academic style, as if she were going to a college alumni meeting. Her short, straight, dark-red hair was never in curlers but was brushed up off her face while leaving two flat curls settling on each cheek.

When we first moved into the Braintree house, Mum told me she really didn't know what to do with me. So she tied me to the clothesline with a halter around my chest like British people used in the Christopher Robin books. Either I didn't care for it or the neighbors didn't, so my mother stopped using it.

One of my favorite things to do was wait for delivery people. Our milkman, Mr. Harvey, came a couple of times a week. He pulled his White Brothers milk truck right up to the back steps. But he always forgot my name—he called me Peggy. No matter how many times I told him my name was Margaret, he still called me Peggy. He made me quite angry.

"My name is Margaret!" I yelled at him more than once, stomping my foot on the ground for emphasis.

I had never heard of the name Peggy, and I didn't want to be called a name that wasn't mine. Other than that, Mr. Harvey was nice.

After selling the cottage on Longell Road, my parents did not lose their love of Cape Cod. Each summer they rented another place in Dennisport for at least a week. Nothing could keep my father from the ocean he loved, and my brother and I were infected by his enthusiasm. As soon as we arrived for our vacation, Dad would buy a *Cape Cod Guide* to see when the tide was high. Then he'd study the weather to find out if the foggy skies would burn off in the morning or if clouds would be coming in later that afternoon. Even on a sunless, rainy day or when the surf was high from an offshore storm, Dad would be planning his next swim.

At the end of our second summer renting a cottage, my parents bought a small piece of land in an out-of-the-way neighborhood called Mild Bay. During that winter, a cottage was built on the land. Although it wasn't complete by the next summer, we moved in anyway. I had just finished first grade, and everything in Mild Bay seemed exciting. Robbie and I played with leftover building materials, explored the woods, and he took me fishing a couple times. And we usually went to the beach.

Only once during that first summer did we go back to Braintree. It was for a day of school shopping at the Quincy Bargain Center's annual August sale. The next morning Robbie and I sat in the living room of the Braintree house watching cartoons for the first time all summer, as we tried not to think of the shots we were going to get from Dr. Fitzgerald later that day.

When I heard sounds coming from the kitchen, I turned and saw Dad coming out of the kitchen door, hunched over, and struggling to walk. As he moved through the dining room, he grabbed the back of a chair to steady himself. Our mother quickly appeared, helped Dad to the bathroom, and then sent us up to a neighbor's house, just before an ambulance arrived at ours.

Dad had a heart attack, a coronary thrombosis. He was only forty-four years old. Robbie and I were allowed to visit him once, but most of the time, the neighborhood mothers watched us. Sometimes Robbie and I sat in the parking lot behind the South Shore Hospital and waited for Mum to finish her visit. When she came out, she always told us Dad was waving from his window, but as hard as I looked, I never saw a hand moving.

We were already back in school by the time Dad was ready to come home from the hospital. Mum told Robbie and me we could never fight again. The doctor had said Dad needed peace and quiet at all times to recover and our fights might upset him. With these orders, I was given the job of not killing my father.

The heart attack transformed Dad from a vibrant, enthusiastic person to a cautious, fearful, much older-acting father. From that time on, our family's sole focus was keeping him alive. His diet was restricted to foods he didn't like. He needed a nap every afternoon. Mum encouraged Robbie and me to spend more time out in the neighborhood or at friends' houses to keep our home quiet.

The next summer our family went back to Mild Bay. The doctor was happy my father had a place to relax. But we couldn't stay long at the beach anymore. The hot sun and too much walking in the sand were taxing on Dad. Each day, I held my breath as I watched him struggle on his way to the beach blanket. He could wade and float in the water, but no more real swimming. And there was absolutely no more diving off his knees or throwing us up in the air for the big splash. If Dad did something he shouldn't, I held my breath until I was sure he was fine again.

My biggest concern was his going to church every Sunday. At our home parish in Braintree, he had to climb a dozen granite stairs very slowly so he wouldn't die. But our summer church was more dangerous to him—the inside was hotter than Hades. Every Sunday Dad, Robbie, and I dressed up in our "Sunday-go-to-meeting" clothes and went to church in the Dennisport summer chapel. We usually got there early enough to find a seat, but when the latecomers arrived and began lining the aisles, my father would stand up and offer his seat to the closest female. She usually protested, but when he insisted and moved into the aisle, she slid into his seat and settled down. For the next hour, I counted the beads of sweat on my father's brow and watched to see if he took off his sports jacket, because that was never a good sign. By the end of the mass his shoulders were drooping, and he'd reach for the back of a pew for support. I anxiously held a continual vigil during the mass in hopes my watchful eye would keep Dad from dropping dead right there.

But that was long ago. I didn't want to think anymore about how life changed after Dad's heart attacks. I shook the thoughts out of my head and turned up the car radio. Dick Summer was playing The Beach Boys' "Little Deuce Coupe" on WBZ, so I turned up the volume and belted out the song as loud as I could with the windows wide open and my hair flying about my face. I drove up and over the Sagamore Bridge and then exited the Mid-Cape Highway at Route 134, "All Points in Dennis" and headed south toward Dennisport.

Chapter 5

THE PAST

As I drove into the entrance of Mild Bay, I passed the old signpost where name plaques were hung to identify each family who lived on the Circle. I loved those little signs. When I was younger, I wanted our name up there to show that we belonged at Mild Bay, too. But my mother said our name sign was fine at the end of our driveway.

Belonging to something must have been important to me, because when a little classmate told me she was an Indian, I wanted to be one. I ran in the back door one day after playing outside and announced, "Nancy Hope is an Indian, and I want to be one too. I'm an Apache or a Blackfoot."

My father looked up from his newspaper and told me I was only a Blackfoot when I didn't take a bath.

Then my mother, always the teacher said, "Margy, you are not an Indian."

"How do you know?" I argued. "Nancy Hope is an Indian. I might be one."

"Nancy Hope may be an Indian, but you are not."

I didn't like hearing I couldn't be an Indian, so I played my trump card.

"I could be an Indian," I yelled. "You don't know what I am, because I was adopted."

As soon as I said it, I knew I shouldn't have. My mother lost that I-know-best look with which I was so familiar. She seemed hurt. I didn't want to hurt her; I just wanted to belong to something like Nancy belonged to the Indians.

As I drove farther around the circle, I thought of how wonderful it was to now have girlfriends. Those early years on Mild Bay had been pretty lonesome. Robbie and I played together sometimes, but eventually I annoyed him and then I'd be alone again. A couple of older boys lived close by, but they had little interest in either Robbie or me. There was no gaggle of kids on the circle like there was back home on Edgemont Road.

Since I had difficulty sitting still those early summers, I entertained myself by repeatedly walking around the circle. Sometimes Teddy and I would end up at the pond, where he'd swim and I'd look for crabs. The water was pretty to look at, but it had a mucky bottom so only dogs ever swam in it. When Teddy came out and shook off the contents of the pond, we knew why it was just for dogs. As Teddy and I continued around the circle, a neighbor might call out and say she had a girl visiting from out-of-town, and ask if would I like to play with her. I always thought that was great, but it was usually for just one evening.

As I drove past Auntie Bessie's house, I thought of how much my parents liked her, but I never understood why. She wasn't anyone's aunt. She just wanted us to call her that, but she didn't seem to like kids much. She was older and wore a two-piece bathing suit when she gardened in her yard, showing pale fleshy bulges around her waist and too much breast in the top. Her gray stringy hair stuck out from under a cap that was cocked to the side. I didn't know anyone who dressed like that. She was not my aunt, for which I was entirely grateful.

Mrs. Howe's cottage was right before ours. It had weathered Cape Cod style shingles with orange shutters. Mr. Howe came down on weekends and sometimes he'd play cards with me. Mrs. Howe liked to fuss around her house and kept it neat and clean. She told me once about her ancestor who fought in the Revolution and the one who had been the Taylor of the department store Lord and Taylor. I loved those stories, although I knew

I'd never have one. My mother was the first one in her family to be born in America and my father's family came from Ireland a generation before that, so I'd hear stories and decided years ago I'd just enjoy them.

As I turned into our driveway, I could see my girlfriends' cars up ahead.

"Hey," I yelled as I jumped out onto the sandy drive.

"What took you so long?" Donna asked with a laugh.

"Hi Donna," I replied. "Hey, Tripper," I called to the other girl.

Her first name was Kathy, but I often gave people nicknames. I began calling people "honey" and "sweetie" once, but it didn't go over so well, so I had to stop.

"Can either of you stay with me tonight?" I asked.

"You know I can't stay in your house," Tripper answered. "You have too many spiders and crawly things. You can't tell the difference between the inside and the outside."

"Hey, it's just a cottage," I said, embarrassed that my mother's haphazard housekeeping was so obvious. I looked over at the cottage with its three wooden stairs rising to a center door, with an unshuttered window on either side. The kitchen and living room were inside across the front, their ceilings opened up into the rafters. The two bedrooms were across the back.

"I'll stay," said Donna. "I'm not afraid of bugs. I'm just not crazy about being out in the woods where you can't see the lights of another house."

I hated that too, and when I was little it petrified me. I'd crawl into bed at night and worry myself to tears as I expected someone to come through the woods and do us all in. If I were out after dark, I'd run home as fast as I could, digging into the sand with my little sneakers, hoping no one would jump out at me or I'd have to hear the persistent melancholy of the whippoor-will, before I made it to the safety of the top step.

Tripper went home after supper. With no TV or telephone for entertainment, Donna and I went to bed early. The next morning, after Donna went off to our summer waitressing job, I drove into the little village to see if there was anything new. I was happy to see my favorite stores were still there—Hazelton's, where I dreamed of buying their dark pine furniture someday, Davenport's for sewing supplies and other knick-knacks, and then House of Hunter, where beautiful wool sweaters and skirts made me wish money were no object.

When I came to the edge of town, I turned in the direction of the ocean and decided to go past the old Longell Road cottage. I hadn't been there for a while, but I still felt strongly attached to it. Longell Road was a sandy lane with a private beach at one end and our old cottage at the other. I pulled up in front of the sweet little, gray-shingled cottage we used to own. I was disappointed to see that the dark-green wooden shutters with the pine tree appliques had been replaced with white plastic, but the cottage's change in appearance didn't stop warm, cozy feelings. I could still picture the little fireplaced living room to the left of the front door. Robbie's and my bedroom was to the right. The kitchen was at the back but we ate our meals on the screened porch, which the new owners had enclosed.

I turned the car around at the dead end and drove back down the sandy road. When I stopped at the intersection with Old Wharf Road, I could still see the weathered rail fence I sat astride, trying to pretend I was on a real horse. I pulled onto Old Wharf Road and drove toward one of the earlier rental cottages before we bought Mild Bay. It was across from Glendon Road Beach. I pulled over into that beach parking lot, and jumped out onto the sand I had waited all winter to walk on. The ocean water was sparkling, and a few hearty souls were testing the still-chilly water. I looked back across the street at our rental cottage, and suddenly realized not all my early memories of Cape Cod were pleasant.

Visions of my parents being quick to find fault and even quicker to punish flooded my mind. Their discipline was harsh. No other parent I knew turned their kids over a knee in public like my father did and spanked with at least six hard hits for what seemed like a minor offense. His "I will pull down your pants in front of everyone and tan your behind" was much more severe than anything I heard from other parents. "Deliberately disobedient," were the words I heard as his hand stung my bottom. Their discipline never made sense to me when I thought of how they had waited such a long time to have children, and then were chosen specially by an adoption agency.

Although my father's spankings made me feel sad, angry, and ashamed, he never disconnected from me. No matter how angry he became, he never abandoned me. My mother didn't hit as often, because her punishment was to isolate me. Eventually I would confess to almost anything just to be allowed back into the family's activity.

I also understood I wasn't an easy kid. I was a challenger and a complainer, opinionated, demanding, and contrary. I was silly and talked too much. I couldn't sit still. I ran rather than walked, and was impulsive. So in a family that valued self-control, I was ripe for the punishment that was being offered.

As I turned back to look at the beach, I no longer felt the joy of being back on the Cape. Sadness had taken over. I had no idea I carried around these old emotions from so many years ago. I thought they had all been put away.

Chapter 6

BOURNEWOOD

*R*estaurant work meant long hours, but I loved it—independence, friends, being out of the house, making money. My parents finally arrived at Mild Bay, and I was glad to see them. I had missed my mother's regular meals and my father's chatty conversation. But after a few days, I sensed something was wrong. My father was getting into his "too excited" mood. I hadn't seen this since last year, when Dad took me to The Hollow Restaurant in Quincy. After we sat down in the pine-paneled dining room, Dad stood up and began visiting other tables.

He didn't know the people, but he'd start conversations with a charming introduction, commenting on the cuteness of their child or a person he thought they both knew. Then he would move about the room, offering his pleasant talk at various tables. For short exposures, people thought he was delightful. But I knew he would linger too long, and then those customers would be looking around the room for someone to rescue them. Eventually, I'd be able to refocus him on eating or paying the bill, before I could direct him toward the exit.

I didn't expect that behavior here on the Cape, but then this morning at breakfast, he startled me with, "Margy, do you think your restaurant might want to hire an ole fart like me?"

I didn't know what to say. Then he told me how he had applied for a summer job yesterday at the same liquor store where he worked years ago before his heart attacks. The store had hired him in the morning but fired him by the end of the day. Now I didn't know how what to think. The use of "fart" had caught my attention. He never used profanity.

When I came home from work that night, I excused myself and went into my bedroom to iron my uniform and polish my work shoes. I could hear my parents' voices rising on the other side of the cottage wall. Then suddenly my father was yelling and cursing. I peered around the corner from the bedroom door.

Mum was standing next to my father pleading, "Dave, don't go."

My father stormed out the front door with Aunt Dot's little beagle dog leashed behind him. His shadow moved into the darkness as his voice carried through the night. "I'm going to walk the dog!" he yelled back at my mother. So full of rage, so irrational—I had never seen him that angry, not with my mother anyway.

When Mum turned and saw me, she must have thought I needed an explanation. "He'll be okay," she said. She seemed to be reassuring herself more than me, but I enjoyed her calm. I wanted to stay, but I could tell she didn't want me to. As I walked back into my room, my mother's panicked plea echoed in my ears—"Dave, don't go." Her usual calm, to the point of looking disinterested, had disappeared.

I climbed onto my bed and peered out the window. I hoped I'd see a shadow of my father in the thick stand of oaks and pines, but I could only see the blackness of the night. I felt a shock of panic when I thought he might have a heart attack. His anger and stress were all the things we tried to keep away from him. The thought of his dying where we wouldn't find him for days terrified me. I only calmed myself by remembering he hadn't had an attack in years. I laid down on my bed that night and waited patiently to hear the front door open and his footsteps on the linoleum floor, but they never came.

In the morning, I climbed out of bed when I heard my mother running water for coffee. She seemed calm as I stepped into the kitchen. I sat down to eat my cereal. I turned when I heard a noise and saw my father framed in the screen door. Pine needles covered his shirt and pants. He let himself in and unhitched the loyal beagle dog from her leash. He walked past us and went into their bedroom.

Mum turned to me and said, "Margy, why don't you get going so you're not late for work?"

I still had time, but I quickly drank my juice and went into my bedroom, where I pulled my waitress uniform off its hanger and slipped it over my head. As I tied my shoes, I thought of the first time Mum told me something was wrong with Dad. It was two years ago in the fall of my sophomore year. I was sitting on the edge of my bed in Braintree doing homework. My brother was away at his first year of college, and I had just finished playing a season of field hockey. Mum called me to come into the kitchen. She was sitting at the table. I sat down across from her.

"Everything okay?" I asked.

"Your father is going away for a while," she said calmly. "He'll be going to Bournewood Hospital in Brookline. He needs some electroshock treatments."

"What? What are you talking about?" I said, trying to understand what she was saying while organizing an argument that said she was wrong.

"He's depressed," she said. "Haven't you noticed that he doesn't do anything anymore?"

"Depressed? What do you mean?"

"He hasn't been himself lately." She leaned back in her chair and looked at me hard, as if to suggest I hadn't been paying attention to my family.

I shook my head a little sheepishly. I hadn't noticed anything. I had been busy with school, friends, and sports.

Waves of guilt crashed over me. I liked to think I was a good daughter. I didn't want to be as self-centered as she was implying.

My mother became distant, immersed in her own thoughts. I wanted her to say something, but she had nothing else to tell me. I took her cue, got up, and walked back to my bedroom. I climbed back on my bed, and pulled out a French book.

As I finished tying my shoes, my mother knocked on my door, startling me out of the old memory. "Margy, you're going to be late for work."

I grabbed my pocketbook and car keys and kissed my mother on the cheek.

"Are you coming home during your lunch break? I'll make you a tuna sandwich," Mum said.

"Yes, I should have time. I have two hours today."

The restaurant was quiet except for the kitchen prep work. I took the chairs off the tables, heated up the chowder and rolls and then distributed the ketchup and mustard bottles. Customers began to arrive when we opened at noon. Donna and Tripper came in for their shifts, and before long the restaurant began to fill up.

"Don't forget my fish and chips, David," I yelled into the kitchen.

"What fish and chips?" David called back.

"The ones I ordered *to-go* for table eight."

"If you didn't give me the order, I don't know about it."

"Damn it," I felt the slip in my pocket and hurried into the kitchen and clipped it to the wire over the deep-frying vats.

"Hey, can someone finish up with my ladies in the back corner? I need to go on break," I called out to no one in particular.

"Sure, I need a table," Tripper said.

"Thanks. I really appreciate it. I'll see you when I get back." I said and added up a check, delivered the *to-go* order, and then stepped out into the midafternoon sun. A cool breeze was coming off the ocean. I tipped my head back and let the sun's rays warm my face. My shoulders relaxed, and I hoped the rest of my body would, too. The events last night were still haunting me. I had heard my father's anger before, but I had never seen my mother's fear.

As I turned up Depot Street, the car radio began playing the Rolling Stones' "Nineteenth Nervous Breakdown." I sang along as usual, never thinking about the irony of the lyrics. I drove past the intersection of Depot Street and Depot Road and then took a left into Mild Bay.

I pulled up next to the clothesline on the side of our yard. It was a hot July day, and my waitress uniform stuck to my legs as I tried to slide off the plastic car seat. I untied my apron, tossed it back into the car, and slammed the door. The heat of the day was rising up from the sand, baking my legs as I walked toward the cottage. My mother was standing on the top step waiting for me. She didn't usually do that. I waved to her. There were no clues that anything was wrong, but I was taking it all in. My mother would have called it my analyzing too much. I liked to look at things from every angle, so with my chatty nature and always wanting her attention, Mum heard too much from me.

I skipped up the three front steps and followed my mother into the cottage. She seemed ill at ease. I was about to ask her what was going on when I heard my father calling to my mother from their bedroom.

"Midgie, Midgie, come on in here."

I had never heard this flirty, come-hither tone before. I glanced over at my mother. A mildly embarrassed look crossed her face. I looked at the front door and wondered if I should leave.

Then I heard his voice again. "Midgie, come on in here." This was a side of my parents I had never seen.

My mother took a step toward their bedroom. "Dave, Margy's home. She came home for lunch."

The forced lightness in her voice made me realize that things were not okay.

My father climbed out of bed and made an unbalanced landing on the floor. He then appeared at the bedroom door and bounced into the living room. "Margy, Margy, I'm so glad you came home!" he exclaimed as he walked toward me, right past my mother. "It's always good to see you. You spend too much time at that old restaurant."

I worried that he might lecture me again about how I never went to the beach with them anymore, but he continued right past me and stopped at the kitchen table. He picked up his pack of Kent cigarettes and took one out. He fumbled with a nasty-looking cigarette holder that was supposed to pull the nicotine out—a gesture to his doctor rather than quitting. He lit the cigarette and took a drag from it. "They work you much too hard, Margy," he complained on the exhale.

His chatty demeanor was not unusual, but something was different. He directed everything at me, ignoring my mother. When he was well, his attention was usually on her, and she liked it that way. They were a close couple, and I often felt squeezed out of their relationship. All my life my mother had been everything to him, but in the last few months, he was challenging her whenever he could. Now he appeared to be on the verge of another emotional outburst. It was like watching smoke pour from a stalled car and waiting for the gas tank to explode.

He took another puff on his cigarette and turned to me again. "Margy, your mother's not happy with me, because I bought a car."

"Yeah, Dad, I saw it. Why would you ever buy a '59 Chevy? It has those ugly taillights," I chided him, pretending nothing about this afternoon was unusual.

"Margy, they gave me a great deal on it. I couldn't pass it up!"

He seemed oblivious to my teasing. I felt as if I were talking to a child. Children don't have a sense of humor when something important to them is being challenged. But this man was not a child, not someone I was baby-sitting. He was my father, my parent. How did I begin worrying about someone who used to worry about me?

"I don't know why your mother won't just let me do what I want, Margy. She interferes with me all the time," my father declared, bringing me back to the reality I didn't want to face… Dad was not himself.

"Dave, we can talk about this later?" my mother said as she moved closer to him. She pointed to a chair she had pulled away from the kitchen table. "Why don't you sit down, Dave? You haven't been feeling well. You haven't been yourself." She was trying to be gentle but straightforward.

"Marjorie, I don't think you want me to be well," his voice was rising. "I felt awful all winter, and now all I want to do is enjoy my house on Cape Cod, go to the beach, and relax. And you won't let me do that."

But that wasn't all he wanted. He also wanted to drive around in the evenings visiting people he had met at the post office or waiting for his morning newspaper at Maloney's Drug Store. He'd be warm and friendly to them. Then these strangers would invite him over to their cottages. Mum had to go with him because she knew the new acquaintances would eventually regret having encouraged the friendly, manic man they had met earlier in the day.

My mother looked at me apologetically, as if she hadn't expected me to see my father like this. Not until that moment did I realize how she had been protecting me over the years from my father's worst manic behavior. When Dad was like this, she would let me take the car to visit a friend or she'd send me on an errand. She had kept this all to herself. This was her fight, her battle. She would handle it on her own.

Dad flicked his cigarette into the nearest ashtray as my mother finally caught his attention. I was glad the focus was no longer on me. This illness, this moment, was not about me. It was about them. They had expected to have a nice life, but their struggle with both physical and mental illnesses had been more challenging than either of them had imagined.

"Dave, you are going to need some treatment." Her words came out slowly, carefully and kindly, just before he exploded. Within a moment, his arms were flailing about him. His face became red, and his eyes went black.

"Jesus, Mary, and Joseph! By God, Marjorie, I am not going to let you take me back to that hospital," he screamed while slamming his chair to the floor. He leapt aside when he thought my mother might grab him. "You are not going to put me away!" he yelled as he kicked the fallen chair in her direction before stomping around the corner. I heard the bathroom door slam, and I thought it either broke or came off its hinges. Through the thin cottage walls, I could hear his angry ranting, all directed at my mother. "You want me sick, Marjorie! You like it when I'm in the hospital. By God, Marjorie, there's nothing wrong with me! I'll go somewhere where I can live in peace. If I want to stay out all night, that's my business. Marjorie, you stay out of this!"

My mother stood in the kitchen like a rock. Her determined face said she was not going to let his terrible words break her down. But the afternoon sun was setting behind the trees, and my father was getting worse with an increasing threat of violence. I didn't know whether I should stay to make sure nothing happened to my mother or leave to keep out of the way. I was frozen in place when a sound outside caught my attention. An unfamiliar dark sedan had pulled into the driveway.

"Mum, there's a car outside."

"They're here?"

"Who is it?"

"I called Bob Laing. He's going to take Daddy to Bournewood."

I watched as Bob Laing and another close friend of Dad's, a janitor from North Quincy High School, stepped out of the car. I had known Bob Laing since I was little as my father's closest friend at work. Bob was always smiling and had something friendly to say. He and his father had built our cottage. Their arrival triggered relief and I jumped down off the top step to greet the family friends. But the men were not here to be greeted. Their words were reserved. Two other men climbed out of the back seat. One had a priest's collar, and the other was a broad-shouldered young man. I took a few steps back.

My mother opened the front door, greeted the two men she knew, and was introduced to the priest and the football player. She went back in the house, and a moment later my father appeared. He bounced down the steps to greet everyone as if they had arrived for a social visit.

But as he began to chat with his friends, a scuffle broke out. My father had tried to move away when someone put a hand on him. Then the football player blocked his path. Another move and another block. The encounter didn't last long, but fear fired every nerve in my body. I had never seen grown men be physical with each other, not in real life anyway. Then I saw my father's head dip down into the back seat of the dark sedan. The priest and football player sat on either side of him. Bob Laing and the janitor climbed into the front.

With my father safely tucked in, a sense of relief washed over me. My mother and I watched the car proceed slowly down the dusty driveway. The rear of the car was visible for another moment, until only the taillights could be seen flickering through the dense woods. And then they were gone.

A lump formed in my throat, and my legs went weak. My stomach felt as if I had been kicked. I gasped for tiny breaths. I didn't want to miss him so much. Then the tears began to flow. "Don't cry," I admonished myself. I didn't even know why I cried anymore. Sometimes I wept like a baby over nothing and other times I had no tears. I tried to squelch the thought that maybe I should be the one going to Bournewood.

I looked at my mother for reassurance. *Are we okay?* My mother seemed to have no sense of my being there or not being there. I walked toward her and then she turned and walked up the three stairs ahead of me. I followed her into the living area. She expected me to go back to work. Maybe she wanted me to leave so she could process what had happened this afternoon. Or maybe in her mind nothing *had* happened. I think it was probably the latter. Reflection on anything that happened in our family had never been encouraged. "Why should it be?" my mother would have said. There was never anything remarkable happening, and I believed her.

When I arrived back at the restaurant, I walked in and tied on my apron as if nothing had happened—because to everyone else, nothing had.

Some who were trying to be helpful said I shouldn't take my father's illness so hard because he wasn't really my father anyway. "You were adopted," they said. But no matter what anyone thought, Dave Meaney was my father—the only father I had ever known—and he was being taken away to a mental hospital, again.

Chapter 7

ON THE BEACH

With the restaurant almost full, I fell quickly into the serving rhythm—cleaned up a table, brought water to another, and then took an order. The rush of customers came hard and fast, but it waned early. The usual long line never formed, so the door was locked at eight. Excitement spread throughout the staff when we realized we'd be getting out early. After-work plans were finalized, and everyone had a place to go, but I wanted to be alone. I'd had many fun times with the girls, and I expected to have more, but tonight I wanted to be by myself.

The beach on Longell Road would probably be quiet, and it was just around the corner. I parked the car next to a small sand dune and slipped off my shoes. I felt the soft, cool sand under my feet. The tiny grains squeezed up through my toes, and I thought of my father reading A. A. Milne's poem "Sand-Between-the-Toes."

The ocean lapped gently at the shore creating a hypnotic rhythm. As the sound was absorbed into my being, I eased myself down onto the sand and scooped small handfuls of the white grains, letting them sift through my fingers. I pushed my feet out in front and my heels dug little troughs. The more I touched the sand and let the sounds and smells of the seaside surround me, the more I fell into a soothing trance.

My mind put that afternoon's episode aside, and I embraced the wonderful memories and feelings of love I remembered from my early years with my family. This beach, this road, the little cottage had been the beginning of my life. I longed for this part of my childhood. But as I absorbed all the goodness of the warm, comforting memories, I wasn't gaining strength. I was losing my defenses. My outer crust was softening, and I began to feel vulnerable. I had hoped coming back to my childhood "womb" on Longell Road would soothe my pain, but the joy I first felt on Cape Cod was no longer in my life. Too much had changed. While it was lovely letting the past envelop me and quench my thirsty soul, it was not giving me the strength I needed to face my future.

"Oh, Daddy…Daddy!" My cries came without warning. "Where are you?" My desperation had no direction. My tears flowed. I wanted to bring back the father of long ago. I wanted to hear his voice and see the man who had become everything to me. Memories flashed through my mind and a special day came into focus. It was a Saturday. My father had taken me to a track meet at his high school before his heart attacks.

We arrived at a field full of high school boys running, throwing heavy balls, long poles, and metal plates, and jumping over fences. When they weren't doing those things, they were crowding around my father to hear instructions. The busy young men mesmerized me, but a loud noise—a gun—startled me. I jumped as I heard it go off and saw some boys begin to run. I wanted to run, too, to get away from the noise. After the race my father showed me the starter's pistol. He held it down at my level, hoping that I'd be less scared. He explained that it wasn't like a real gun. He assured me it was safe.

"Would you like to hold it?" he asked.

My eyes grew large at the thought, and I took a step back. I was stunned as I nodded in acceptance. I couldn't believe he was giving me such a responsibility. I took the gun and held it down at my side. We didn't have guns in our house, and I didn't know anyone who did.

"Now, don't give it to anyone," my father said.

I was stiff with responsibility. I held it at my side, by the handle, with all the awkwardness of a person in a completely unfamiliar situation. I began walking toward the cinder track, keeping the gun at my side, convinced I had the most important job in the world. Boys were running fast and then jumping into a pile of sand. Another boy picked up a heavy ball and threw it with all his might. The most interesting was a boy who stuck a pole in the ground and while holding the other end, went flying in the air high over a bar. As I became more and more fascinated with the activities, I hadn't noticed how far I had wandered. A young man came running up to me.

"I need the gun," he said breathlessly.

"What?" I couldn't believe anyone would be asking for something so precious for which I had total responsibility.

"Can you give me the gun?" he asked.

"No!" I exclaimed. "My daddy told me not to give it to anyone."

"Well, he asked me to get it," the young man replied as he patiently smiled at me.

"No," I stood firm. In my mind, I was to take care of it, to protect it from someone like this boy, even though he was wearing the red and black uniform of North Quincy High School.

This young man's patience was waning. "Go ask Mr. Meaney. He will tell you."

"Fine," I thought, with a little haughtiness that I kept to myself.

I looked across the football field and realized how far away from my father I was. I began walking carefully with the gun still held close at my side as the young man continued asking me to give it to him. I finally arrived at my father. I tugged on his jacket.

"Daddy, he says I should give him the gun." My eyes looked over at the young man standing next to me.

"Oh, yes, give him the gun," my father said offhandedly.

I was dumbfounded. My father had given me what I thought was the most important job in the world, and then he casually took it away with a wave of his hand and a nodding gesture. My expression could not mask my disappointment.

My father bent over and said, "Margy, you were such a big help, holding that gun for me. I can't tell you how much I appreciated it. Now stay close because they're going to start the races. You might want to block your ears."

I warmed all over. He not only knew me, but he cared about my feelings. I stood a little closer to him as other men and boys came and went, receiving instructions each time. Every conversation with him ended with a laugh or smile.

Suddenly, a car door slammed, bringing me back to the quiet sounds of the beach. A couple appeared in the dim evening glow and walked over the small dune past my sand boundaries. The ocean, with a hint of moonlight sparkling on the ripples of the rising tide, held my attention for another moment, and then the father of my memories disappeared.

I was dumped back into the reality that my father was gone. But the place in my heart and soul, which had been made for him so many years ago right here on Cape Cod, had been getting smaller. He was like a friend who had disappointed you once too often and now needed to be less important. I wanted him back, but he was never going to be my complete father again. He had become more like an uncle—someone you didn't really need, but you were happy to see. Someone who needed you more than you needed him. It all hurt. It hurt so much.

I climbed back in my car and drove home to Mild Bay. My mother was sitting under the wooden bridge lamp, reading a book when I walked in. She asked if I needed any supper. I told her I was fine. I babbled about a customer who didn't leave a tip. Nothing was mentioned about the man who was missing from our midst.

Chapter 8

Aunt Dot

*T*he next morning, as the sun's rays crept around the sides of my window shade, I scooted under my blanket, pretending the day had not arrived. Why *not* just stay in bed? Everything was more easily handled under the covers. When I got up, I'd see my father's empty chair at the kitchen table, my brother's empty chair after he joined the Army, and the empty place in front of the screen door where my dog Teddy used to lie. Teddy died last year, a month before my Aunt Dot. I still couldn't believe Dot was dead.

I rolled over in my bed and stared at the spackled, unpainted wall. It was the end of July, and that was when Dot always came to spend her week of vacation with us. Every summer she'd arrive with all kinds of sweet goodies and her loving, fun personality. It was like Christmas in July. My mother was always thrilled. My father loved Dot, too. Dot couldn't wait to go to the beach with us. Then sometimes she'd do things just with me. We especially liked going gift shopping, and on Cape Cod there were lots of choices.

Dot had bright, red-orange hair in a style that had never changed. She was a soft place in my life. I never doubted that Dot liked me. She brushed my hair gently and said nice things about the clothes I picked out. Dot even liked me when I annoyed her, although I only remembered doing that once. If I didn't behave, she never punished me; she just told me a better way, and then we were fine again.

I never expected Dot to die. I didn't know anyone who had died. Sometimes my parents talked about Dot having a bad heart, and I remembered overhearing them say that she had purchased a cemetery plot. Even though I cried when I heard that, I didn't think she'd need it.

Dot was fifty-three in March of my high school junior year. I had never visited her without my parents. But on a beautiful warm evening in March, when I was driving myself to Quincy Symphony practice with my new driver's license, I thought I might stop by her house when practice was over. Dot lived just around the corner, so I made plans in my mind to visit her when I was let out. I knew I'd be surprising her, but I'd just stay a moment. I hoped it would be the beginning of a closer relationship.

At the end of rehearsal, the symphony secretary asked us to stay and look for a piece of missing music. The first bassoon had misplaced his Sibelius. By the time we were excused, it was too late for me to stop at Dot's. She was probably in bed anyway. My disappointment stayed with me the whole drive home.

When I pulled into the Braintree driveway, I assured myself that I still had a few more Wednesday nights to visit Dot before the end of symphony season. I opened the back door and walked through the small hall. I called out to my parents, but no one answered. I stepped into the dining room and squeezed past the dining room table and saw my father sitting in the living room. He stood up when I came in. I could tell something was wrong. Then Dad told me—Dot was dead. She had died earlier that evening. My mother had been worried when she couldn't get Dot on the phone, so she drove over to her house and found her.

"Mum found Dot sitting on her sofa with Tippy curled up next to her. She left a note on the kitchen table with instructions for everything," Dad said. I began sobbing and headed toward my bedroom. I didn't tell Dad that I could have been the one to find her.

As I tried to shake those memories, I pushed my face deeper into my pillow. My mother was making more noise out in the kitchen. That was her way of trying to get me up. But it was too early. I didn't have to get ready for work yet. But I was grateful to hear Mum sounding stronger. She seemed to be finally recovering from her operations.

Right after the funeral and Dot's burial, my mother had a serious gallbladder attack and was taken to Quincy City Hospital. When the doctor opened her up during the emergency surgery, he found not only the diseased gallbladder, but also a large cluster of malignant tumors the size of a grapefruit attached to her kidney. I heard about it when a nurse friend of Dot's called. I was the only one home, so she decided she'd tell me. As I began to understand what Dot's old Army buddy was saying, my body began to crumble and then full-blown panic took over. I shook and then collapsed. I got up and ran from room to room, finally falling on the living room floor. "Please, please, dear God, don't take my mother. I can't lose my mother," I yelled to the empty house.

In my mind, Mum was never supposed to die. Every day I thought my father might, but not my mother.

A month later when Mum went back to have the kidney removed, the doctor assured us that people lived on one kidney all the time, and the good news, he said, was that he didn't think her tumors had spread.

"Margy, come on, get up." I heard simultaneously with a knock on my door. "Come and have your breakfast."

I dragged myself out of bed and made my way to the kitchen table. I poured myself some cereal and looked over at my mother. She seemed almost normal now. The doctor said it would take a year for her to feel anything like herself again. It was a little over a year now. But the word "malignant" meant death to me, so I never stopped thinking about losing her.

Chapter 9

MAINE

By Labor Day weekend on Cape Cod, the color of the sky, the smell of the air, and the way the sun reflected off the water in Nantucket Sound, had all changed—as if a switch had been pulled—and summer instantly turned into fall. A twinkle of light now appeared across the top of the waves that hadn't been there in the hot humid days of July and August.

The tourists began leaving the Cape and the time had come for us waitresses to leave, too. Most of us were starting our first year of college. I packed up my things, closed the cottage and began my return to Braintree. As I drove west along the Mid-Cape Highway, I thought of how lucky I was to be even going to a four-year college. My guidance counselor had many doubts.

At the beginning of my senior year, my guidance counselor called me into her office. I was excited to talk with someone about where I was going after I graduated. She opened up a folder in front of me, which contained my complete school record, dating back to Thomas A. Watson Elementary School. On the inside flap, she pointed to my most recent SAT scores. She explained that with scores as low as mine, I probably wouldn't be accepted to any college. Even the University of Massachusetts, she said, where many of my friends were applying, probably wouldn't take me.

"That doesn't make sense," I raised my voice. "I'm in classes with kids who are applying to really good schools, and my grades are as good as theirs. Why wouldn't U. Mass take me?"

"Well," she said, "it's your SAT scores. Your achievements aren't bad, but colleges are looking at SATs." The counselor closed the folder, sat up straight, and looked me in the eye. "You could always go to a nice secretarial school."

"No," I blurted out. "I've worked too hard. I have an A in International Relations. I taught a class on socialism in Sweden. I don't understand."

"Well, you can always apply to the University of Massachusetts," she said. "But I doubt if you'll get in."

When my first set of disappointing SAT scores arrived a year ago, my father urged me to take a prep course, but my mother nixed the idea. The topic was never raised again.

That night after supper, I told my parents what the guidance counselor had said about secretarial school. I tried to make it sound as if the woman had lost her mind, but my mother immediately embraced the idea. I hadn't expected that. All my life, my parents had talked about Robbie and me going to college. They had both gone. My mother graduated from Tufts, and my father from Boston College. Three years ago, although my brother's grades weren't as good as mine, my parents only discussed college for him.

"You know you really don't need to go to college," my mother said. "You'll probably get married."

"What do you mean? You went to college," I responded sharply.

"That was different. I had to, to become a teacher."

"Well, maybe I'll become a teacher. Mr. Archikowsky asked me if I were going to be a math teacher."

"Being a teacher isn't a very good idea for you, Margy. Your father and I are both teachers. It's a difficult profession. You need too much immediate gratification with everything you do. Teaching doesn't give you that. Why don't you go to secretarial school like your guidance counselor recommended?"

"Because I want to go to college," I retorted loudly. "How can I be a secretary? I got a C in that college typing class."

"But what would you study in college?"

"I don't know. I like lots of subjects…I like doing research."

"Well, you don't just major in research," Mum replied.

At that point my father interrupted. "You can be a teacher, a secretary, or a nurse. Those are the professions open to girls."

"What about a social worker?" I challenged. My parents didn't answer. Their silence meant the discussion was over. But I was seething, and I couldn't hold back. "You don't want me to *be* anything!" I yelled.

Tears flowed. My voice was on that "high G" my mother hated, and I hated when she pointed it out to me. I just couldn't keep my emotions under control. They had no idea how frustrating it was to do well in school and then be saddled with SATs that yelled "not college material."

"When I was in the eighth grade, Mum, I wanted to be a lawyer, but you told me I couldn't because I didn't write well."

"You are not a good writer, Margy. You have to be a good writer to be a lawyer."

"Well, you're an English teacher. Why don't *you* teach me how to write?" I yelled.

"I told you before, no one can teach writing. To become a better writer you have to read more, and you don't read very much."

"I can't read. I read too slowly."

"Well, then it doesn't do you any good for us to tell you that you can do something you can't."

I could see her point.

"Well, maybe I can't, but at least you could encourage me. Kathy's parents expect her to go to college and do something special."

I wanted my parents to have hopes and dreams for me so that I could hope and dream for myself without feeling I had nothing to offer. Then I remembered something. "You told me the adoption agency let you adopt me because you both had college degrees, and they expected me to go to college, too."

"Well, things change," my mother said. "If you think you still want to go to college, you can apply to a state school."

I didn't understand why they no longer expected me to go to college. Yes, my SAT's were bad, but I was a good student. I loved learning. Was their change of mind because my biological mother hadn't gone to college? But they had both gone to college. Why didn't they think of me as the daughter of two college-educated parents?

Those memories quickly left my mind as I entered my old Braintree neighborhood and drove past my school bus stop. I couldn't believe I'd never be standing there again, waiting for that yellow bus to pick me up. I was going to the University of Maine in the morning.

As I walked in the back door, I wondered how my father was doing since he had just come home from Bournewood. I passed through the dining room. I could see Dad sitting quietly in the living room. He pepped up when he saw me.

"Margy, you're home! It's so good to see you. Your mother and I have been waiting for you." I detoured into the living room and sat across from him. This wasn't the man I had known all my life. His manic state had calmed, but in its place was a drug-induced, hyper-connecting demeanor. "Margy, did you know that it took four Boston College football players to get me under control when Bob Laing took me back to Bournewood?"

"No, Dad…I didn't know that," I said. I thought again of that day and contrasted my experience with the excitement I was hearing in his voice. Dad had graduated from Boston College in 1934, the vice president of his class. The college and their sports had been important to him for as long as I could remember.

"What do you think about that?" he asked.

I didn't know what to think. I didn't know whether I should cheer him on or just let the sadness overwhelm me. I told him it was great that he gave them such a hard time, and then I excused myself to my bedroom.

In the morning, goodbyes to my father were unsettling. "Dad, I'm heading out now."

"Well, what kind of a father do you have who isn't taking his daughter to college? Your mother just won't let me go, you know. I don't understand her. Doesn't she realize a daughter needs her father and mother at a time like this?"

"Yes, Dad, but it's okay. Rob is taking me. We'll be fine."

"Well, I want you to remember, Margy," and then he quoted some Latin about being forewarned and forearmed. He quoted Latin more often in his manic moments. I had no idea what he was saying. But if Dad were quoting Latin, it was symptomatic. If he had said, "Have a great year and be careful—can't wait to hear all about it," I would have sighed in relief.

Robbie drove and I rode in the 1966 Impala, our family's first-ever new car. He was home on leave before his next Army assignment. Robbie immediately squelched any connecting chatter I was planning with loud music and his silence. I understood. For some reason we had never become close. I liked having a brother. We played catch and shot baskets together sometimes, but our lives seldom overlapped. We never attended the same school at the same time. Since he started school young, he and his friends were three years ahead of me. But what truly separated us were our distinctly different natures. We were opposites. I never liked breaking rules. Not because I was so virtuous—I just didn't like getting punished. I knew I wasn't an easy little sister. I continually annoyed him, and I was the worst tattler.

The one thing we did have in common was being adopted, but we never discussed it. It was the only life we knew, and talking would have exposed our differences even more. We came from two separate biological families. When someone heard we were not blood-related, they often decided we weren't siblings at all. I told those people they were wrong. Robbie was my brother, I'd insist, but it didn't do any good. They had made up their minds. "Oh, so he's not your *real* brother, is he?" they'd say.

People didn't always view adoptive relatives the way they did biological relations. Some referred to my parents as "your step-parents" or "foster parents" instead of just "your parents." I never understood why anyone cared so much about how I was related to someone. It must have been important to them, because the topic was discussed often enough.

My brother exited the interstate just after Bangor, and we traveled along the Penobscot River until we passed through the former lumber town of Orono and onto the University of Maine campus. My dormitory was relatively new. York Hall was four stories tall with a large picture window in each room. We climbed up the granite front steps, weighed down by my two overstuffed suitcases. The front hall was hospital-clean but completely devoid of people. As we walked down the sterile corridor toward the stairs, I could only hear the clicking sounds of my loafers echoing off the cement block walls. An image of a *Twilight Zone* episode came into my mind in which Rod Serling was announcing from the lounge below, "Town overtaken by aliens…only two survivors walk abandoned corridor looking for signs of life."

On the fourth floor, I opened the door marked 434 and found a room for two, outfitted with beds and bureaus for three, but no one was around. I went into the communal white-tiled bathroom. Multiple sinks, toilets and showers, but no one was there. I never imagined my arriving for band practice would land me in an empty room, dormitory, and campus. And now Robbie was anxious to get home. He gave me a perfunctory "Good luck," and then he was gone.

Later that afternoon, as I walked to band practice, I saw other members walking along, too. I was excited to see new people, but I realized quickly they were all preoccupied with friends. My heart sank. No longer was I alone, but worse, I was alone in a crowd.

As I walked back into my room that first night, I felt abandoned. Not a soul was around. I thought I was ready for this adventure, but a horrible sinking feeling was squeezing the life out of me. I needed a connection to someone…to anyone.

On Sunday the campus exploded with the arrival of all students. With a full schedule of classes on Monday, I began to feel better, but the whole episode had frightened me. I didn't understand why I couldn't tolerate being alone.

During the next few weeks on campus, I met more people, found my way around campus, and began thinking of groups to join. Notices about the Maine Outing Club's annual climb up Mount Katahdin were posted everywhere. I had never climbed a mountain before. This was a mile-high mountain, second largest in New England. It was the kind of adventure I was hoping to have at Maine. My mother often talked about her climbing activities when she was in college. She and her friends climbed mountains in New Hampshire and even skied down them. I had never seen her do anything like that, but her wooden skis were in our garage, along with a never-used-again tennis racquet and golf clubs.

Another girl from my dormitory floor and I arrived at the Steam Plant parking lot at the appointed time with our sleeping bags and a couple of extra socks. My tennis sneakers looked pathetic next to the Limmer hiking boots other climbers were wearing. The other girl and I made it to Baxter Peak the next day—the top of Mount Katahdin and the end of the Appalachian Trail. We even hiked across the Knife Edge, but on the way down to our campsite at Chimney Pond, my sneakers proved to be less support than I needed, and I fell hard on my tired, turned ankle and tore all the ligaments. The only way for me to get back to camp was to scoot on my bottom the rest of the slope back to the campsite. The next morning the pain was severe. I couldn't put a drop of weight on the foot, so two young men took turns piggybacking me down the last 3.5 miles to the parking lot.

At the school infirmary, a doctor put a cast on my leg and handed me crutches. When I understood my new limitations, I called the band director to tell him I thought I should quit the band. He was not happy with me. I was letting everyone down, he said. I wasn't a serious musician, he concluded. He wanted me to sit in the stands during football games with the other band members, even if I couldn't march on the field. The thought of sitting on those metal bleachers, with people I still couldn't call friends, made me feel the sadness of my earliest days on campus coming back.

I called my mother to tell her I would not be playing in the band. Rehearsals were a much larger commitment than I expected, and the timing of them kept me from going to dinner with my dorm friends. Mum was not happy either. She had made me practice every day since fourth grade, and in her mind I was throwing it all away. She reminded me that I had just bought a new oboe with my own money. I guess the director was correct. I was not a serious musician. I wanted to live a new life with new activities and friends at Maine.

I joined a sorority later that fall. The sisters saw in me things I had never seen in myself. They encouraged me to take a leadership role, and soon I was appointed pledge trainer.

At the end of freshman year, I was chosen to be a Maine Eagle, a group that helps incoming fall freshmen. I felt alive, connected to friends and to the university. I told my father that I had "found myself" at Maine, but I didn't let his response—"I didn't know you had been lost!"—puncture my bubble.

Chapter 10

Dad

By junior year, Maine felt like home. My major was psychology, so I took an internship at Bangor State Mental Hospital. Every week the matron opened up the tall, antique door with her nineteenth-century key and let a group of us onto the female ward. The patients had been diagnosed with schizophrenia twenty to forty years ago and had lived in the gothic-style mental hospital ever since.

Each week I was exposed to a new perspective of psychosis. Foul odors from bodily fluids, having been absorbed by the walls and floors over the last century, attacked our nostrils each week. The ranting and screams of the patients created a horror story, in which my father could have been the main character. My mother insisted my father be treated in a private hospital. Now I knew why.

By the first week of November, nightfall seemed to arrive by midafternoon, and the cold air from Canada made us reach for our winter coats. As I tried to shake the chill from the first cold snap, I thought of the poem my father used to read to Robbie and me.

And there sat Sam, looking cool and calm,
In the heart of the furnace roar;

And he wore a smile you could see a mile,
And he said, "Please close that door.
It's fine in here, but I greatly fear
You'll let in the cold and storm—
Since I left Plumtree, down in Tennessee,
It's the first time I've been warm."
"The Cremation of Sam McGee" by Robert W. Service

The dorm felt especially cozy as I walked into the entry of Penobscot Hall later that Thursday afternoon. I continued up to the third floor and strolled into my room. Both roommates were on their beds reading.

"Anybody ready for supper?" I asked.

"I have a sorority meeting tonight," Mary Lou said.

"Your mother called," Joanie added.

"She did? What'd she want?"

"I don't know. She just said you should call her back."

"She never calls me at school," I muttered, as I lay my books on the desk. "I hope there's nothing wrong with my father."

"You thought that last year, but nothing was wrong with him. It was your great aunt or something. She died, didn't she?"

"Gret," Carol called my college nickname from the doorway. "We have a sorority meeting. Are you coming?"

"Oh no, I forgot. Wait, I need to call home," I said, as I grabbed my coat, and we hurried toward the stairwell.

"You can call over at the sorority room," Carol insisted.

I stopped at the telephone booth outside the sorority room and called home. The busy signal surprised me. My mother was seldom on the phone. I followed the other sisters into the room and waited for the meeting to begin. The discussion was about how our national sorority governing board was still angry with us for initiating an African American student last spring. We really didn't care what they thought, and were excited about our new sister.

When the meeting was over, I hurried out of the sorority room and called home again. "Hi, Mum, did you call?"

"Margy…oh, Margy," she stammered. "It's your father."

I felt my legs go weak. My mother's pained voice was foreign.

"Margy…Dave's dead. Your father's dead."

It took only a moment for the information to settle in, and then my whole body and soul collapsed.

"Oh, no…no, no, no." I yelled. I moaned. Tears poured. I always knew the call was coming. I had been bracing myself for it since I was seven years old, but now it was here, and I wasn't ready at all.

"What happened?" I asked.

"He died in the teachers' room," Mum said. "They took him to the hospital, but they already knew he was dead."

"I'll try to get home tomorrow. But I don't think can get a ride."

"Why don't you fly, then you'll be home sooner."

"Ok, I just have to tell my professors."

"Well, come as soon as you can."

I pulled myself off the floor, and Carol helped me hang up the phone. "I have to fly home tomorrow," I whispered. "My Mum needs me." My voice was echoing in my head as if it were rattling in a vacuum. But the words, "My Mum needs me," repeated over and over like a mantra. I had never put those words together. My mother had never needed me, but now I felt she did. She wanted me home right away.

My sobs were loud and uncontrolled. Carol walked me out the door, and we moved slowly under the lamp-lit campus walkways. I felt no shame from the awkward stares. Evening strollers must have thought no boyfriend was worth all those tears, but my body refused to stop shaking. We walked and walked. Carol and I covered the campus until I could walk no more, and then she put me to bed.

Someone drove me into Bangor the next morning. As I sat on the wooden, bus-station-style bench in the waiting room of Bangor International Airport, I repeated to myself that my mother needed me. Between sobs, I began readying myself for my new role. I had always wanted to be important to my mother, and now I expected to be.

A friend of my parents picked me up at Logan Airport in Boston and drove me home. My mother was stoic when I arrived, focusing only on the business of wakes and funerals. She broke down periodically, but for the most part she was "holding up well," as people would say. She told me the whole story. My father had gone to school as usual that morning, but during the last period, Bob Laing stopped by Dad's room.

"Dave, you don't look so good," he said. "Why don't you go down to the teachers' room? I'll watch your class."

My father walked down the corridor. He opened the door to the teacher's room and received greetings from old friends and colleagues. He began to counter their cheer with one of his jokes, but he never made it to the punch line. He fell to the floor, dead from a heart attack, right there in the teachers' room at North Quincy High School.

People brought food to our house, accompanied by their sympathetic wishes, just as they had during Dot's funeral preparations. I liked all the comings and goings, although none of my friends from college could make it. My mother had nothing special for me to do, so I wandered around visiting with whomever had stopped by. My mother's focus was mainly on whether Robbie and his wife, who were overseas, would make it home for the funeral. They never did.

In the quiet of my bedroom, I began regretting that I had not worked on Cape Cod last summer—my father's final summer at his beloved Mild Bay cottage. It was the first time, since I was adopted, that I hadn't spent at least some time on the Cape. My mother did not understand why I wanted to be a waitress at Westchester Country Club in the heat of a New York summer, when I could have been on Cape Cod. I had seen working at the club as a great adventure. A friend had arranged the job in Harrison, New York, and I couldn't let Lyn down.

After working one month, I drove up to Cape Cod to visit my parents over the Fourth of July weekend—their anniversary—and they were delighted. My mother told me my father was having a "good summer." He didn't need a trip to Bournewood for the first time in many years. I was glad to hear that. I wondered if it might have been more relaxing with me away. He had begun his psychotic episodes when my brother went to college and ended them when neither of us was home. I didn't know what to make of that.

When the first night of wakes ended, and the last visitors left the funeral parlor, I had a moment to walk over to my father's open casket. I knelt down and looked at his familiar face—the bald head, the mustache, the half-rimmed glasses—I couldn't believe a joke was not passing his lips.

"Margy, how about a game with your old man here. Come on, Margy, sing with me:

Ohhh…it's…nice to get up in the mornin',
When the sun begins to shine,
At four or five or six o'clock in the good ole summertime.
But when the snow is snowing,
And it's murky overhead,
It's nice to get up in the mornin',
But it's nicer to lie in your bed!"

He looked so peaceful as I knelt next to him. I thought of how he would have been astonished at the number of mourners who came to pay their respects. Three mayors attended—one current and two former. Students lined up outside for hours. Former students brought their children. Some were now his students. Many had a story to tell.

I was amused as I thought, if Dad were alive, he'd be introducing me to everyone. When I was little, he'd say, "Margy, this is Miss Gooch. Miss Gooch, this is my daughter, Margaret. Margy, can you say, 'Hello, Miss Gooch'?" At which time I would repeat the person's name and say hello. Then Dad would tell me something about the person I had just met. "Margy, Miss Gooch teaches Latin at my school." He was always trying to teach me something. If you didn't like learning new things, living with my father would have been torture.

I gazed at his peaceful expression. He looked so normal lying there in a suit jacket, so familiar. My hand was near the rim of the casket, and I let the tips of my fingers slide onto the fabric of his suit. Suddenly I touched something hard, wooden, and inhuman—the arm of a dead man.

I pulled my hand away. The fantasy that my father was just resting vanished. My dream that he would get up and finish his day was smashed. My father was gone. He was really gone. My legs buckled. One of the funeral workers reached out, and I dissolved into uncontrolled sobbing. My father had not been just a father. Even with all his mental and physical issues, he had been everything to me. His unconditional love was always offered, and I didn't know how I would survive without it.

During the funeral mass at the old, cathedral-style church in Weymouth Landing, I thought of how glad I was to have seen my father a week ago. I had never come home from college before Thanksgiving break, but last week I came home for Tripper's wedding on Cape Cod. After the reception, I drove back to Braintree in time to take Dad to the Maine vs. Boston University football game.

My father and I parked a short distance from Nickerson Field, and as we walked toward the field, I noticed he was moving much slower than I remembered. At halftime, he climbed gingerly over the metal bleachers and moved at a staggeringly slow pace to the men's room. Each step was more labored than the previous. I had never seen anyone walk that slowly who could still make the distance. I wanted to run after him and help, but I pretended there was nothing wrong. I didn't want anything to be wrong.

The next day, my ride came for my return trip to Maine. As the car pulled away from the house, I looked back over my shoulder and saw Dad waving goodbye from the top step. He looked pale and fragile, but I knew nothing about the progression of heart disease. I never expected that he'd be dead in four days. He was fifty-six years old.

Chapter 11

THE FOREVER FAMILY

When I came home for Christmas break, Dad's death became more painfully real. The emptiness of the house sucked the life out of me. Memories of his humor, love, and charming entertainment were everywhere, but they were only memories, and they gave me little solace. I was grateful to know he was no longer in pain. Even with the shock treatments, he had still suffered for years. At least now, he didn't want to kill himself by driving into the ocean at Wollaston Beach, an urge he had admitted to me last year. He told me he felt so low during his depressions that even if he stood on his tiptoes and reached up as high as he could, he could not have touched the belly of a snake.

Our family Christmas celebration had been reduced from the original five members to two. My "forever family," as I heard non-adopted people call families like mine, hardly existed—Dot and Dad were both gone. My brother was away in the Army. It was just Mum and me. Since we had no decorations in the house, and Mum had no interest in presents, she decided we'd visit her sister Irene in Connecticut and I didn't disagree.

As I began driving us south on Interstate 95, I hoped my mother and I might chat about the relatives we were about to see. I had never been completely comfortable with them. Aunt Irene and her family seldom showed much interest in my brother or me when we were little, and they got angry when I played with the wrong toys, asked the wrong questions, talked too much, and bothered everybody in ways I didn't understand.

We only saw them every few years. After Dot died, Irene and her daughter came up to Braintree to help my mother sort through Dot's estate. My cousin Helen was allowed to help out and miss a day of high school, but my mother made me go. That night Mum told me how they distributed the estate, and I heard that my cousin received the items I wanted. I wish I could say I hated arguing with my mother over something as silly as Dot's possessions, but I wasn't that nice a person. My longing for my mother to acknowledge me far outweighed any empathy I felt. I feared I was hurting her, but she acted as if nothing were wrong with her health, so I treated her that way and perhaps pushed when I should have pulled back. I just wanted us to be a normal mother and daughter, a normal family.

"What happened to all Dot's pierced earrings?" I asked.

"We split them up evenly between you and Helen. Helen picked out the ones she wanted and I brought you the rest." My mother handed me a small box. I knew Dot had some very attractive earrings from her time in Rome, but when I opened the box, none of them were in it.

"Mum, Helen got all the good earrings, and she doesn't even have pierced ears," I whined.

"Well, Helen is going to get her ears pierced soon, Margy. You can't have everything," my mother said caustically. This sounded more like something Irene would say.

My mother was the oldest of the three sisters, and she seemed to have wielded the power when they were all younger. Stories were legend of bike rides where my mother and Dot left Irene behind. Then there was the story about my mother knocking Dot's head against a wall while telling her not to say something. But as adults, Irene lived more comfortably than we did, with her four bathrooms to our one, and Mum began to defer to her sister regularly.

As Mum and I crossed into Connecticut, she wanted me to think well of my aunt and uncle and reminded me of how much they had enjoyed my visit with them last spring. At the time I had been in their area with a friend looking for a summer rental for the Westchester job. I thought maybe they would give us a place to stay that night, although I had never visited my aunt and uncle before without my mother. Uncle Bob answered the door, and he seemed pleasantly surprised. Irene was out for the evening so he invited Mary Lou and me in. After some light conversation, he began making us whiskey sours. He was an attentive host, and we had a sociable time.

The next morning my uncle declared to my aunt that I had changed miraculously from my annoying, younger days and was now a lot of fun. "Really? Okay," I thought. I had never known I was that bad. My uncle went on about how much he enjoyed my company. I didn't remember the evening being exceptional. He was affable, unlike my memories of him, and I learned to like whiskey sours. My friend and I went to bed with a big buzz on, just like we did after fraternity parties, but I didn't experience the evening as my uncle had.

After breakfast, Irene was finishing up a chatty episode with me as we cleaned off the table. While her connecting was foreign, it was enjoyable. Then an honest, earnest look appeared on her face, and she said, "I sometimes forget you were adopted."

Her words came out slowly and thoughtfully. Her voice had regret. Forgetting I was adopted was the way it was supposed to be, but I had never been able to do it, so I didn't expect anyone else to. I understood what she was saying. My feelings weren't hurt. I appreciated her honesty. She could only feel what she felt, and apparently, she decided something was missing from our relationship because of the adoption. I was just sad for us both.

The Christmas visit was pleasant enough. My mother never stayed anywhere more than three days and two nights, so we were soon on our way back to Braintree. During the drive home, my mother told me that she and Irene had talked about what I might do with my life. I was fairly surprised to hear that. I didn't know the topic interested my aunt, and besides, I still had a year and a half left at Maine.

"Irene and I thought you should think about leaving Maine. Your psychology major needs a master's degree to get a job. And you won't be able to get a master's degree." I couldn't tell if Mum meant I wouldn't be able to afford it, or I wouldn't be able to do the work, but I didn't disagree. I didn't know anyone who had a master's degree. I just enjoyed studying psychology.

My mother suggested that I come home for good after final exams in January, and I didn't have the strength to keep her suggestions from becoming my plans. Maybe she was right. Her implied message was something I had wanted to hear—she needed me at home. I hardly heard the part that I should go to secretarial school. All I heard was that she thought it was time for me to come home, and on some level I welcomed the invitation.

I wasn't sad. I wasn't upset. I was stumbling around in an emotional fog, not focusing on what I might want, but what my mother thought was a good idea. She made the decision, but I allowed it. After Christmas break, I went back to Maine to finish three weeks of classes and to take my final exams. My father had only visited the campus once, so I didn't see him everywhere like I did when I was home. At Maine I was relieved from the sadness I felt in Braintree. But the lack of sadness was replaced with guilt for not thinking more about him. Grief gets you coming and going.

As I prepared for finals, I pinned the front page of the student newspaper above my desk. Stephen King's editorial was a picture of a fierce-looking character in black and white with hair in disarray. His eyes and the business-end of a shotgun barrel were aimed right at the reader. Two words were under the picture: "Study, Dammit!" I loved this sort of thing, the quirkiness of Maine, and it made me sad to think I'd be leaving it.

I made a list comparing reasons to stay at Maine with reasons to go home. On the "stay" side were my studies, friends, acquaintances, organizations, honors, and just being on my own. On the "leave" side was my mother needed me, and that was enough for me to give up all the others.

Most who knew me expressed shock that I was leaving. Sue, a big-sister type I had met at the beginning of my freshman year, asked, "Why are you going home?"

"I need to help my mother. You know my father died."

"I know, I'm so sorry. But you're doing so well here. You were an Eagle. You'll probably be an All Maine Woman. Why would you leave this?"

I had no answer. We had both known students who had lost parents, and none of them left school. Going home to be with a fully functioning mother made no sense to anyone. When Sue realized my mind couldn't be changed, she reminded me of how far I had come as a person at Maine. When I was a freshman, I was too anxious and uncomfortable with myself—a person too needy when making connections, too verbose. Talking to Sue was like talking to an older sister—kind, loving, and helpful. She saw me now as a confident young woman who had come a long way. I knew what she meant. I appreciated her thoughts. I *had* come a long way. But rather than think of how much more I could grow at Maine and be the person others saw in me, I wanted a chance to have what my mother and I had never been able to create—a real mother-daughter relationship. I had always needed my mother, and now I felt she needed me. I had no difficulty changing the trajectory of my life for that.

Chapter 12

BACK TO BRAINTREE

$\mathcal{A}$s I unpacked my suitcase in my childhood bedroom, I couldn't help but think of what I had left behind in Maine. My thoughts then turned quickly to how a new relationship with my mother was worth it all. I would have been leaving college in a year or so anyway, I told myself. Maybe it was time for me to grow up, see what the real world was about, get a job, and enjoy living near Boston.

My mother and I settled into an easy rhythm. She seemed more interested in me than I remembered, and we chatted over the supper table each night about the comings and goings of life. Without my father, her attention was now on me. I loved being her new focus. Then after a few days, while we were finishing up the dinner she prepared each night, simple but balanced, Mum brought out a plate of brownies. As I munched on dessert, she announced, "Now that you're home, you'll need to start paying rent."

What? I couldn't believe I had heard correctly what she was saying. I hadn't even been home one week. I felt like she was turning me into a boarder. What was she talking about? Of course, I had planned on getting a job. I was nervous, but excited, to work in an office. I didn't understand why there was such a rush. She had never mentioned my paying rent while encouraging me to leave Maine. I thought I was coming home to reorient myself after my father's death, maybe go back to school, find a career, while I kept her company.

Then she qualified it. "But if you go to secretarial school, I won't make you pay rent until after you finish."

An unexpected flash of anger rose in me. I would have given her anything. But charging rent for my bedroom made me feel as if I didn't belong in my own house. She then explained herself by reminding me that her sister Irene had charged her sons rent when they lived at home. I didn't understand the comparison. Irene's boys were working full-time at permanent jobs. Then my anger dissipated when I remembered I was alone in Braintree. Any old friends from high school were at college. My Maine friends were six hours away. My mother was the only one I had.

In hopes of getting me into the work force, my mother called my father's oldest and dearest friend, Barry, to see if he might have a job for me. Barry held a senior position at a local manufacturing company. I loved the idea of working for a family friend who was more like an uncle. Barry and my father were only-children in families who lived next to each other and were more like brothers, going on vacation with each other's families. Mum set up an appointment.

Barry stood up from behind his desk and greeted me pleasantly but in a more businesslike manner than I expected. No one seeing us would have thought my father and he had been best friends. Quickly, he let me know he didn't have a job for me. I was surprised. I thought that was why I was there. His familiar, friendly manner was missing. I had seen this man many times in my life, and he was always jovial and joked around with us kids. His family was one of four who came to our cottage each summer for a day at the beach. I expected to see in his greeting some understanding of how much we both missed my father, but instead he acted as if nothing had happened. Our meeting seemed more a courtesy to my mother rather than finding a job for his best friend's daughter. I wondered if he no longer thought of me as the daughter of his best friend now that his friend was gone. Could I only be Dave Meaney's daughter while Dave Meaney was alive? Was I simply the embodiment of Dad's parenting experience? And now that death took the parenting away, my relationship with my family's friends was gone, too?

Although Barry didn't have a job for me, another worker came into the room and took me away to give me a typing and arithmetic test. I had avoided interviews like this because my nervous, shaking hands embarrassed me every time. But I didn't want to be uncooperative. I was still hopeful Barry might find a job for me. During the test my hands shook on the keyboard, and my mind went blank on the math.

When I was finished, I was escorted back into Barry's office. He seemed irritated to be in the position of finding me a job. This was not the man I thought I knew. I was disappointed. I thanked him for the interview and then drove home discouraged. Not getting a job that I thought was waiting for me was bad enough, but never again being able to think of Barry as family made it worse. I hadn't expected him to be a father substitute, although I certainly could have used one, and I'm sure my father would have liked him to be. I resolved right then, I would never take a job from someone who was unenthusiastic about me. I was not a charity case…not yet anyway. My experiences at Maine showed me I had something to offer.

By the time I arrived home, Barry had already called my mother to tell her I had done an unremarkable job on the tests, and he didn't think he could do anything for me. I told my mother I had been trembling when I took the tests. Mum looked at me quizzically. Either she never had a nervous moment in her life, or she knew how to avoid them, because she showed no understanding of my situation. That was strangely reassuring though. If she had coddled me, it might have made it worse. I needed to pull myself together. I needed to exhibit confidence, if I were going to be looking for a job.

Every night, I spread out the Quincy Patriot Ledger on the living room floor and first turned to the women's jobs section. Then I searched through the combination men's and women's listings. I had no idea who might hire me. I could type a bit, but I wasn't ready to be someone's secretary. Two and a half years of college hadn't given me much training for the work world, and most employers required prior experience.

The advertisement said, "Order Expediter: Manufacturing company in Boston looking for someone to process orders." I called the next day and found that a men's shoe manufacturing company—French, Shriner & Urner—had placed the ad. The company had been in Boston for about a hundred years. They still made hand-stitched leather shoes for men in sizes 8 AAA to 16 EEE. Except for the less-than-ideal location, behind a Sunoco station and above a printing company, the job sounded interesting. There were no typing tests—just a couple of interviews. Before I left, they offered me the job. Since I had no other prospects and it sounded interesting, I enthusiastically accepted.

My mother was happy to hear I had found a job, but I was still unsure why she pushed so hard to get me working. Most mothers seemed to worry about their daughters' getting good jobs or doing something they liked. My mother's focus seemed entirely on getting me out into the working world. There was no room for who I was, who I might want to be, or who I could become.

No sooner had I begun my new job than my mother reminded me I needed to go to secretarial school in September, or I'd have to start paying rent. I was surprised by her tenacity, but I wasn't against going to secretarial school. Women didn't seem to be hired directly from college for interesting jobs. They often had to start out as secretaries. Maybe secretarial school would help me get a good job in business. And Mum's encouragement suggested she had some ambition for me.

A month after beginning work at the shoe company, Barry called. He now had a job for me. My mother was thrilled and wanted me to quit my job immediately and take the position Barry was offering because he'd had to "pull some strings." What I had thought was a wonderful idea a month ago, now felt like someone's charity. I couldn't imagine working where people were unsure of my capabilities. So I reminded my mother, if I took Barry's job, I would have to quit in six months to attend secretarial school. She dropped the subject immediately.

As I sat on my bed night after night, the reasons I left Maine became less clear. When I wasn't at work or eating supper with my mother, I was sitting on my bed reading books I should have read in high school. Mum's life seemed full enough. She and her friends went to the theater. Her bridge club met. She seemed to be just as busy as she wanted to be. The only difference was that she was missing her best friend, my father. I thought I was home to help her adjust, but she seemed to be fine. A couple of times I drove her and her friend Margaret to a theater performance in inclement weather, but their tickets were purchased so far in advance, there wasn't an extra for me. I suggested once that I could fill in at bridge if she taught me the game, but she said it would be too difficult to teach me.

My social life became exceptionally quiet. I thought often about Maine—the ambiance, the people, the classes, and the high level of activity I had there. I even thought of going back the next fall until I discovered I'd be considered a transfer student. Transfer students were housed in the old Air Force barracks near the Bangor airport. I had visited a student there once and experienced that wind-whipped, treeless tundra. I knew I couldn't tolerate the feelings of isolation in such a remote location, so I gave up thoughts of returning to Maine.

At night my mother and I continued to chat over supper. I told her about my interesting job, but difficult boss. I heard about my cousin Helen and how well she was doing in secretarial school and how much she liked it. I also heard about my brother, his wife and little girl at his new Army post. After dinner I would retire to my bedroom, where I flopped onto my bed ready to tackle another book. I had finally read *Jack and Jill* by Louisa May Alcott, but not *Little Women*. I read *Beau Geste* and *The Count of Monte Christo* for a second time. When I read them the first time, my parents were puzzled by my taste in that kind of book. Now I was working on *Lord of the Flies*, but when I thought of the boys ganging up on the victim, I wasn't sure I wanted to finish it. I looked around my room for another book and thought how strange it was that I was sitting in the same position, feet dangling over the edge of the same bed, just as I had in junior high and high school. My mother was in the same place too, right outside my room sitting on her end of the sofa.

I stood up ready to grab *East of Eden* off my bureau, when I saw a couple of leftover notepads from high school. I began rifling through the first one and saw a marked-up draft of a letter that I had sent to my tenth grade principal. My mother was furious when I told her I had sent it.

My letter was a multi-paged opus about things I thought were wrong with my new high school, mainly discipline for minor infractions. The next morning, full of confidence, I slinked into Mr. Roger's empty office and put the letter directly on his desk. That night I panicked. The idea that the principal might become unhappy with me turned my confidence to abject fear. I didn't like people being upset with me, but my impulsivity— about which my parents regularly warned me—had taken over.

I walked into the living room that night seeking assurance, "I gave Mr. Rogers a letter today. I told him that I didn't think the kids in my class were being treated fairly."

"What *ever* made you think you should write to Mr. Rogers? And why didn't you let me read the letter before you gave it to him?" she demanded.

"I don't know. I was afraid you wouldn't like it," I said honestly. "Mum, I had to write it. Everyone is so unhappy. We all loved East Junior, and here they treat us like we're all delinquents."

"If it were that important, someone else could have written him," she said. "You didn't need to do it. Now you could very well be in a lot of trouble." She was stunned by my temerity.

By fourth period the next day, I was beginning to relax. It was almost time for lunch, and no one had called me to the office. My letter must have been lost among all the administrative papers on Mr. Roger's desk. Maybe it ended up in the trash. Then, just as I was waiting for the bell, the PA speaker in Mrs. Riley's geometry class crackled.

"Mrs. Riley," called a voice over the paging system, "will you send Margaret Meaney to the office after class?"

"Yes, Mr. Rogers, of course," she responded. Her eyes scanned the room trying to remember who Margaret Meaney was, and then they landed on me. Panic shot through my whole body right down to my fingertips. I had never been sent to a school office. "Now look what you've done to yourself," were the words I imagined my mother would say. "Margy, you must think before you do things. You can't go off half-cocked all the time."

She was right. I was impulsive. My life would be much easier if I followed her advice, but I lost perspective when I saw a lack of fairness.

My walk to the front office was like a death march to Judge Parker's gallows. I stepped inside the outer office door. The secretary told me to take a seat. I'd never known anyone who was sent to Mr. Rogers's office and left without a major punishment. I berated myself as people came in and out, each looking down at me, wondering what kind of trouble I was in. I finally saw my mother's point of view.

A short man with white, thinning hair came to the door of the inner office and called me into his space. I was never so unhappy to see anyone. He didn't seem angry, but you never knew with principals. They could hide their true feelings until they closed that door behind you. He gestured for me to take a seat in front of his desk, so I would have to look right at him. Then he closed the office door and walked slowly over to his chair, and lowered himself in. I sat on my shaking hands.

"I received your letter," he began. He held it in front of himself, as if reading it one more time. "Did anyone help you write it?"

"No," I whispered.

"Well, you know, when you write a formal letter, it should be on white paper, not lined," he began. "And always use a pen."

I had not anticipated an English lesson. I never thought of this man as a teacher, only a stern, unapproachable principal. Now he seemed quite nice.

"You made a number of good points," he continued.

My eyes widened in disbelief as I processed what he was saying. When was he going to tell me how he really felt and give out the punishment? As I braced for the worst, he told me he appreciated my letter being respectfully written. He told me I made my points well and that he would take it all under consideration. He wanted me to know I could approach him anytime, and said some other nice things—none of which I remembered because my nerves were frayed to confetti.

There was no joy in being vindicated. I was just glad I didn't get suspended. Raising a passionate point at home with an adult always went badly, with threats and punishments. No matter what Mr. Rogers thought of my leadership traits, my parents would never have agreed with that perception of me.

When I got home from school, I reassured my mother that Mr. Rogers was not upset. In fact, he said he appreciated what I had done. But that made no difference.

"Don't you ever do something like that *ever* again, Margy, without first getting our permission," my mother demanded.

I put the old marked-up letter back on my bureau and heard the evening news finishing up on the TV in the living room. My mother still watched the *Huntley-Brinkley Report* every night, just as she did when Dad was alive. At the end of the broadcast, David Brinkley said, "Good night, Chet," and Chet responded, "Good night, David." When my father was alive, he was usually dozing by then, but he would sit up straight in his chair when he heard his name, and respond "Good night" to no one in particular. My parents thought this was very funny.

Tonight I heard the goodbyes, and then I heard my mother crying softly. My first thought was that the news broadcast had triggered a memory. Now I understood why I came home from Maine. It all made sense. I slid off my bed, skirted the dining room table, and scooted past the TV, before lowering myself onto the sofa next to my mother. I ached for her. The love of her life was gone. She took no solace in thinking my father was in a better place. She never mentioned that life was easier now that worries over his mental illness were gone. She missed him terribly. I leaned over and began to wrap my arms around her shoulders. But just as our bodies brushed, she pulled away, abruptly sitting up straight. She did not try to reassure me that she was all right or appreciated my concern. Her stiff body language and the look on her face were like a slug to my stomach, but I waited to make sure I understood her correctly, and I had. She was in full composure. She said nothing, but she had said everything.

As I walked back to my bedroom, confusion settled in. I had been dismissed, but why? For being me? The realization hit hard that she did not need me for what I wanted to give her. I gave up Maine for this? My mind was racing. My hands were shaking. I felt completely disconnected from her and from everyone. All the joy that carried me at the university had been drained out. I needed a different life, but I didn't know how I'd find one. I just knew I could no longer be my mother's fool, ready to entertain her, to keep her company, while she wouldn't accept me into her life.

Chapter 13

KATIE GIBBS

My mother was delighted when I received an acceptance letter from Katharine Gibbs Secretarial School. Mum had insisted on paying for one more year of schooling, but when that year was over, she wanted me to be done with my education. Returning to college would have required more than a year for me to graduate, and she refused to co-sign a student loan. As much as I wished I were going back to college, I went along with her plans. Keeping my mother happy reduced my anxiety.

The night of my acceptance, my mother and I were sitting down to our usual dinner. She told me again how thrilled she was I had been accepted to Katharine Gibbs. "Well, commuting into Boston shouldn't be too difficult," she remarked, as she fluffed her linen napkin on her lap. "People do it every day."

I sat up straight and braced myself for her response. "I'm not commuting, Mum."

"What do you mean you aren't commuting?" she said incredulously. "You have to commute. How are you going to get to Katie Gibbs every day?"

"I'm going to live in Boston."

"I don't have enough money for that," she scoffed.

"You don't have to pay for it. I've been saving up."

"But you don't know anything about where to live."

"I've been looking. I found a place on Beacon Street."

Ever since my mother had pushed me away in her moment of grief, I had been saving all but a couple of dollars each week. By September I'd have enough for half the rent on a Boston apartment. My mother was not happy. Her plans for my secretarial education included my living at home. Knowing I had disappointed her raised surfable waves of guilt. I looked at my shaking hands trying to steady my fork. She frightened me when I disappointed her. I didn't know what was wrong with me. It wasn't as if she were going to hit me.

"Mum, you can't expect me to drive into Boston every day. The traffic was bad enough going to South Boston. The Back Bay is that much farther. If I live at home, I'll miss out on everything."

She began to argue with me, but I was not giving in. Not this time. The reason I returned home from Maine was to relieve her grieving and be needed, but I accomplished neither.

The apartment I found was in an old brownstone on Beacon Street between Hereford Street and Massachusetts Avenue. It was a few houses away from a bridge that crossed the Charles River to go to MIT. The unit was tiny, just the front section of the third floor, but the living room had a pretty fireplace, parquet floors and a bay window overlooking Beacon Street. I loved it and found a roommate who was coming down from Maine to finish up her degree at the pharmacy school.

On my first day at Katie Gibbs, I walked the seven blocks in my low heels, professional dress, stockings, and accent scarf to the Marlborough Street address. A few years earlier, I would have needed a proper hat and white gloves to conform to their dress code. The school was housed in a century-old Back Bay townhouse. The first floor had been the former family's living area, but it was now the Gibbs administrative office with high ceilings, tiled foyer, ornate plaster moldings, and tall windows in the classic French style. I climbed up the stairs to my new classrooms on the top floor, which might have been the original maid's quarters a century ago. Now they housed the typing and shorthand rooms.

I took a seat behind one of the latest IBM Selectric typewriters and watched the other students do the same. We had all attended at least two years of college. Unlike me, most of them had already graduated with a four-year degree. Their families were sending them to Gibbs for additional training. They wanted their daughters to be able to compete for what were limited business opportunities for women. Many of the girls came from wealthy Midwest families and had already been to Europe a few times. In the end, we became a congenial, fun group who wanted to succeed in business and enjoyed supporting each other.

Our school day was highly structured, with plenty of time devoted to practice and repetition. I had taken typing in high school and knew the keyboard, but I was far short of the Gibbs accuracy and speed requirements. Katharine Gibbs certification hung over us like the Sword of Damocles. A college degree was not enough, the school asserted. There were no exceptions to the benchmarks we had to attain. We knew the rules and the consequences—the pressure was on.

By November, we were becoming more proficient at shorthand. One day our teacher dictated a letter in shorthand class, which we were expected to type out in the next room. As we left the shorthand room, we kept our notebooks closed. There was to be no talking. After we settled behind our typewriters, the teacher gave the signal. We all picked up a piece of paper and placed it in the typewriter carriage. In unison, we turned the knobs to put our papers in position. Little ratcheting noises sounded throughout the room.

"Now, ladies, type your names."

Tap, tap…tap, tap, tap. The sound of people typing their names on the blank paper filled the room, and then suddenly stopped. The tension was as thick as a Nantucket fog. Before the instructor could give us our next instructions, everyone froze. The sound of a classmate ripping her paper out of a typewriter filled the room. No mistakes were allowed when typing your name. We all sat stone-still.

As the classmate inserted her new piece of paper, the tension continued to build. As we waited, we worried we wouldn't be able to read our own shorthand. The turning of the roller and the ratchety-ratchet sound broke through the dead silence. Then *tap, tap….tap, tap, tap* came from the one machine, as the girl retyped her name. Everyone was sitting up straight, facing front with fingers lined up on the home keys. We were like competitive swimmers standing on the block, waiting, waiting, waiting for the signal. Then…*ding*.

"Open up your notebooks, and begin typing."

I opened my shorthand book and immediately knew I was in trouble. The symbols were not translating into words. My fingers were ready to type fifty words per minute. I read shorthand about one word per minute. With all the pent-up tension, my hands began to shake. I tried to calm them, but the symbols made no sense. I looked harder. I took deep breaths. My whole body was now shaking, and nothing could stop what my hands had started.

The teacher saw I was in trouble. She walked quietly over to my desk and gave me permission to stand up and follow her out the door. I was weak with nerves. Another teacher and an administrator met us. Their kindness brought me down to simple panic. The director gave me the address of a mental health professional with whom I might talk and hopefully feel better.

As I stepped outside into the cool autumn air, some relief came over me. The afternoon reminded me of Maine. But at Maine, there was always a congenial companion to chat with in the Bear's Den. Now there was no one, just strangers passing me on the street. The sinking sun left behind only a dark sky, and a shadow of gloom passed over me. Another day was ending. At this time of day, fear took over me, but I didn't know of what—afraid of dying, a catastrophe, being alone, abandoned, knowing no other earthly soul who would be there for me? I wasn't sure which one bothered me the most. Maybe it was all of them. I walked toward Beacon Street and found the building.

Many psychologists rented the front or back rooms of these old brownstones for their offices, but this six-story building was the man's office and home. He invited me into a comfortable living space with tall bookshelves, stuffed chairs, oriental rugs, and high ceilings. He was kind and welcoming. I blurted out everything that had happened to me the past year and added my fear of flunking out of school. He listened carefully, and I felt a little better as the hour progressed, but in the end he said he didn't expect to see me again. Maybe it was my lack of money, maybe he didn't have time, or maybe he thought I was a lost cause. He never said why. But it was okay, I told myself. I was used to having my plans changed.

As I walked back up Beacon Street toward my apartment, my nerves began building again. I couldn't kid myself. Nothing had changed. I had to go to school on Monday, or my mother would lose all the tuition money. But I had no idea how to stop my hands from shaking.

Back in the empty apartment, I thought of how when I wasn't doing well at Maine, I just studied more. But I couldn't study my way out of this mess. It seemed people were either capable of taking shorthand or not. Even on a good day I could hardly read my own handwriting, let alone make sense of those shorthand squiggles. Gibbs told us without shorthand we'd never get a good job. If I couldn't get a job, I couldn't work; I'd have to live at home. My mother and I would become roommates forever. "Oh, my God, please help me," I prayed.

I sat on the apartment sofa and stared down at the culprits, my shaking hands. Their poor behavior was not new to me. They had kept me from playing the solos expected of me in symphony. They almost lost me my summer job at Westchester Country Club. When I delivered my first drink that summer, my hands shook uncontrollably. I tried holding the glass in different positions, but my hands kept shaking. Finally, I placed my hand over the top of the tumbler with my fingers down the sides. I knew no one wanted my hand all over the rim of the glass, so I did it quickly and hoped the club member wouldn't notice. Then I did it a few more times. No one said anything. And then my hands suddenly stopped shaking, as if they had been playing a trick on me. I served the next Dewar's on the rocks without the rocks flying onto the floor.

The next morning was Saturday. I didn't know how I could go back to Gibbs on Monday. I called my mother to tell her how badly I did on the shorthand letter and what an emotional mess I was. She told me the same thing she always did—"Oh, Margy, I never worry about you."

I wished she did sometimes. Saying she didn't worry wasn't the same as telling me I could do anything—she never said that. In fact, my failures seemed to reinforce her preconceived notions of my limited abilities.

Walking was helpful when my nerves were frayed. So after my roommate went home for the weekend, I began walking down Beacon Street. I crossed the Public Garden and the Common and stopped at stores over on Washington Street. I walked all afternoon, in and out of stores, crisscrossing my path many times. The presence of strangers comforted me, but the weight of worry was overwhelming me. My mind seemed hell-bent on making panic and disaster-thinking my norm.

Monday morning came. Nothing had changed over the weekend. I had no idea how I could continue at Katie Gibbs. My panic level was as high as ever. My stroll down Beacon Street made me feel like a dead man walking. All my attempts at reprieve had been spent.

My feet could hardly make it up the beautifully turned school staircase, as I ascended toward my classroom. I had begun to accept that past was probably prologue, but I hadn't given up. I continued to take deep breaths and quietly release them.

The shorthand class began and the dread of failure continued to overwhelm me. I prayed that my body would suddenly relax, but the opposite was happening. At the end of the class, I stood up on wobbly legs, and crept into the typing room. I placed my notebook next to the typewriter. Suddenly a new panic froze me, when I remembered that I needed to type my name with no mistakes. What if the class had to wait while I pulled out my sheet of paper? How many times would I have to retype my name before I got it right? None! Because I would have melted into the floor and disappeared.

Breathing, breathing…*paper in carriage, turn the knob, paper in place, hands on keys*. Letters appeared on the paper in front of me. I hardly dared to look. I couldn't believe it, but there was my name—no mistakes. A momentary lightness lifted me.

A thought came to me—typing out shorthand was not like a typing test where you could never erase mistakes. With shorthand transcription you could erase any mistakes on your letter. My mind was racing now. What if I let my fingers go anywhere they wanted as I read the shorthand? I wouldn't try to control them. If I made a mistake, I could erase it. Oh my God, I could erase tons of mistakes! Even if it took all morning, I could erase everything that wasn't right. With the number of mistakes I could make, the paper might develop a hole. That certainly wasn't "Katie Gibbs acceptable," but it was the best idea I'd had since last Friday, and I had nothing to lose.

I sat up straight, opened my notebook when instructed, took a deep breath, and let my fingers find the home keys. They were not cooperating, but when they were close enough, and before they could shake themselves loose again, I gave my fingers permission to begin typing. I had no idea what keys they were pressing. I expected the letter to look like a two-year-old had been banging on the keys, but I kept reassuring myself that I could erase any incorrect letters. I could erase whole words, whole sentences.

My fingers began moving like an old jalopy, first starting, then stopping, jerking, then pushing hard, and then too soft. After a minute or so, I knew I had produced some typed material. When I got the courage to look at it, I was shocked. Most of the words made sense, and some were spelled correctly. I didn't have to erase every word, only a manageable number. Immediately, the tension drained from my body, and I relaxed. My eraser began eliminating the mistakes, and as each one disappeared, I gained more confidence. It was like successfully delivering the drinks at Westchester. I knew I was never going to be the best waitress. I certainly wouldn't be Katie Gibbs's best, but I was not being sent home today.

By springtime, most of the students had completed the one-year program and had gone home. But I still hadn't certified and the end of the semester was coming quickly. On one of the last tests, I miraculously passed shorthand and became Katharine Gibbs certified. It happened so suddenly—one test I failed, the next one I passed. But before I could en-joy the moment, the school wanted me packed up and gone. It was fairly humiliating to be one of the last students left in the class. As I collected my belongings, I felt sorry for one particular student still waiting for cer-tification. She had graduated from college the spring before with Phi Beta Kappa honors. None of that seemed to matter in business or the world of Katharine Gibbs.

Chapter 14

COUSIN, MOTHER

Soon after I completed the Katharine Gibbs program, the controller at French, Shriner & Urner called. He invited me to lunch at the Hampshire House on Beacon Street. His offer to resume my old job was generous, and I accepted without hesitation. My mother was perplexed— all that money and training in secretarial school, and I was going back to French, Shriner & Urner.

But she had never seen the job as I did. I felt fortunate to have it. My work was interesting and challenging enough that I didn't miss being in a fancy downtown office. I had enjoyed the job and didn't want to leave it in the first place.

I started back to work immediately and stayed in the apartment until the end of June when I ran out of rent money and had to go back to Braintree for the summer months. My mother was happy about my coming back, although she planned to be on the Cape for the summer. Before she left, her doctor wanted to remove some colon polyps. My mother described it as minor surgery; she'd be home in a day. I visited her the day before her operation. Lying in her hospital bed, she was chipper. When I came back the next day, she looked as if she were dying. Tubes and machines were everywhere. Her face was ghostly pale, and she wasn't conscious of anything.

I stood next to her bed, trying to hold back tears. I was sure I had lost her. I touched her hand and talked to her, but she was not aware of my presence. I wanted to run, to go home; I wanted her pain to stop. I wanted *my* pain to stop, but I didn't want to leave her.

The hospital recovery floor was dead quiet. Not a soul was around. Mum seemed to be the only patient. I found a nurse who reassured me my mother was simply recovering from an operation, which I learned was more extensive than my mother had let on—her incision was the length of her torso. I had never seen anyone look so ill. The nurse encouraged me to go home, and reluctantly I did. But as I drove down the vacant, dark streets, my body seemed empty—hollowed out like the town, the street and our house.

For the next few weeks, I visited my mother every evening after work. During one of those visits, Mum suggested I go down to another floor and visit with my father's cousin Ruth, who had just been admitted for a non-life-threatening condition. The last time I had seen Ruth, she had come up to Maine with my mother to move me back home. I had been surprised to see her because Mum never had much interest in Dad's relatives.

Ruth and her mother, Ann, were the only relatives on Dad's side of the family that I knew. He told me he had many cousins all over Quincy, but I had never been introduced to any of them. At the holidays, we usually visited this aunt Ann and cousin Ruth. Then every summer Ann and Ruth rented a cottage in Dennisport for three weeks, where Ann's sister Margaret and her adopted son John would come from Michigan and join them.

John was a teenager when I first met him, and I was about seven. My brother and I were thrilled with him. He was nice to us kids, and he was adopted too. The female relatives oohed and aahed over John—his friends, his fun, his good looks, just about everything—and I didn't disagree. He was Hollywood handsome with his dark summer tan.

When I stepped into Ruth's hospital room, she greeted me with genuine warmth and love. I felt I was seeing her for the first time, although I had known her all my life. She was even my godmother. I wished I had stayed in closer contact during high school and college. My visit was much more enjoyable than I had anticipated. Ruth was sweet and had a joyful, playful way about her. I vowed to visit her more often when she got out.   Ruth never made it home. The jaundice wasn't too bad, and the doctor expected her to recover. But within a couple of days, Ruth was dead. Everyone was shocked.

With my father gone, my mother in the hospital, and my brother in the Army, Mum designated me the family representative for Ruth's wake and funeral. She conferred with me about some of Dad's relatives who I'd be meeting for the first time. John would probably be coming from Michigan, she thought, so she told me more about him.

I walked into the funeral parlor and introduced myself to the other visitors as Dave Meaney's daughter. I was surprised when everyone seemed glad to meet me. After I paid my respects, I saw John come in the door and move through the funeral parlor. He chatted with some of the same people I had spoken to. He was just as handsome as I remembered him. He knelt down next to Ruth's body and blessed himself, as we Catholics were taught to do. I wondered if he really knew for whom he was praying. Ruth was not John's cousin, my mother had recently told me. Ruth was John's mother. Ruth was John's biological mother, and today he was saying goodbye to the woman who had given birth to him.

Ruth became pregnant by a man she had met during her first job after high school. He was handsome and charming.

"Ruth had very little dating experience," Mum said.

Then, because Ruth's father had died years before, my father became the family representative to speak with the young man. Ruth went to Michigan to her Aunt Margaret's to have the baby, and then Aunt Margaret kept the baby and raised him as her own.

John was devoted to his adoptive mother, Margaret. Every summer Margaret brought John back east where he spent time with his biological mother Ruth and his grandmother Ann. Nothing about those visits gave away this secret. As I watched John move about the room chatting with other visitors, I had no idea if he knew Ruth was his mother. Maybe he did. I was surprised at how normal it all was. I had been told that letting the biological mother and the adoptee have a relationship caused too many problems. But John had an adoptive mother and was able to see his birth mother every summer. Today, he saw his mother, Ruth, one more time. I was happy for John. He seemed to have the best of both worlds.

Chapter 15

COMING TO TERMS

By the end of the summer, my mother had recovered from her polyp operation, and I went back to my Boston apartment. The shoe company had been treating me well, sending me to conventions in Chicago and New York City and business in Louisville. Shortly after Chicago they gave me a significant raise, which brought my income closer to what a man might earn for the same job. Life was great, and I was dating my future husband.

Jed Hendrick and I had been reintroduced while I was finishing up at Katie Gibbs, and he was graduating from Providence College. The previous winter, his mother and my mother were at a social gathering. My mother encouraged Jed's mother to have Jed write to me. I received a letter from him and wrote back saying he should stop by the next time he was in Boston. A couple of months later Jed and three friends called my apartment after a Red Sox game and I invited them to come by. When Jed walked in, I recognized him immediately as the grown-up version of the boy I had known from summer get-togethers. His family was one of the four families who came each summer to Mild Bay for a day at the beach. The first time I ever saw Jed was when we were nine years old. The last time was when we were both entering high school.

We began dating that spring while I was still in secretarial school. In September, Jed started law school in Boston. Within six months, Jed and I became engaged, and we married the next June. Our first apartment together was in Medford, just north of Boston. My salary was sufficient to support the two of us while he finished his last two years of law school. He had an adventurous spirit, was conscientious about school, and made me laugh. I had fallen in love with a good match.

We delayed our honeymoon until the end of the summer, so Jed could finish up his seasonal job. Then the week before he began his second year of law school, we drove up to Montreal for our wedding trip. On Sunday night we returned, full of excitement and enthusiasm for our new life. As we were unpacking, I received a call from a co-worker at my job. She wanted to warn me—my office had been emptied. Everything had been cleared out. The company had been sold. I'd be out of a job within a week. My secure, fun position, where I felt valued, was gone. And the rent was due.

I became desperate to find a job and quickly took one at an engineering firm north of Boston. My new boss convinced me I'd have lots of independence in their company and no typing. But on my first day and for the next few months, I was given typing each morning, and the man who hired me seemed to enjoy my discomfort. Before long I learned that none of the opportunities I had been promised at the company would be available to me. The all-male firm didn't allow women in their meetings unless they were serving coffee. "Women here can only be secretaries," the office manager told me. At that point I wanted to find a new job, but I was the sole support of Jed and me. I knew they would fire me if they found me looking for another position. We couldn't afford a week without a paycheck.

I tried to make the best of it, and asked to attend an in-house seminar. I thought my boss would be happy I was taking initiative, but instead he told me I wasn't educated enough to benefit. Then to prove his point, he asked me what the derivative of x squared was. I told him $2x$. After the annoyance left his face, he said I could attend.

The morning after the seminar, a colleague rushed into my office. "What did you do last night? Harry wants to fire you."

I had some idea why. "He's probably mad because I wouldn't make coffee. He called me to the front of the room last night during the break 'to get this coffeemaker going.' I just said, 'Steve, you know I'm not very mechanically minded.' I guess he got mad."

I didn't understand myself. While I was anxious most of the time, sitting on my hands to keep them quiet, I couldn't stay silent even when I knew someone would end up angry with me.

A new man was hired over me, and I was expected to train him in the job, which some thought should have been mine. I had worked a year trying to create a career at that company, but I finally gave up, and went into Boston one day and looked for a new job. New England Merchants Bank made me an offer. The job description showed I'd be mostly collecting loans in the heavy-equipment department.

The upper management of the bank wanted a female in what had been a male-dominated area. But the department head didn't think a woman could collect a loan secured by a Peterbilt or a Kenworth truck. So while the upper management was happy I was on the job, the department head was hoping I'd fail. Within a short time I began to have the same success as the male collector, and everyone, except the head of the department, became supportive.

After a year collecting loans secured by trucks, backhoes and loaders, a branch manager approached me and suggested I should become an assistant branch manager because of my collection experience. This was the kind of position I'd wanted. But when my department head heard I was interested in another job, he took it personally, and he began orchestrating my departure. Devastated at being pushed out, I went to my immediate boss who had always been supportive. "You know I've always done a good job, Max. Why did Hal send me that memo telling me to correct my work or I'd be fired, when half of the clients he mentioned aren't even mine?"

"Well, you know when Hal gets something in his head…."

"But what about the work I've done for you? I uncovered two embezzlements. Remember the guy in New Hampshire who took out a loan, and then never bought the car, and the other guy who was a former employee. The FBI even interviewed me. Doesn't any of that count?"

"Look maybe it's time for you to go home...start having babies. Your husband passed the bar exam and has a job now. You don't need to work anymore."

On my last day of work at New England Merchants, I felt shattered. I was out of another job, and the colleagues who had filled my days with laughs and challenges were going to be gone. I had worked hard to be needed and valued. I wanted a career, but I had no idea how to climb the corporate ladder. Whoever I was, I was not what companies wanted.

The firing from New England Merchants devastated me. Unresolved issues with my mother, losing my father—and what seemed a hundred other things—rubbed my emotions raw. My anxieties climbed to a screamingly unhealthy level. Uncontrollable worries about dying dominated my daily thoughts. I became afraid of things that never concerned me before. The most pressing was fear of a terminal illness. My doctor examined me and kindly said the issues were not in my body, but in my head. I didn't want to admit it, but I knew he was right. I was too anxious, too scared, too worried—and I had no control over it.

On the corner of Commonwealth Avenue and Hereford Street in the city's Back Bay was the Boston Evening Clinic, a beautiful multi-room Victorian mansion. It was the only place Jed and I could afford. On the third floor, I met the resident doctor and two of his students from Boston University. The doctor asked very pointed, challenging questions in a harsh tone of voice. I thought therapy was supposed to be gentle and reassuring. But as I walked out the door, I was even more shaken than when I arrived. I still begged him to see me again. I needed to get better. I would try anything.

He assigned me a graduate intern. Every session lasted longer than the usual fifty minutes. I was exhausted. The more I talked about my important relationships, the more I was confused. If my mother wanted me so much that she adopted me, why didn't I feel it? The love everyone told me was there, I didn't recognize. I didn't know what was wrong with me. It must be my fault. I saw what other mother-daughter relationships looked like, and I felt cheated—and then I felt guilty.

My mother once told me that her mother never hugged her or kissed her or told her she was loved. But, my mother said, she always knew she was loved. When I heard that, I wished I saw things like she did. I knew I needed a hands-on mother. I needed to hear loving words with physical connections. Mum was giving me love the only way she knew, but I needed it differently.

When I was younger, I knew I needed a different kind of love. I watched my friends kiss their mothers on their way out to play. I began kissing my mother too. She didn't seem to mind and I even heard her tell a friend it amused her. I guess I took what I needed.

Within a couple months, the young therapist told me he wouldn't be seeing me any longer. He was graduating. I didn't want to hurt his feelings, but I had been getting worse. My hypochondria was now in full force, and it was debilitating. He told me his supervisor was available to see me.

During my first visit with the supervisor, I told him how my worries were keeping me up at night, preventing me from thinking about anything but my next catastrophic illness. During the second visit, I told the doctor I was feeling worse, but he told me I didn't need to see him anymore.

"What about the hypochondria?" I pleaded.

"What do you want me to do about it?" he slammed back.

At the end of the session, I dragged myself down the two flights of ornate stairs out onto Commonwealth Avenue, defeated and helpless. My body and soul were crumbling. I didn't know how much longer I could go on. I kept hoping my obsessive thoughts could be eased, if only for a moment, but instead every new health issue shot panic throughout my system, as if I had received the actual diagnosis. Every bump, pain, or discomfort became a deadly illness. All I wanted was one moment of peace, but it never came.

Chapter 16

STABILITY

After Jed left for work each morning, I went outside and walked. I had no destination. Walking brought on a momentary relief from the panic, and sometimes I could convince myself that I was not going to drop dead momentarily. I often walked to the center of Medford, and one day I took the long way home. It was then that I saw an unattractive, gray-shingled building in the middle of a thickly settled community. There was no neat yard or newly painted trim. In fact, what little yard existed was dirt. As I moved closer, I realized it wasn't a house. It was a stable. I didn't understand how anyone could have horses where houses were no farther apart than a driveway, but I turned toward some noise and saw what looked like a trail ride coming back.

I stood motionless as the four-legged animals crossed my path. These were the animals I dreamed of as a child, and they were right down the street from our apartment. Maybe I'd go for a ride someday. Just before I started to walk home, my childhood dream reawakened. Maybe I could work at the barn? The thought of being around horses every day brought on overwhelming joy.

I walked over to the stable doors, and I asked if the owner was around. I was directed to an office. A middle-aged man with dark, slightly balding hair was sitting at a desk, and two teenage girls were leaning on the wall behind him. I introduced myself and told him I was interested in working at the stable. He glanced at my suburban-style clothes, and a perplexed look crossed his face. I told him he didn't need to pay me. I just wanted to learn about horses and how to take care of them. The man looked at me hard, as if he could see the emotionally battered person I'd become. I didn't know any better than he why I was there, except being around horses had been my life-long dream. And now they were pulling me in like the gravity of an unseen planet.

"Fine," he finally said, as if any of his concerns had been put aside. "Can you come in tomorrow?"

"Yes, I will be here," I heard myself say, as I thought how my mother would think I had lost my mind. Wasn't I just working at a bank, wearing Katie Gibbs outfits? I even held a federal security clearance at the engineering company. But I was now in heaven.

I raced back to the apartment that Jed and I had moved into three years ago. It was at the back of an old colonial-era tavern. The road in front was the same route Paul Revere had taken to warn the citizenry that the Redcoats were coming.

Jed's first thought was that maybe a real job might be better to get me on my feet and back into the working world. But he knew how fragile I was and agreed doing something I really wanted might be in my best interest.

I dove into the back of our closet and found the paddock boots my Aunt Dot had bought me when I was in the fifth grade. They squeezed my toes only a little. They had been with me through every move because I always hoped for a chance to be on a horse again. Dot understood my dream about horses. When I was in the fifth grade, she bought me boots and jodhpurs and signed me up for my first riding lesson. But that would be my last lesson, too. My parents couldn't afford lessons, and I outgrew the jodhpurs before I used them a second time. I kept the boots, hoping that someday I'd have a chance to ride again.

The next morning Jed went off to work, and I rode my bike to the stable. It was already bustling when I walked in the door. Horses had been fed, but now stall cleaning had begun. The smells, the sights…it was wonderful. Mucking stalls was foreign to me, but I was ready to learn. I walked into the assigned stall with the instruction to get the horse out first. I had never moved a horse anywhere. The few times I had been close to a horse, someone else was in charge.

As this horse nibbled at his leftover hay, I leaned over and took hold of his halter and began to pull his head closer to me. He moved easily. His whole body came toward me until he wanted more hay, and then his head whipped back down for another bite. My hand was holding tight to his halter so my whole body followed, and I went down into his urine-soaked shavings. Someone told me not to let him do that, so I took hold of his halter again and braced for the pullback. He rearranged his feet for balance and then followed me into the aisle.

My hands didn't shake at the barn. My large muscles were all I needed to pick up the manure and throw it into the wheelbarrow. When the contents of the stall mounded out, I was shown a ramp, which led to the back of a dump truck. A long head start was needed to push the heavy wheelbarrow up the ramp. The first time, I lost momentum and the manure dumped onto the floor. The old racetrack trainer, in charge of the dump truck, laughed, but then he helped me clean up and offered some tips. The next time I got a faster start, ran the wheelbarrow to the top of the ramp, stopped quickly and let the contents fly forward into the truck.

Later that day I learned how to brush a horse and pick a hoof. I cleaned out more stalls. I even heaved heavy Western saddles up on the horses and tied the girth knot for the trail riders. My finger went into the side of the horse's mouth to remind him to open for the bit. I helped people get into the saddle and watched as everyone marched down the street toward the MDC woods. By the end of the day, I had no need to go riding. It was enough just to be around those beautiful animals.

I rode home on my bike that first night happier than I remembered being in a long time. I was finding peace. My prayers had been answered.

A few months later, when the schools were all closed for the summer, there was a greater demand for trail rides. I was instructed to ride along and take up the rear position. Sometimes, they gave me a dappled gray horse and sometimes a Tennessee Walker. The gray horse had an unsmooth gait and jumped whenever something frightened him. But every time I came into the barn, he put his head over the side of his stall as if to give me a personal greeting. The horses evolved into those connecting companions I so desperately needed.

By the middle of the summer, my worries were getting under control, and I began to think about my future. Jed convinced me I'd never get the job I wanted unless I finished the undergraduate degree I had started at Maine. So I enrolled at Salem State College, the closest and most afford-able college. It was in the same town where the 1692 Salem Witch Trials were held. My major would be psychology.

As I began my evening classes, other changes came into our lives. We were moving to a smaller town farther north, where Jed had grown up. He opened up a law practice there, and I was pregnant. With all the changes in my life, I had to leave the stable, and the healing horses who had become soul companions—silent friends who knew my pain and gave me the inner peace I so desperately needed. My life had been unsustainable last spring, and those horses saved my life.

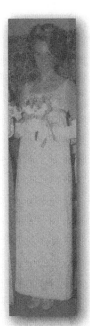

The Dress for Senior Prom 1967

Marketing Picture, one of a dozen provided
by Adoption Agency—6 months old.

Dave and Midge Meaney

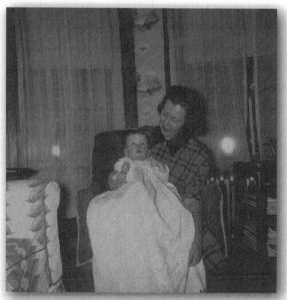

Mum and me, Baptism Day

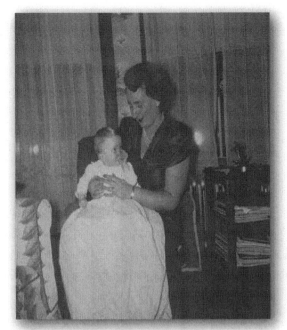

Me with Ruth, godmother

Winter Walk on the Beach, Mum and Dot; Me and Robbie

Independent Spirit—10 months

Adoption Day, April 1950

Longell Road Beach,
Dad and me, 1950

Dr. Seuss before bed in Longell Road cottage

Longell Road cottage, Dennisport, Cape Cod, Massachusetts

Teddy, a gift from Aunt Dot

Aunt Dot

Edgemont Road, East Braintree, Massachusetts

Mum and Dad, outside Mild Bay cottage, Cape Cod

My First Lesson

Wishing I were on a horse—4 years.   Me—3 years old

Chapter 17

FIRST BORN

Our son, Matthew David, was born on the Fourth of July in 1976, two hundred years after the Declaration of Independence. He was due on the second, but he waited two more days and ended up with a celebrated birthday. How funny, I thought, for a child of mine to have such a historical birthday when I had no history of my own.

But none of that mattered. I looked into his beautiful, round, pink face and saw my first-ever blood relative. I never thought I'd meet a blood relative, but here he was. As far as I knew, Matthew and I were the only two people who were descended from the same complete strangers. I laughed at the exclusivity of our club, but I knew of no one else who wanted to join. I had no idea where the other members were, or if there were any, but it didn't matter. I was not alone in it anymore. Matthew was with me. We were the two original members. Perhaps others would join us in the future, but probably not. Information that would connect me with my birth relatives was sealed and kept away from adoptees like me. Right now as I looked at his perfectly formed body, his pale-blond hair attempting to sprout, his curious eyes darting from light to light, he was all I needed. We were one.

When Jed opened his law practice and I started at Salem State, we had just moved up to Reading. The pregnancy was a complete surprise.

I had always identified with my adoptive parents, who were never able to get pregnant. I never thought I'd get pregnant either. Maybe it was a defense to disappointment, but I certainly didn't expect to be pregnant so quickly.

During my first doctor's appointment, I was delighted to learn that all my strange physical sensations were because of a pregnancy. Dr. Bettencourt then inquired into my mother's pregnancies. When I told him I was adopted and didn't know anything about the woman who had given birth to me, he seemed disappointed. A flood of shame came over me as I left his office. I had worked hard to convince myself that I was no different from those who weren't adopted. The doctor changed everything. His question confirmed I was an outlier. I was not like everyone else. I was different. I was one of those few people who did not know who put them on this earth.

After my appointment, I found myself thinking more about the woman who gave birth to me. The doctor's questions seemed to have unlocked a thought process I had put aside many years ago. During high school and college, my family's illnesses and deaths kept my attention. There was no time or emotional energy to think of birth relatives. But now, being pregnant, the woman who put me on this earth seemed important, and thoughts of her interrupted my daily musings. They were not like my obsession with illness. These were pleasant, and they grew every day right along with the baby inside.

These yearnings seemed focused on where I belonged in the human race and where my baby would belong. Within the vast array of people in my town, in the park, at the mall, I began needing to know with whom I might have a biological bond. My adoptive family, both close and extended, probably felt they had given me that connection, but I didn't always feel it. They made me feel like an outsider, like I was barely hanging on to any relationships.

My adoptive parents never acknowledged that my adoptive life was complicated. But I knew I was viewed differently at times, and sometimes treated as an outsider. One night Jed and I were entertaining another couple for dinner. The wife and I had been talking about having babies in the future. I mentioned that I might not be able to get pregnant because my parents never did.

The woman looked at me strangely and in a louder-than-conversational voice said, "Then how did you get here if your mother didn't get pregnant?"

"Oh, yes," I said, "I was adopted."

"You weren't adopted!" the woman exclaimed loudly, as if she were correcting me. Her husband nodded in agreement.

I was startled by their aggressive tone. I couldn't tell whether they were thrilled to have met an adopted person, or whether they had drastically changed their opinion of me—and it wasn't for the better.

"When were you adopted?" The question came inquisition-style.

"I was seven months old."

"When did you find out you were adopted?"

"I've always known."

"Do you know who your real parents are?"

There was that question again. Everyone seemed more interested in my birth parents than I was.

"My 'real parents' were the ones who raised me," I said defensively, trying not to feel somehow less important now that I couldn't produce the relatives they wanted to know about.

I wasn't sure where this discussion was taking our relationship. This couple knew all about their ancestral heritage, which was deeply rooted in colonial New England. They seemed to assume I belonged to that same heritage, too. Now they didn't know where I belonged, and that seemed to trouble them.

"Would you ever like to meet your parents?" This question seemed more curious than accusing.

"Yes, maybe if someone told me my 'mother' was going to be at a certain place at a certain time, I would go see what she looked like from across the room. But I'm not going to seek her out. I don't want to upset her life."

This couple was similar to many people I had encountered who had difficulty with my lack of ancestral knowledge. I dated a boy once whose parents were uncomfortable about my not knowing where I came from. I was uncomfortable too, but I couldn't do anything about it. But they could, and the boy stopped calling me. When each of my adoptive cousins was married, I heard long discussions about who the new in-laws were and who they weren't. Everyone wanted to know about the families into which the children were marrying. I only knew who my adoptive family was, and for some that was not enough. That history telling me from where I came had been taken from me. I wanted to be reconnected to it. I loved history. I wanted to know all about the people who came before me.

My own mother-in-law once said, "I wish we knew where you came from." I didn't disagree, and I didn't take it personally. I enjoyed her honesty.

I had watched people over the years take pride in their ancestors. I often heard, "I'm Irish," "My folks were from Italy," or "My ancestors came over on the Mayflower." I always used my adoptive parents' heritage of English and Irish in those conversations, but I always braced for the person who would say, "But you were adopted, weren't you? You don't really know." Some suggested I could take on the history and ethnicity of my adoptive family, but I knew someone would say, "You're not really my cousin because you were adopted."

I loved being pregnant, and I was sad to think that the woman who gave birth to me probably didn't. I wondered whether she'd had the same emotional issues I had, like my obsession with illnesses. In the beginning of my pregnancy, I worried those "crazies" would come back, but they didn't. I was generally happy, calm, productive in school, and surprisingly joyful. The only discomfort I had was when my fingers began to swell, and I needed to take off my wedding band.

One morning I looked down at my ringless finger and wondered if the woman carrying me for nine months ever felt uncomfortable not wearing a wedding band. The stigma back then of being pregnant and not being married was even harsher. As I left my wedding band on my bureau and went about my day, I felt a strange sense of camaraderie with the woman with whom I had shared the most intimate relationship. My bare finger became a badge of connection between me and a complete stranger, who

I'd probably never know. I took comfort in our coming together in a bond of motherhood, even if it were only in my mind.

Mum expressed happiness for my expanding belly when I visited her in Braintree. I was happy that she was happy for me. This was her fourth grandchild, and she really did enjoy her grandchildren. She already had three girls from Robbie. During one of these visits, I told my mother about the names we were considering for the baby. I thought she would be excited to hear we were planning to use a family last name for our child's middle name. I had always admired my aunt Irene's use of family names. Jed and I had chosen Marshall, my mother's mother's maiden name. But Mum was immediately against it. She didn't exactly say why, except that my aunt had used it already, but that was the generation before. So I didn't understand why that should keep us from using it. Then my mother changed the subject, and I knew the name was not mine to use. My oppositional self wanted to use the name anyway, but my rational self knew my anxiety levels would explode with her disapproval.

When my mother stood up and walked into the kitchen, I followed. Names were still on my mind. I always wondered if I had a name before I was adopted. "Mum, did I have a different name when you got me?"

"Why do you want to know?" She seemed a bit startled, maybe because I had not asked her anything regarding my adoption since the prom dress discussion ten years ago.

"I don't know...I was just wondering." It was hard for me to lie and sound casual.

"You're not thinking of using it?"

"No, of course not. No, I was just wondering."

"Well, yes...yes, you did have another name," she answered.

I didn't expect that. How interesting. She surprised and delighted me all at once.

"Really?" I said. "What was it?" I tried to tamp down my intense curiosity.

My mother looked thoughtful for a moment, and then she turned and faced me directly. "Well, I'm not going to tell you."

I tried to suppress a laugh. *She can't be serious*, I thought as I released a giggle. How could she not tell me? "What do you mean you aren't going to tell me?" I smiled as if the joke were on me. "Why wouldn't you tell me?"

"I don't know," she said casually, which contrasted with my intensity. "I'm afraid that you might like your other name better," she said.

I couldn't believe what I was hearing.

"That's ridiculous, Mum," I exclaimed. "Are you kidding? I've had my name for a long time now. Sometimes I like it, and sometimes I don't, just like everyone else. Right now I like it just fine."

"Well, I'm not going to tell you," she stated firmly.

"Mum!" my voice was rising to those upper octaves she hated. "I am twenty-six years old. I am not going to change my name. I just want to know what my other name was."

When she turned back toward the sink, I knew the conversation was over. I walked back into the living room and sat down in a chair. As I thought more about our conversation, my actual name seemed less important. She had just told me that someone cared enough to give me a name. Maybe they spent a lot of time thinking about it, or maybe they didn't, but at least someone thought about me long enough to name me. I'd take that. I wasn't picky.

Chapter 18

AGENCIES

As spring blossomed, I was beginning my sixth month of pregnancy and my second semester at Salem State. Sunday dinners at Mum's house had become difficult. Her refusal to allow me to use our family name for the baby and not telling me my birth name was building a wall between us. For the first time in my life, I did not care. The Margy who wanted and needed her mother's approval was now a pregnant woman and a mother-to-be. For the first time, my mother's happiness was less important than mine.

Each time Jed and I sat in my mother's tiny living room, the questions about my origins lingered in my mind. It was during one of those visits, when a combination of pregnancy-driven curiosity and my basic impulsivity increased my boldness and I pressed my mother one last time for information about my past.

"Mum, I always wondered what agency I came from. Robbie used to tease me and say I came from the Home for Little Wanderers. Did I come from them?"

I thought she would shut down this query too, but I had nothing to lose. It was my final request. "An agency" had always been the answer to the question, "Where did I come from?" It seemed particularly important now. I wanted to imagine myself in a specific place on this earth at the very earliest moments of my life.

"No," she said without hesitation. "You didn't come from the Little Wanderers. Robbie came from them." I was surprised by her forthrightness.

"Well, where did I come from then?"

She paused a moment, and I didn't like the look on her face. It was the one grown-ups used when they were annoyed by a child's question. Then she said, "You came from a small defunct Catholic agency. It's no longer in existence."

"Really?" Why hadn't she told me this before? I felt like the family dog running around licking up crumbs off the floor.

"I wish you could think a little more about it, Mum. Maybe you'll come up with the name."

"It doesn't matter what the name is. It is no longer in existence," my mother replied abruptly.

Okay, I thought. My mother's dismissive demeanor still intimidated me. There was no regret in her voice. I knew I was supposed to accept what she was saying, but I couldn't do it.

The next day, as my thoughts turned to colors, cribs, and curtains, they also wandered to what my mother said about my agency being closed. If it were closed, then where were all the records? Were they tucked away somewhere? Or maybe they were left on some dusty shelf. Or maybe they had been discarded. Suddenly *I* felt discarded.

"A small defunct Catholic agency"—that phrase repeated itself over and over in my mind while I studied, drove to classes, and ate my tuna sandwiches. I just could not accept that the agency my parents told me about years ago was gone.

Maybe Mum was wrong. Maybe someone else knew more about it than she did. But I didn't know who that would be, and I wasn't really brave enough to ask. As soon as I thought about pursuing information outside the family, I froze. I couldn't do it. I was breaking the rules. I was not accepting my place in life. People weren't going to like me. And what if my mother ever found out? She'd be really upset—I couldn't do that to her.

The records are closed for a reason—for people like you who would upset the system, to keep people like you from finding out things…things you don't need to know. Who do you think you are anyway? Haven't you been listening? You don't need to know!

I hated that inner voice. My head was spinning. I was breaking all the rules by just wanting to know a little more about myself. I was that horrid little girl in the poem my mother used to recite to me:

There was a little girl,
Who had a little curl,
Right in the middle of her forehead.
And when she was good,
She was very, very good,
But when she was bad, she was horrid.

I felt like a traitor for even thinking about pursuing this information—so ungrateful, so selfish—but something was pushing me forward. I was only taking small steps, although they seemed gigantic. I could not turn back.

The next morning I reached under the counter and pulled out the Yellow Pages phone book. I flipped through until I came to social service agencies and then ran my finger down the columns looking for something Catholic—Saint something, Blessed something, or something about Mary. My eyes went up and down the column a couple of times, but I could only see the big one, Catholic Charities. My mother must have been right this time. My heart sank. My emotions were on a roller coaster. I needed to get them under control. One minute I was sure I should pursue this, and the next minute I was a nervous wreck thinking about how upset every-one would be. Upset people weren't happy people. They rejected you. They abandoned you. I slammed the book closed as if I needed to squish a bug between its pages.

I pulled out the phone book again and ran my finger down the list of social service agencies. The only Catholic agency listed was that big, well-known one, Catholic Charities. Everyone had heard of them. So that couldn't be what my mother was talking about. Then again, they might know of a small defunct Catholic agency. In fact, maybe they absorbed all the files of the small agency when it went out of business. I sat up straight. My heart began to pound, and hope rushed back in. Why didn't I think of that before? But then I froze. I wasn't ready to talk to anyone who might be upset by my call. I was sure rejection was one phone call away. I sat back down...maybe I could handle just one rejection.

In another minute, my finger went back to the page and moved along the agency names until it rested on the number for Catholic Charities. I picked up the phone and put my index finger in the dial hole, but of course, my hand shook and my finger fell out of the hole. I laughed at myself. Even in my own house, with no one watching, my hands betrayed me. I hung up and tried again.

"Catholic Charities," a woman answered on the other end of the line.

"Hello, my name is Margaret Hendrick. I was adopted twenty-seven years ago, and I'm trying to find the agency I came from."

I was listening for the rejection in the receptionist's voice and held my breath waiting for a dismissal. Unexpectedly, a pleasant voice asked me to wait a minute. She didn't say she wouldn't talk to me. She didn't tell me it was none of my business. She asked me to wait a minute in a very kind tone of voice. Then another woman came on the line.

"Were you adopted through us?" she asked.

"No, I don't think so. I was told I was adopted through a small defunct Catholic agency. Do you know of any?"

The woman paused, as if to give my question a thorough examination. It absolutely never occurred to me that people would want to be helpful.

"I can't think of any offhand," she said. "What is your name again? Let me see if you were adopted through us by any chance." The social worker put me on hold.

I stood up next to the kitchen wall phone in stunned amazement. This must be an aberration. I was asking for information, which I thought would make everyone angry with me, but now someone wanted to be helpful. I sat down and hovered in a state of disbelief.

After a few minutes, the woman came back on the line. "I'm sorry," she said. I felt my body go weak.

Then I heard what I expected: "You were not adopted through us, and I don't know of any small agency that has gone out of business. I am truly sorry. Actually, I don't know of any small Catholic agencies at all. I even ran it past one of our workers here who has been with us a long time, and she doesn't remember any either. Sorry, I wish you luck."

"I wish you luck." The words repeated themselves over in my mind as I hung up the phone. I stood up and walked around the kitchen in a dumbfounded daze and then continued into the dining room and living room. I didn't know what to think about the whole experience. I felt over-whelmed. At the living room window, I looked out onto the quiet street. I was trying to make sense of my interchange with the agency. I had visions of my mother and all her teacher friends standing over me, wagging their index fingers, telling me how disappointed they were and how ashamed I should be.

Then my heart sank again as I remembered what Catholic Charities told me. They had no record of me. They knew of no small defunct agen-cies. I slumped into the rocking chair we had bought for the baby. I pushed it back and then it came forward, back and forward, back and forward. I stopped rocking. I wasn't going to give up that easily. A new wave of deter-mination lifted me out of my seat and I hurried back to the phone.

The New England Home for Little Wanderers was the only other agen-cy I had ever heard about, and even though my mother said I didn't come from them, maybe I *was* from them, but she didn't want to tell me. I knew she didn't like my digging into the past.

"You know, Robbie has no interest in finding out any adoption infor-mation." That was her way of telling me I shouldn't either.

The telephone number for Little Wanderers was right there in the phone book. I took a deep breath when I heard ringing on the other end of the line.

"New England Home for Little Wanderers." The woman sounded cheerful, but I was afraid again she wouldn't be when she heard what I was calling about. So many people over the years were against adoptees knowing anything about our pasts. I didn't understand why searching seemed so personal to some non-adopted people. "Why aren't you grateful for what you have?" people had said to me in an angry tone. "Your life is much better now than where you came from." They seemed to think they knew more than I did.

The first time I heard adoption being discussed publicly was on TV. It was on the show *Father Knows Best.* I was seven. The story was about Kitten, the family's youngest child. She was afraid she might be adopted. I didn't understand why Kitten would be upset about being adopted. I was adopted, and I wasn't upset. Before that show, it never occurred to me adoption could be a problem, so the episode made no sense. Did she know something I didn't? Maybe adoption wasn't as great as I had been told it was, and that thought scared me.

One of Kitten's friends on the show was portrayed as adopted. She had beautiful, long blond curls, and her school dress looked like a party dress. She told Kitten that being adopted made her special. The adoptive girl's mother and father had picked her out from all the other kids at the agency, and the agency specially picked her adoptive parents, too. The girl concluded this made her whole family very special. Kitten didn't want to be that kind of special, which surprised me because I thought it sounded pretty good. I followed my mother into the kitchen to clarify that point.

"I didn't know you picked me out of all the other kids at the adoption agency." Hearing this, my mother turned around from washing dishes and stated the facts.

"We didn't pick you out," she said. "You were just given to us."

"What do you mean? I thought there were other kids around, and you picked the one you wanted. That's what happened to the girl on *Father Knows Best.*"

"No, you were just given to us. Your father and I drove to the agency, and they handed you over to us. We wanted a girl because we already had a boy. That was our only choice."

My mother gave me the facts, but I didn't feel good after hearing them. I decided to go into my room and think more about it. No one in Kitten's family wanted to be adopted. Kitten clearly didn't, and when Kitten's family found out she had been worried about being adopted, they comforted her. Apparently no one on the show thought adoption was such a great idea. I didn't understand. I *was* adopted, but no one wanted to comfort me. I had to just put it all out of my mind.

"Hello, my name was Margaret Meaney," I said to the social worker at Home for Little Wanderers. "I was adopted twenty-seven years ago. I was told my brother was adopted through your agency. I don't think I was, but I don't know. I'm hoping you might be able to help me." My anxiety was painful now that it had built up to such an intense state, because if these people had nothing for me, I had nowhere else to go. I had come so far. Four months ago I was hesitant to ask my mother, and now I was begging strangers.

"Just a minute, I'll be right back," she said. She kept me on hold a few minutes, but when she came back, my heart sank. "You were not adopted through us," she began. "But your brother Thomas was."

"Thomas," I repeated to myself. That wasn't my brother's name. I was ready to correct the nice lady, when I caught myself. The woman had just given me my brother's birth name. She had the correct family. My parents' names were correct, as was Robbie's birth date. Then her words repeated in my mind—"You were not adopted through us," and I felt myself hitting that brick wall of secrecy again. My heart and soul began sinking. Then her last sentence repeated itself in my mind, this time in its entirety— "You were not adopted through us… you were adopted through Boston Children's Friends up on Beacon Hill."

What? I fell back on my heels and leaned on the doorjamb to steady myself. That was it! That was my agency. My agency had a name. I could hardly believe it. There was a real agency that handled my case.

I thanked the helpful woman and called Jed.

"You won't believe this. I found my agency!"

"You did? That's great."

"And it isn't even a small defunct Catholic agency. It's up on Beacon Hill. It is one of the oldest and largest in Boston." I was practically jumping through the phone lines with excitement. "How could my mother have confused a small Roman Catholic agency with a bastion of Boston Brahmins and the Catholic agency was so small even the Catholics didn't know about it?"

"Midge always surprises me," Jed said.

It never occurred to me that my mother had lied, but even if she had, I would have forgiven her. Fear does terrible things to people, and for her to lie about the agency, she must have been very afraid. For better or for worse, I needed her. She was all I had left of my family, and my need was so primal, so raw, that I'd do almost anything not to interfere with it.

"What are you going to do now?" Jed asked.

"I guess I'm going to call them. I've come this far. Maybe they'll have some information to give me, or maybe they'll tell me to go home and stop being such an itch. But can you believe it? I belong somewhere. I belong!" I yelled into the phone.

"Good luck. I'll see you tonight," he said.

My stomach heaved sideways as if I were carrying an undersea monster, and then a huge kick came up under my ribs. My hand moved reflexively onto my swollen belly. At that moment, I knew I could never go back.

Boston Children's Friends' phone number was right in the Yellow Pages. I had seen the name numerous times without realizing its importance. This call was going to be the real thing. They had my records. I came from them. This was the end. I lifted the receiver and put myself back in the position of being rejected. What if they wouldn't talk to me? Then I would beg and plead. I had no shame. I would do almost anything now to find out something about myself. I dialed the number with all the confidence of a mouse anticipating a pounce from a cat. A receptionist answered.

"Hi," I stammered, "My name is Margaret Hendrick. I think I was adopted through your agency." I felt like a person who had been suffering from amnesia and now needed to be filled in on everything that had been forgotten.

Again, I was surprised. There was no unpleasant tone of voice. No one to say, *this is none of your business. Go home, and be grateful.* This receptionist was a little more reserved than the other two, though.

"What was your adoptive family name?" she asked briskly.

"Meaney," I said.

"I'll be back in a minute."

Before long I heard the voice of an older woman come on the line. Oh no, this must be the rejection I had been waiting for.

"Hello," the woman said. "My name is Mary Burns. I was the social worker on your case. I knew both your mother and father."

The social worker! "Really, you knew the Meaneys?"

"Well, yes, I knew the Meaneys, but I'm referring to the ones who gave birth to you."

Mother and father, I repeated to myself incredulously. I wasn't comfortable referring to the parents who gave birth to me with the words I only used for the parents who raised me, but here was an adoption professional using those same terms. This social worker was giving me permission to think of my birth parents as real people. An immediate sense of disloyalty to my adoptive parents came over me.

"I had a number of meetings with them when they were making plans for your adoption," Mary Burns added.

I sat down on that little kitchen chair and was surprisingly speechless. This social worker knew me, and she knew everyone else who knew me. She had my history. I was dumbstruck. She didn't sound as enthusiastic as the other social workers, but Mary Burns had what I wanted.

"I have quite a bit of information on you, but of course, I can't give you any identifying information." She didn't sound disappointed when she said that. But instead of getting angry, I reminded myself that some information was better than none. "I will be happy to meet with you and give you what I can," she said.

"Yes, I would love to meet with you."

"My office is on the corner of Beacon and Joy Streets. I can meet you next Wednesday at 2 p.m."

"I will be there."

The days crept by as I waited for our meeting. I had no idea what to expect. I knew only a few adoptees, and none of them had my interest in learning about their pasts. When the topic of searching came up, they usually responded, "I had great parents. I've had a good life." I always said that too, because if you didn't, non-adoptees wanted to know what was wrong with you. But my searching had nothing to do with the life I led. I never thought I had a bad life. It was mine, and I didn't want another one. My search was about my roots, my history—what had been taken away from me. My parents and their friends talked about where their families came from. I wanted ancestors that no one could question because I was not a blood relation. I didn't understand why I couldn't have both my adoptive family and my birth history.

The next Wednesday, I climbed up the old metal-edged stairs out of the Park Street subway station and into the bright sunlight. Early afternoon on a clear spring day in Boston was a delight after the long, cold, damp New England winter. I walked toward the gold-domed State House. The walking paths, lined with gaslight lamps, crisscrossed the new spring grass. On my left was the bench where Jed proposed to me, with Brigham's coffee-fudge ice cream cones in hand. The directions led me up the granite steps across from the State House and out onto Beacon Street. Down the hill, I found Three Joy Street. The building was larger than the narrower townhouses along Beacon, which all had brass hardware on their shiny black doors and matching black shutters. I opened the oversized front door at Boston Children's Friends and walked into the foyer. Oak wood floors and walls created a utilitarian atmosphere. There was a bare, open stairway to the right that looked as if it had replaced something more elegant.

Descending the stairs was an older woman, almost nun-like in her plain appearance. Mary Burns greeted me pleasantly, but not effusively. I followed her back up the stairs, and we entered a tiny meeting room with a glass-topped door, an empty old wooden desk, and two hard chairs. She seated herself behind the desk, and I sat across from her. She opened a thick manila folder.

Those were my records! Mary Burns had all my information right there. The key to my identity was less than an arm's length away—the family I came from, my ethnicity, my ancestors, even the names of my birth mother and father. I was starving for that information, and she was full of it. How could she sit there in front of me and share only crumbs of information?

I gave myself an imaginary backhand. I needed to get my perspective in order and be satisfied with the crumbs or I wouldn't get anything at all. I tried to suppress any resentment. I'd be the good girl I had been raised to be, but I hated groveling. My sudden impulse to grab the folder and run down the stairs and out the door amused me. I had never stolen a thing in my life. I settled into my seat and waited for whatever Mary Burns wanted to share.

She began by saying, "You look just like your father," as if he had stopped by earlier. "He had light-brown wavy hair like yours." I hadn't realized my natural curl was showing.

"Your mother was of English-Irish descent. She was a very attractive girl. Her family was not doing well at the time of your birth. Her own mother and father were divorced, so they could not give your mother the support she needed." Mary Burns described my birth mother as having an older sister who had married and had a baby a few months before I was born.

"Your mother worked as an au pair until she became pregnant with you. She had a couple of brothers and just the one sister who was married and had a new baby. The sister worked as a telephone operator."

I sat quietly but euphorically as I heard each detail. Information that would have sounded dull to a disinterested soul was creating a strong response in me. My feelings were out of proportion to the simple statements Mary Burns was sharing. I was hanging onto each comment about height, build, color of hair, and education. Each new bit of knowledge was bringing on highs of excitement, as if she were giving me directions to the Holy Grail.

Mary Burns continued, "Your father was of German ancestry and from the Midwest. He was attending MIT and studying mechanical engineering."

I sat up straight upon hearing the name of his college but said nothing. This meant we had something in common—I always liked science and math. Did she know she had just given me the name of his school?

"He had been in the Army during World War II and was in Boston to finish his education. He was of average height." She went on to say he played the clarinet in his school band. The clarinet had been my first instrument. His parents were still alive. His father was an electrical and mechanical engineer and also had a college degree. My birth father had two aunts, an uncle, and an older sister. "Your father paid all your bills."

Mary Burns worried she might be giving me too much information. "No," I reassured her. There could never be too much.

"You lived in a foster home before you were adopted. You were very attached to your foster mother and the three teenage girls in the family. You were very happy in that home. We tested you and concluded you were quite bright. You were a pretty little thing with delicate features. Your mother married another man while living with her sister, and with her new husband, she hoped to keep you, but his mother was not in favor of that. Your mother finally decided that putting you up for adoption was for the best."

Toward the end of our meeting, she asked about my adoptive parents. I told her my mother was still living but had been treated for cancer a few times. I told her my father had died seven years ago and before that he had received electroshock treatments for manic depression. She nodded in polite recognition that she now had information she had not previously had, but otherwise she expressed no interest.

After listening to Mary Burns share details about my earliest months and the people who had put me on this earth, I was experiencing emotions I'd never felt before. All this information made me suddenly feel very different, like a real person. I thought I had just *wanted* this information. I had no idea I *needed* it. Hearing I was someone who had been cared about, thought about, planned for, worried over and even loved was wonderful. Even if I had been born to people who had no interest in me, at least I now knew where I came from. For the first time, I felt connected to the world.

As I stood up to leave, Mary Burns said I could contact her any time. She had started her career working with my families, and now she was ending it when I came back seeking more information. While I wondered what she thought about that, she never gave me the impression she thought about it at all. She just seemed to be doing her job. I was happy she considered meeting me a part of that job.

I floated down the agency stairs feeling light and airy, not dismissed, not rejected. The agency had treated me as though I were a person who was simply missing something and they were happy to give me what they could. My husband met me halfway across Boston Common, and he listened to every word about who I was and where I came from. As I walked with my arm in his, it was as if I had fallen in love all over again. Feelings of overwhelming love and joy waved over me, but this time they were bigger than just one person. I was in love with everyone—the people walking toward me, my relatives, the family I could never meet. They existed, and I loved them all. I was a part of them. My baby, when it arrived, would be part of them, too. And no one could ever take that away from either of us ever again.

A few months later on that hot July 4th, I delivered Matthew David. As I lay back on my maternity ward bed, I tucked him close to my side. My eyes never left his sweet, sleepy face. I snuggled and kissed Matthew's beautiful blond head. Overwhelming emotions swept over me, and I held him closer. Then I burst into tears. *What if I had to give up my Matthew tomorrow? What if I had to put him up for adoption? What if I could never see him again, not know whether he was dead or alive? What if he needed me, and I wasn't there?* I sobbed for the birth mother I had never met and for all the birth mothers who felt they had no choice except to never see their babies again.

Chapter 19

ANOTHER MOTHER

*M*atthew was a beautiful, sweet baby. I studied him carefully to see if he held any secrets about our shared ancestry. Then my mother-in-law showed me baby pictures of Jed and I could see that Matthew was the image of Jed as a baby. None of me was in his little face. Oh well, it really didn't matter. I laughed at my disappointment.

Matthew was a hungry baby, demanding to be fed every couple of hours. He had been a big boy at birth—eight pounds, thirteen ounces—so I was always pulling a breast this way or that trying to move it into a comfortable position for him to latch on. One morning as I adjusted myself, I felt something. What was that? A lump? No, that couldn't be a lump. I moved my hand around and felt for it again. Oh my God, there was a lump. That couldn't be cancer.

My dormant hypochondria came back full force. I tried to reassure myself that I didn't have cancer. Suddenly my thoughts flashed to a woman in town, about my age, who had recently died of breast cancer. I called Dr. Bettencourt. "Doctor…I have a lump in my breast."

"Are you nursing?"

"Yes, all the time."

"Well, lumps can come with nursing. Is there any pain in it?"

"No, not at all."

"Then I think I need to see you."

Dr. Bettencourt said he wasn't concerned. I was only twenty-seven. In his experience, women my age didn't get breast cancer. "Has your mother had breast cancer? Or anyone in her family?" he asked.

There was that mother question again. My body stiffened. "I don't know," I said. "Is it important?"

"Well, breast cancer can run in families." I suddenly thought of all the women who had been asked that question and gave a simple "yes" or "no" answer.

"I was adopted," I reminded him, feeling ashamedly apologetic, knowing I had just failed to provide him with something essential in his decision-making.

"Well, I don't think there's any problem," Dr. Bettencourt said. "Let's watch it, and we'll see if it gets any bigger."

"Yes, I'll let you know if it gets bigger." I shut the door behind me.

As I drove home, the fear that I might be carrying around a terminal time bomb paralyzed me. My hypochondria, which had been quiet for a year, was rearing its ugly head.

I called my agency, Boston Children's Friends, thinking that a medical condition might allow them to contact the woman who gave birth to me so I could find out if the family was prone to breast cancer, but the agency said they couldn't help. The person I once was and the family I had before adoption, no longer existed in the eyes of the law. I only began to exist after the adoption, so those pre-adoption records were sealed. I couldn't figure out who they were trying to protect with all this secrecy. It certainly wasn't me. I always thought that adoption was about the "best interest" of the child. So how could keeping this information from me be in my best interest?

I tried to settle back into my daily routine, but the lingering worry that I might be harboring a deadly illness began to take a toll. I couldn't let it go. I called a specialist in Boston.

"It isn't very large," he said as he moved his fingers over the lump. "Has your mother had breast cancer?" he asked offhandedly.

There was that damn question again. "I don't know," I said. "I was adopted."

"Well, some people who were adopted know these things," he said in a casual, cavalier tone of voice. His lack of knowledge on the subject, while pretending to be so well-informed, irritated me.

"I don't know how they could," I said. "The records are sealed."

"Oh, I don't think that's true anymore," he said, as he kept pressing about my lump.

I was incensed at his ignorance. I hoped he wasn't spreading that misinformation around.

He told me to put my clothes back on. "If you learn anything about your mother, let me know, but we will just watch it," he said.

"Thanks," I said with no enthusiasm. "I'll let you know."

Driving home, the reality that I would never know the information I needed was ripping me apart. The only one who might be able to tell me about breast cancer in my family was the woman who put me on this earth—the one I was never supposed to know.

As I pulled in our driveway, I began to think about breaking the rules—the ones that were keeping me from my own personal information. I was not much of a rule breaker in general and I had always said I would never look for my birth mother, but I was beginning to rethink that decision. I was tired of being the good girl, the good adoptee.

As I delved into why I couldn't obtain my adoption record, I found that access to original birth certificates in Massachusetts had only been closed for a short time. And the records were not closed in all states, or in most countries. England and Canada had never closed their records. Massachusetts' records had only been closed since the early 1970s, so if I had requested my records when I turned twenty-one, I would have the information now.

Within a week, an article appeared in *The Boston Globe*. A hearing was being held at the State House on reopening adoption records. If the records were reopened, I might be able to find out if my family had a history of breast cancer. I didn't hesitate. I attached Matthew to my front in the Snugli carrier and climbed onto the next train to Boston.

In the hearing room, Matthew slept on my chest while adoptees, not much older than I, stood up in front of the audience, which included government officials, adoptive parents, and other adult adoptees. The adoptees testified they wanted their "full identities" back. I heard their pleas and thought how much I agreed with them. I had never heard the issue discussed so thoroughly and sincerely.

But the adoptive parents in the audience did not agree. A busload of them had arrived from western Massachusetts for the sole purpose of keeping the records closed. They saw us adoptees as destroyers of their families. If the records opened up, they imagined their families would crumble. They did not see any semblance between their children's future and our current needs. I didn't understand how they could adopt children, yet have so little empathy for us. Weren't we just like their children? The only difference was that we had grown up, but their children would also grow up someday.

I went home discouraged, and the lump wasn't gone. It was on my mind much too often, although I was trying to keep my obsession under control. I was busy with my new baby, going to school, and I had begun keeping the books for my husband's law practice. If the doctors were really worried about my lump, I told myself every day, they would have done more. Then that unwelcomed inner voice piped up, *but what if you are the exception? Doctors can make mistakes.* Then I was back chasing the tail of my damn neurosis again.

For years I had assured myself and anyone who asked about my adoption that I was never going to search for my biological mother. I was quickly becoming less confident about that decision. If I were truly honest, I had always wanted to know who my birth mother was, but I never let myself be honest because it made me feel disloyal to my adoptive parents. After much thought, I finally came to the conclusion that a medical issue justified searching for my birth mother.

One morning a TV talk show hosted an adoption organization, which was sympathetic to searching. I called the station and asked if they had contact information. They directed me to the head of the organization. She was part of an underground network, which could circumvent the secrecy barrier of sealed adoption records. They had people who could find out the information I was looking for. She would call someone, and I would eventually receive a call back. The phone rang one afternoon.

"Hello?" I heard a woman on the other end of the phone. "Is Margaret Hendrick there?"

"Yes, this is she," I answered, trying to place the voice.

"Your name was Marcia Lynn," the voice said. "That is Marcia with a C, not an S-H. Your mother's married name was Ann Holbrook."

I couldn't believe what I was hearing. This woman had seen my original birth certificate. I stood silently, taking in what she was saying. "What is my father's name?" I asked.

"There is no father's name. They didn't allow fathers' names on unmarried birth certificates back then, even if they asked to be."

"Oh," I said, "I didn't know that."

Although my immediate quest was to find my birth mother and her health information, I was beginning to have thoughts about my father, too. This biological father and I seemed to have a lot in common, but I had to stop thinking about him. No way was I going to find a man whose name wasn't even in the record.

Just thanking the stranger on the phone for the information seemed hardly enough, but she was gone quickly. *Marcia with a C*, I repeated to myself. Why would someone use a different spelling? I laughed to myself when I remembered how I hated the name Marsha when I was growing up.

I felt strangely empowered with this new information and I suddenly had a strong urge to see that original birth certificate. I wanted to hold it, to see my first name in print. The only birth certificate I had ever seen was the revised one with my second name, Margaret Helen Meaney; even that one I didn't see until I was applying to colleges.

One afternoon during my senior year of high school, I was putting the finishing touches on a college application packet and inserting my revised birth certificate. I looked down and noticed my place of birth. It was listed as Brookline, Massachusetts.

"Hey, Mum," I yelled into the kitchen. "I thought I was born in Boston. My birth certificate says I was born in Brookline." I kept yelling because I was too lazy to get off my bed and walk into the kitchen.

"Oh, yes," she called back. "You were born in Brookline."

"But you always told me I was born in Boston," I yelled back.

"Boston, Brookline—it's all the same," she called from the kitchen.

"Not to the people who live there," I muttered to myself.

Not to me either, I thought, as I stared at the paper in front of me and realized after all these years, I had never known where I was born. Brookline was an attractive, desirable community just outside of Boston. Boston was a city and complicated, like any large city.

"Mum, why did you tell me I was born in Boston?"

"Oh, I don't know. What difference does it make?" she yelled back. I guess it didn't make any difference to her, but it wasn't her birthplace we were talking about. It was mine.

Chapter 20

An Era Ends

Erik Erikson, the great psychological theorist whose work I studied in college, found that processing emotional milestones was an important part of healthy human   development. Somehow the identity milestone was only important for those people who weren't adopted. No one seemed to care if we adoptees suffered the neurotic consequences of an unprocessed identity. I didn't understand why I was less important than other citizens. I paid my taxes, didn't I?

I felt sorry for my mother, though. Not every adopted child was as focused as I was on her adoption history. Many adoptees were accepting and less questioning. I wished my mother had been given a girl who was more like the one she wanted—quiet, petite, a book reader, a doll player, not a challenger. Maybe the first baby she turned down would have been a better match.

The non-identifying information the agency gave me and identifying information the woman on the phone gave me were a good beginning to start a serious search. If I used both, I might find where my birth mother was living after I was born and perhaps piece together where she now lived.

I heard about the state Vital Statistics office, where the state birth, marriage, and death records were kept in downtown Boston. The outside of the building looked like any early twentieth-century architecture, but inside was new construction of steel and cement. I stepped into the brutalist-style hallway and felt colder inside than I had outside in the dark, drizzly November day.

The name on the door said Vital Statistics. I stepped inside. A woman was sitting at a desk. I told her I was interested in doing some genealogical research. She recited the rules of the stacks—if I were interested in any births or marriages, I needed to show her those volumes before I looked at them myself.

"Why?" I asked.

"Because there are illegitimate births mixed in with those records and I have to check to make sure the one you are looking for is not missing a father."

"But if you can't show me one of the records, then I will know that the person I was looking for was illegitimate, won't I?"

Her look made me realize I should stop asking questions, or she might not allow me in the stacks at all. Why was this clerk able to see my birth certificate when that book was open to my page, but I would never be allowed to see it?

She led me into the records area, where other curious folks were opening and closing books. The rows of shelves were filled with what appeared to be record books. I pulled out the marriage index, but neither my birth mother's maiden nor married name appeared. That was a surprise. It never occurred to me she hadn't married in Massachusetts.

I didn't know what to think. I hit a dead end before I even knew I was on a road. Maybe she wasn't even born in Massachusetts. I flipped through the birth index to see if I could find her birth, and there it was. She *had* been born in Massachusetts. I went to the appropriate volume and page and saw the certificate, which had both her mother's and father's names. Her mother's name was Margaret! I laughed when I saw it. My adoptive family had named me after my birth grandmother, but they didn't know it. I looked back at my birth mother's name and moved my finger across it. I stood quietly and thought how this was the woman who gave me life. She had been the most important person in the world to me, until she wasn't.

Since I knew my birth mother's parents' names, I decided to look up her sister's birth. She would have been a few years older than my birth mother and had the same last name and parents. Then I found it—the sister's birth record was right there. I put the book back on the shelf and wondered if the sister's marriage record was also here. I pulled out the marriage index again. Mary Burns had told me the sister had been married before I was born. There it was—the sister's marriage. She married a man from a different town than where she had been born, and it looked as if the wedding took place in that other town.

Finally, at closing time, I stood up and retraced my steps toward the front door. The raw November wind whipped off the harbor now. I ran to the subway entrance for cover. A few names and dates raced through my mind on the train home, but when I pulled out the notes, nothing of importance caught my attention.

I exited the train in Reading. As I walked down the wet, shiny, tree-lined sidewalk, I wrapped my coat tighter. The rain had stopped, but the wind and cold air went right through me. I laughed when I thought of how I had been warmer in the dry, cold air of Maine than I was now in the damp of Boston. Shadows moved under my feet as the streetlights shone through the upper branches. I watched as windows lit up in the houses along the street. People were arriving home and settling in with their families. A wave of isolation made me feel disconnected from everything. I thought of all the people on this street, in this town, everywhere, and I could never know whether or not I were related to any of them. I felt like a pinball bouncing off the game's obstructions, and never finding the right hole.

As the drizzle began to fall again, I picked up my pace, rounded the corner, and then I saw our porch light. I hurried up the steps and pushed open the heavy front door. My husband was in the kitchen with Matthew in his arms. Jed handed him over to me for a feeding. I sat down at the kitchen table as Jed kept preparing supper.

"How'd it go? Did you find anything?" he asked as he stirred the spaghetti sauce.

"I don't know. I have to sort through my notes, but nothing jumped out at me. I had hoped to find my birth mother's marriage, but I didn't. I found her birth, though." I put Matthew on my shoulder and coaxed out a burp. "But that doesn't really get me anywhere."

"Don't worry. You'll find what you're looking for one of these days."

"Or I might not. If I can't find any of these people, I might never know where I came from or anything about family illnesses. I thought I would find my birth mother easily once I knew her name, but now I'm beginning to think I may never find her."

I stood up, put Matthew in his infant seat, pulled a couple of plates from the cabinet, and put them on the table. "Do you remember the sister the agency mentioned? I think I found her marriage record. She may have married a man who lived just west of Boston. Maybe she settled down where they were married," I said, as I watched Jed pour the heated sauce over the noodles.

I grabbed the forks and knives out of the drawer, sliced some pieces off a loaf of Italian bread, and put it on the table.

"Maybe they still live there," Jed said.

I moved three-month-old Matthew into position so he could join us at the table. "I don't know. That'd be too easy. Then again, if they don't live there, I don't have anything else to go on. It's the only lead I have."

After I sprinkled the Parmesan cheese on my spaghetti, I paused to feel for the lump on my breast. It was still there, but it didn't seem any larger… or maybe it was. I chided myself about whether I would let myself have a normal night or focus on that damn lump. For the moment, the medical obsession was pushed to the back of my mind as I wondered if my biological mother's sister might live right in the area.

"I don't want to bother her," I said to Jed. "I don't know what other choice I have. She did know me, you know, so I wouldn't be a total surprise. Unwanted, perhaps, but not unknown."

"Why not keep looking?" Jed said. "There's no real rush. I know you're worried about that lump. Don't you think the doctor would have done something if he thought you had cancer?"

"I don't know. That woman who died went back to her doctor a number of times before the doctor finally figured out what she had. I keep telling myself that's not me, but you know me. I worry about everything." I buttered another bite of bread. "You know, I wouldn't be running around like a weirdo looking into people's business if the records were accessible. If one of those Massachusetts legislators were adopted, those records would be opened in a nanosecond," I said.

Jed laughed. "Are you going to stay on your soapbox?" my husband asked with a smile that said he had listened patiently to my latest "fairness" speech.

"Maybe," I smirked. "I know I get a little pushy."

I walked up the stairs to get Matthew ready for bed. I hadn't decided whether I'd contact the aunt if I found her in the phone book—in fact, I had no desire to at that moment—but I was curious to see if she still lived around here. After Matthew fell asleep, I rushed downstairs and pulled out the local phone books. The large one was for Boston, but the three smaller ones were for the north, south, and west suburbs. There was no "east" phone book. If you lived east of Boston, you'd either be drowning in Boston Harbor or living on an inhospitable island. I looked at the maps on the phone book covers. I opened the "west" book, and ran my finger down the A's. Oh my heavens, the sister's married name was *right there!* It wasn't even her husband's name. It was hers. That must be her, but this was too easy. It couldn't be her! I was bursting, but I didn't know if it were from excitement or fear. A real blood relative could be living nearby.

"Jed," I yelled into the living room. "She's right here in the phone book." I rushed into the living room to show him what I had found. I knew about her town. It was in the Bay State League just like Braintree. I played field hockey and basketball at that high school. I marched on the football field with the band. I could have played against a first cousin in sports and not even known it. My mind was racing with excitement as I wrote down the aunt's number, but when I thought about actually making the call I feared I wouldn't be able to keep a coherent thought in my head. If I stayed on this anxiety level, I wouldn't even remember my own name, so I wrote out a script.

"Hello, my name is Margaret Hendrick." I laughed to think I needed this prompt. "I don't want to bother you. Are you Marie Allen? Do you have a sister named Ann Holbrook? My name is Marcia Lynn."

I took a deep breath. I picked up the phone and dialed the number. An older woman answered. I began reading my script. I even read my own name because, in fact, I had forgotten it. The woman listened patiently to my questions and answered "yes" each time. I had the fleeting thought that I should just skip to the end, but then I was suddenly there.

"My name is Marcia Lynn," I said. It sounded unnatural, as though I were pretending to be someone I wasn't.

Then I heard, "Oh…Marcia! It is so good to hear from you. I'm so glad you called. I always wondered what happened to you. Could you wait just a minute while I change phones?"

I waited, and almost immediately the woman came back on the phone. She seemed delighted to hear from me—I wasn't ready for that. This was not what I had anticipated. I thought I might get an answer or two before she hung up. Or if she did talk to me, by the end of the call, I'd know it was the last. She seemed so open and friendly, as if she had been anticipating my call.

As soon as I had the chance, I asked her about any family breast cancer. She paused a moment, "No, I don't think so. I don't know of any." The tension, which had frozen me so often in a paralyzing state of anxiety, began to melt.

The thought crossed my mind that I didn't have to bother this woman anymore, but I didn't feel I had control over the conversation. This aunt wanted to tell me all about the family, and I wanted to hear it. She covered details about my mother, her mother, her brothers and their children, and her children, whom she called "your cousins." I asked about whether her children played sports or had been in the band, but our interests were not similar, and I felt a bit disappointed. She asked about me and my family. I couldn't believe how normal the conversation was.

"Your mother will be so happy to hear from you," she blurted out.

I was stunned at her conclusion. She told me where my birth mother was living and what her family looked like. The man she had married right after I was born was no longer her husband. Now she was happily married to another man.

"I'll call your mother," Marie said. "I know she will be delighted."

"You don't want me to call her?" I asked.

"Oh, no, that's all right. It might be better hearing it from me."

"Thank you," I said. I was glad because I was in no condition to make that call. If I had found my birth mother's number instead my aunt's, I might have hesitated to make any call. Fortunately, this aunt seemed excited. If I had stopped her and told her I didn't want to pursue it any further, I was afraid I would hurt her feelings.

I began to worry that we might be catching my birth mother at a bad time. The aunt reassured me we weren't. Then I thought of how life often catches us at bad times. It certainly wasn't a good time for me to find a lump on my breast when I was in the middle of new motherhood bliss. It wasn't a good time to lose my father when I was trying to finish college, and it certainly wasn't a good time for my mother to get sick and my aunt to die when I was a junior in high school. By all the crying I reportedly did when I was removed from my foster home, that must not have been a good time either.

When my aunt removed the anxiety of calling my birth mother, I felt an immediate sense of relief. I hadn't really been ready to make the connection. I never imagined even knowing her, and now she was only a phone call away. I didn't know when I'd be ready. I was overwhelmed.

My husband and I settled into the living room with TV for a distraction, trying not to focus on the aunt's call to my birth mother. The worry of being rejected by this birth mother was running very high, but I didn't want to lose the chance that I might hear from her. As soon as I allowed myself to think honestly, I knew I wanted to make the connection.

As a half hour turned into an hour, I became afraid the sister might have been wrong. My birth mother might have been horrified to know I'd found her. I tried to prepare myself for rejection. I could handle it, I told myself. I knew the family medical history. If the phone didn't ring, that was okay. I didn't want to rush anyone. I began to create excuses of why she might not call—she might not be home, or she might not want a connection tonight, next week, in a month, or ever. I was trying to see how it would feel if she never called—relieved and devastated at the same time.

Then the phone rang. Jed and I both jumped. I panicked and told him he had to answer it—I wasn't ready. Hadn't I just wanted medical information? Now I had it. I didn't anticipate a whole new family forming in one night. I didn't know what to make of it. I had grown up in a small family with people who were more disconnecting than connecting. This aunt was the opposite. She made me feel like part of the family, and I hadn't even met her.

I listened while my husband talked to someone on the phone. He shared pleasantries with what sounded like a man. "Well, I don't know that she is looking for anything in particular. I know she has had some medical concerns and was wondering about your wife's medical history."

My heart sank from a place I didn't know it had risen to. The conversation sounded as if the man was hesitant about my contacting his wife. The aunt had been mistaken, and I had been fooling myself. There was no connecting theme here. The person on the other end of the line was more questioning than conversational. My birth mother must be upset. I feared the opportunity about which I had been thrilled and terrified might be slipping away. I needed to talk with this man, whoever he was. My birth mother was so close, and I couldn't just let her go.

I signaled to Jed that I wanted to talk. He handed me the receiver. The man repeated the same questions I had heard Jed answer, and I gave him the same answer, "I really don't want anything except some medical information."

While we talked, he excused himself every so often to speak with what sounded like an emotionally distraught woman in the background. That must be her. *Oh my God, my birth mother was right there.*

It was almost too much to believe—she was so close. Her emotions were melting me. I wanted to reassure her that I would never bother her again. I just wanted to hear her voice. I wanted to hear the answer to the medical question one more time. "Could I talk to her?" I finally asked her husband. I wanted to alleviate the pain I was hearing.

Her husband went away from the receiver, and when he came back, he said, "Well, yes…yes, of course, you may."

A moment later, I heard a woman's voice come on the phone. She was crying so sadly, and between sobs I heard, "I'm sorry. I'm so sorry." I ached when I heard her pleas.

Every time she said she was sorry, I said, "It's okay. There's nothing to be sorry about. Everything is fine. I'm fine. All is good. Please don't be upset."

I tried to find the right words to take her pain away, but nothing seemed to be working, so I just repeated what I had said before. "Everything is fine with me. You have nothing to apologize for. Please don't be sorry. I've had a good life."

As I already knew from my own experience, Mother Nature wouldn't let you cry forever, and my birth mother was eventually able to control her sadness, and then we talked. She asked me about my life. She told me about her son, my half-brother, and what was happening in her family. I asked her about the breast cancer. She said she didn't know of any. Relief calmed me once again. We shared stories as if I were talking to an old friend. It was a wonderful, light, lovely conversation. We talked about meeting sometime. She was living out of state but making plans to move back to the Boston area. We both decided that when she came up the next weekend to look at houses, we would meet. She wanted to come to our house. She thought it would be better for me to meet her in a familiar place.

"Why don't you come for dinner?" I suggested.

"Oh, no, dear, you will have enough on your mind with us meeting for the first time. We can do that some other time." How wonderful—she was thinking of my feelings and "another time" too.

Our conversation finally ended. I was spent. Yesterday, I didn't know where I belonged in the human race. Now I knew precisely who my mother's side of the family was. Emotions I had stuffed deep inside were bubbling up uncontrollably. It was as if someone had left the gate open, and I had the joy of escaping. My mind threw caution to the wind. Everything I could possibly feel was rushing to the surface.

Throughout the week, I thought of my birth mother every moment of every day. I had that strange yearning like when you haven't seen someone in a long time, except I had never met her. I wished there was a book about what to expect in these reunions because I could never have anticipated the intensity of emotions I was feeling.

I worried that my mother Midge would make her weekly call and notice my unusual excitement. She'd want to know what was going on, and I couldn't tell her. She'd never understand, and I couldn't hurt her. I knew I'd calm down eventually. Someday I'd have control of my feelings again.

Chapter 21

THE MEETING

A couple of days later, I received a lovely note and a picture of my birth mother and her husband after their wedding outside Trinity Church in Newport, Rhode Island. When Saturday arrived, I knew she had been right. I was in no condition to make dinner. The week-long wait had felt like a year, and all day Saturday I was like a child anticipating Christmas.

After supper, Jed and I settled into the living room, rising intermittently whenever a set of headlights passed by. Maybe she wasn't coming after all. I began pacing between rooms. A car finally halted in front of our rented duplex. A tingle of nerves ran up my spine. *Was I really meeting the woman who knew me before anyone else—the person who put me on this earth, who was actually there on the day I was born?* All the past musings about her were unimportant now. The actual person was coming. We had been as close as two humans could be…attached and inseparable, until we weren't. Our long, twenty-seven year separation was inconceivable now. I heard footsteps across the porch before the bell rang.

Jed hurried to answer the door; I couldn't move. Sounds of pleasantries were audible, and then…there she was, appearing around the corner and moving into the living room. My history, my identity, and the confirmation that I belonged to the human race walked in.

My body relaxed rather than tensed, which surprised me. My eyes scanned her for the anticipated resemblance that said we truly belonged to each other, but there was none. We looked nothing alike. She was shorter and without the blond hair I anticipated. If she had been watching closely, she would have thought I was disappointed. But after all these years, I had imagined a tall, blond woman. Whenever I saw a woman like that, I always had a reflexive reaction—could that be my mother? Now I realized I had been looking for the wrong woman.

Ann walked toward me, relaxed and poised, as if she had walked into many rooms where new people were waiting to be met, and immediately put me at ease. Neither of us had an outburst of emotion. We smiled. We hugged. We glowed with warmth, but there was none of the "Where have you been?" kind of thing. Her first words after the greeting, hugs, and pleasantries were "You look just like your father." And then she added, "You should know who he is."

I was shocked. I had been afraid she might not give me information on my birth father. I had heard of biological mothers who kept that information to themselves. Her demeanor was reserved, and I wondered if she worried about where this new connection was going. She may have been unsure of how I was feeling and didn't want to jump into my life. That was smart of her—close connections made me anxious. I always assumed people were likely to leave me, and I had a low tolerance for that. Coming together after so many years was a recipe for a complicated relationship, and all of this was happening so quickly. We were two people who had once been so close, but were now strangers.

Ann couldn't take her eyes off Matthew, so I invited her to sit on the sofa and hold him. We sat next to each other, and I looked more closely at her features. I would never have identified her as my mother. Her face was oval and mine angular. While our physical appearances were dissimilar, our body language, use of language, and tone of voice were highly familiar and recognized by both husbands, who sat across the room astonished. We also shared the same taste in clothes and house decorations. I loved the match-ing dress and jacket she was wearing. She complimented me on my choice of fabric in the living room.

As she sat on the sofa, cooing and talking to Matthew, we shared stories about long labors and new babies. She thought I should have been born by C-section, as Matthew had been. She had studied natural childbirth methods like I had. She signed up to work in the nursery after my delivery so we wouldn't be separated. At the end of that first week, she still had no permanent place for us to live, but she had no intention of putting me up for adoption. A social service agency became involved, and I was placed in a foster home. Ann was very fond of my foster mother and visited me often. The foster mother let her take me out in a carriage, hold me, and feed me, but Ann was desperately sad with her situation.

After a few months, Ann moved in with her sister's family. She was planning to take me home and raise me herself. The agency gave her an IQ test, which she thought was to help her find a job or schooling, but the agency had no intention of helping her. The test was meant to determine how bright I was, not her. From the beginning, the agency had always planned on her putting me up for adoption.

While living with her sister, Ann met and married a young man. Their plan was to go back to the agency and take me home with them. But what they heard from the agency was the same speech given to most birth moth-ers: *You need to let this child be adopted. It is selfish of you to keep this child. You cannot give this child what a more mature couple can. We have a wonder-ful couple ready to adopt. You will forget this baby and have other children.* Mary Burns herself told me that last statement.

Ann wanted to know about my life, and she was a good listener. I probably told her too much. My relationship with my mother Midge was strained. With the multiple family deaths, I feared my life sounded dread-ful, as if the decision Ann made many years ago had not been a good one. That wasn't my intention. My life had been my life, but I couldn't sugar-coat some of the things that had happened to me.

We talked and shared and agreed that when she moved back to the Boston area, we would see more of each other. The evening ended as pleasantly as it began, but now we were looking forward to more contact. She promised to send letters and photos, and she did.

Ann and her husband did move back to the Boston area, and I drove down to see her regularly. She talked to me in motherly tones. "What do you think you'll wear? I'm so proud of you for finishing up college." She worried about me at times, not obsessively, but I had to get used to being the object of worry. She never failed to introduce me as her daughter. We shopped for wedding gifts for her niece, my cousin. At the wedding, everyone looked wonderfully familiar.

During one of those early visits, I was sitting quietly in Ann's kitchen when a thought came to me—"You were born. You were really born." It seemed strange, but for the first time I suddenly had no doubt I came into this world like everyone else. I hadn't been plucked out of a cabbage patch.

After the euphoria of meeting, Ann and I became two people with a common bond, keeping in touch and sharing stories about our families and activities. As I spent more time with Ann, the problem of balancing the two mothers developed. I was overwhelmed by feelings of guilt and disloyalty when I thought of my mother Midge, but I didn't know what to do about it. The bell had been rung, and it could not be unrung. I did not regret finding Ann. I sensed a whole new strength in me, and my husband saw both an emotional equilibrium and a true sense of peace he had never seen before.

Chapter 22

DISCLOSURE

Except for the time I rubbed poison ivy all over myself in an attempt to imitate my brother, finding my birth mother was the only other secret I kept from my adoptive mother, Midge. This made our monthly Sunday dinner gatherings increasingly uncomfortable. Every time I saw my mother, I felt I was being deceitful. Even when I realized she had kept the agency information from me, it only made her seem more fragile. I knew she could never see through her pain to my joy, so I kept it to myself. I wanted to protect her. She was still my mother, after all.

On a Sunday in March, Jed, Matthew and I were at Mum's house for our combined birthday celebration. For years, the Sunday between our birthdays was when we had our cake and ice cream. I still had no plan to tell her about Ann.

After dinner, we cleared the table and settled down in the living room. Mum picked up a magazine and brought it over to me. She opened it to a particular page and gave it to me saying, "I thought you might be interested in this." I was excited that she wanted to share something with me. I looked down and saw the article was about adoption. Of course, I wanted to read it. I would never turn down a chance to chat with my mother about something.

The magazine was one of her favorites, *Woman's Day*,[1] and the issue had been published on my birthday. The author was a well-known psychologist, Eda LeShan. As I began reading, the theme of the article quickly became apparent—any adopted child who looked for birth parents was emotionally deficient, unstable, and in need of psychological help. I had felt emotionally deficient all my life, so in some perverse way, I wanted to see what a professional said about it.

In the beginning, the author sounded sympathetic toward adoptees. LeShan mentioned that "wanting to find biological parents seems entirely natural." She then described how the courts and agencies were being stressed by helping adoptees find their pasts. She suggested that it was not right to stress the courts.

Early in the article, LeShan declared that she was an adoptive parent and said, "Some people might think I could be biased, but I don't think that is true." She felt an adoptee's need to know about his or her past was "an unchecked impulse" that should not be given in to. "If psychology has taught us anything, it has made clear that we are almost constantly bombarded by impulses to which we must learn *not* to give in." She continued by saying an adoptee's interest in his or her identity could be compared to people who steal or want to hit someone (other impulses). Her conclusion surprised me. I had never read anything in my psychology books condemning impulsivity. In fact, some schools of psychology promoted it. Then she continued, "A search for biological parents is one of those thoroughly understandable, absolutely human impulses. But it seems to me that in most circumstances it's an impulse that needs to be controlled."

"For most adoptive parents, the most delicate and stressful issues about 'search' come up during the adopted child's adolescence." That was news to me. When I was a teenager, I had no interest in searching for anyone, but why did the article suddenly switch to *her* stress? Wasn't this about adoptees?

---

1 LeShan, Eda, "Should Adoptees Search for Their 'Real Parents,'" *Woman's Day*, March 8, 1977, p. 40.

She surprised me by assuming to know the innermost thoughts of *all* adoptees—"How do I find out who I am? Why do I feel so alienated? What is it about my family that makes me feel so angry? What makes me hate myself so much?" The last one really puzzled me. I had never hated myself, and I knew people who thought I liked myself much too much. The other questions didn't make sense either. I only felt alienated when I was treated in a way that would make anyone feel alienated. I didn't worry about who I was, but I did want to know where I came from. I was often sad, but LeShan never mentioned that.

Her presumption, that she knew how her daughter or other adoptees felt, was patronizing. She wasn't the one adopted, so how could she know how we felt? LeShan expressed strong sympathy for the adoptee having to process early "rejection." But I never thought my birth family had actually rejected me. I thought of myself as inconvenient. Then she seemed to sympathize with us adoptees by saying we must be scarred from our early experience, and we should work on our "anguish" so that "disastrous searching" would be avoided. Who was she to evaluate adoptee searches as disastrous? Was mine disastrous? If adoptees were so scarred by adoption, why weren't the professionals finding better ways to help unwed mothers so we children would be less harmed?

LeShan worried about the results of "bad searches." Her definition of a bad search was when the adoptee might be rejected, but I didn't think that indicated a bad search. If the adoptees found out who gave birth to them, they at least knew from where they came. That had to be a good thing. Adoptees were then free to find their ancestors and maybe relatives who might be more welcoming. At least they had retrieved what had been taken from them—the foundation of their identities.

She continued with her observation, "It has been my experience that such needs and feelings can almost always be handled in therapy." That was news to me. When I was in therapy, the urge to search never came up. When I later felt the need to search, I didn't have money for a therapist.

Then the real reason for the article suddenly became clear. "Our daughter assures me that she doesn't want to search for her biological parents.

We'd have insisted that she have an opportunity to explore her needs and feelings with the help of a counselor or psychotherapist…for introspection." Okay. Now I got it! The author's fear of her daughter searching made her take this bully pulpit to report to the world that all searching adoptees were needy and mentally unstable. How dare she use her reputation to say searching was symptomatic of an emotional illness with no science to back her up? How unprofessional of her. She didn't write that article to help anyone but herself. Of course, her daughter would never search with an article and a diagnosis like that hanging over her head. LeShan's attempt to scare not only her daughter, but all adoptees, with the stigma of mental illness was shameful.

I sat back on my mother's sofa, not sure why Mum wanted me to read the article. Did she want me to think I was emotionally unbalanced?

I closed the magazine and looked up at my mother, who was now standing over me. As my eyes met hers, I said in a calm voice, "I found my birth mother."

"You did?" she paused. "How'd it go? Were you glad you did it?"

"Yes, it was fine."

"Well, I was worried that you might get hurt."

Hurt. That was strange. There had been so many times when I was hurting that she told me she never worried about me, but now she was. She turned away, trying to hide some emotion developing on her face. She stepped back into the dining room. I wanted her to stay with me, but I also wanted her to go. I felt so unsettled, but it was not from searching.

Chapter 23

Searches

By the next fall, our beautiful new son Michael arrived. It was two years after Matthew was born that he came to us on a cool, colorful October morning. The leaves were the brightest oranges, reds, and yellows outside my hospital room. We were thrilled to have two sons, and grateful for a less traumatic birth experience.

Matthew's birth was still unsettling in our minds. After a long labor, Jed had been sent out of the delivery room, and then Matthew, a large healthy baby, spent the first day of his life in an incubator. I wanted things to be different with this baby, so I requested Jed be allowed in the delivery room, as fathers were allowed to watch C-sections in the major Boston hospitals. I also insisted that this baby be with me after the birth. My doctor called it the "infant-mother bonding experiment." The nurses called it "let's watch the husband faint in the delivery room." He didn't.

Both of my mothers were delighted by Michael's arrival. While I didn't talk to Midge about Ann, Ann asked about Midge quite often. Ann even expressed an interest in meeting Midge. She seemed to have warm feelings about the woman who was the mother of her birth child and wanted to express them directly. But Midge had no interest in a meeting.

In June before Michael's birth, I had graduated with a degree in psychology *summa cum laude* from Salem State College. My life was too complicated to think about a career. My husband's job was not flexible. I enjoyed our boys, and my birth and adoptive families were keeping me busy. The rest of my time I volunteered and fixed up the old house we bought.

A friend of mine, who knew I was adopted and worked at the state adoption agency, asked me if I would talk to a group of social workers. Although these social workers were in the business of placing children with people other than their birth family, they had never met an adult adoptee. My adoption wasn't a secret, but I was nervous. I found professionals often wanted to tell me what it was like to be adopted. "Well, you were lucky. Look how much better your life has been. Look at the wonderful parents you got." Then they told me how much more important nurture was than nature, although no studies had ever been done to support that. I didn't understand why they wouldn't accept my experience of being adopted as a "professional opinion." My friend assured me it was a nice group of people, and they were simply interested in the whole picture.

The meeting went well. Everyone was cordial and curious, and they seemed appreciative. They enjoyed the way I presented myself, even adding humor. Before the meeting was over, one of the social workers asked if I could speak at an upcoming conference. I warned the organizer that my personal opinions might not match everyone else's. She assured me the group would be welcoming.

During the morning session of the conference, I sat in front of a large group of people and wove humor through my presentation. Many people came up to me afterward to thank me for being open and helpful. A panel discussion was planned in the afternoon. Four of us were on the panel. I was the only adoptee, and that meeting didn't go so well. A social worker in the audience who had either adopted or planned to adopt was angry that I had searched. A high level of tension filled the room, as she accused me of hurting my adoptive family. From then on I decided to stay away from the adoption controversy.

My life was busy enough with regular visits to both my mothers. Some people commented they were surprised that my new relationship with Ann wasn't full of wonder, bells, and whistles. I tried to explain that it was more like any other mother-daughter relationship. We talked. We visited. We enjoyed each other's company.

In fact, I had learned that it wasn't the "bells and whistles" that were important. Meeting my birth mother Ann did much more for me in a quiet, subtle way. The reflection of myself in her was one of the most important experiences in my life. Most girls have the luxury of seeing themselves reflected in their mother over a lifetime. It was why I heard girls say, "I love my mother, but I'm never going to be like her." I never said that because I wasn't anything like Midge. But with Ann I saw lots of things in her that I also saw in myself. We enjoyed the same activities and taste in clothes, but I also saw a reflection of traits that I never acknowledged until I saw them reflected in Ann. They were the same things all daughters see in themselves through their mothers. I had just never seen them before.

So Ann and I continued our visits and phone calls. During one of our regular calls, Ann told me my birth father's name. I didn't even have to ask. She just said, "You should know who your father is."

I was startled but grateful. Looking for my father wasn't in my plans at that moment, but I was glad she wanted to give me the information. I hadn't looked forward to asking her or being put in the position of begging, which I would have. Between kids, meetings, new relatives, and other activities, my life was full enough. I didn't know if trying to find a biological father was even prudent.

I leapt quietly with excitement when I heard, "Your father's name is Charles Wilson." My searching was now over! My identity might be complete sooner than I expected. My excitement at hearing his name made me realize how much more interested I was in him than I had allowed myself to think.

I hoped she was comfortable giving me this information, but she must have been. She seemed confident and relaxed, but she always seemed confident and relaxed, a trait we didn't share. Since he had such a common name, I immediately thought of how easy finding him would be. College alumni books were filled with the names of anyone who had ever attended a particular school. I knew his college and I knew his name. I couldn't hold myself back.

I raced between stop signs on Beacon Street in Boston's Back Bay. My old apartment was on the left, just before I turned right onto Massachusetts Avenue. I couldn't believe how close I had lived to my birth father's school when I was at Katie Gibbs. How funny when I thought about a bunch of us going over to MIT to dances on Friday nights. Halfway across the Massachusetts Avenue Bridge, I could still see the old "Smoot" measurements, left over from an MIT prank, measuring the bridge by the length of a boy named Smoot. As I crossed the Charles River, the round dome at the center of the MIT campus was prominent, and I thought of another student prank that had transformed the dome into R2D2's head a few years ago. The school was always very interesting.

I walked into the library, wondering if my mission was detectable, and became fearful that I would be stopped at any moment and declared an outsider. The front desk directed me around the corner to the gray metal shelving where the alumni and yearbooks sat. "Yearbooks…how exciting," I thought. When I found out the year he graduated, I could look up his picture too. Everything was coming together. Soon I'd be seeing that light-brown wavy hair and the face, which was supposed to look like mine. My excitement was difficult to contain.

I pulled out the most recent alumni book and began flipping through the pages to the end of the alphabet. My finger went down the column of W's and located a number of Wilsons and a few Charles. But as I looked closer at the Charles Wilsons and the years they graduated, none of them were in the class I expected to find my birth father. In fact none of them graduated even close to 1949. One graduated in 1934 and another in 1956. It occurred to me that maybe my father hadn't graduated at all. But I hadn't graduated from the University of Maine, and I was still in their alumni book. Maybe he never allowed his name to be published in anticipation of my trying to find him, or maybe the agency and my birth mother were wrong. Maybe he told people he was going to MIT, but he was just one of those hangers-on at the Phi Gam house.

I went to the 1949 yearbook and the ones before and after, but there were no Wilsons. I thought maybe I didn't have the right name after all, and wondered why Ann would give me the wrong name. Did I hear it wrong? I couldn't imagine that, but stranger things have happened. She had given me his name over the phone, and I didn't ask for any clarification. It seemed straightforward. None of this made sense, but I didn't have the courage to call and ask her.

From that day in the MIT library and for the next couple years, I spent too much time chasing down the name Charles Wilson and coming up with nothing. I searched for either him or his father hoping to find a lead by looking through old professional engineering magazines.

I wished the system made it easier for me. I had two little ones at home. I couldn't be taking time away from them. Also on my mind were the people who told me I should just be grateful for what I had. I heard that a number of times. *Haven't you had a good life?* That comment always amused me. No one ever asked my biological children if they had a good life or suggested that they should be grateful. Of course, my children appreciated what they had, but "grateful" was appreciation with a little guilt or shame added. I didn't think that was necessary from either me or my children.

After spending too much time and having no luck finding my birth father, I started to give up. It was frustrating to know his name and not be able to find him. Perhaps it was time to do my last search and look for my foster family. I had always wanted to know them and thank them, but I thought I'd begin searching after I found my father. Now it seemed as if I was never going to find my father, so maybe it was time to move on.

Everything Ann and the agency had said about the foster family had been positive, so I began to permit myself to be interested. My birth mother Ann said they had been very kind to her and allowed her to visit regularly. I hated to admit that when I was growing up, my foster family was never much in my thoughts.

When I began having children, I thought a little more about my foster care experience. Before that, living with a foster family felt like a holding pen for adoption. When my own children neared seven months old, I realized how wrong I was. Seven-month-olds were lively and aware of everything. They engaged, giggled, loved, and "mama" was on the tips of their tongues. They were inconsolable if anyone but "family" cared for them. My children were completely bonded to me at seven months. Suddenly, seven months seemed like the worst possible time to have been taken from the family with whom I had fallen in love.

Finding this foster family suddenly became a priority. The woman who was my "mother" for the first seven months came alive in my mind in a way I had never allowed her before. I asked Midge what town they were from.

She didn't remember, but asked, "Why are you so interested in them?"

I didn't have an answer. Ann was surprised too when I told her I was looking into my foster family. "They're not your family," she said.

I didn't know who they were, but I was feeling a strong attachment to them and I wanted to find out more. I wanted to know everyone who had been part of my past life. I wanted all my history back.

I called the agency, Boston Children's Friends, and asked for Mary Burns. The receptionist politely told me she had retired. She put me through to the new director. A kind voice answered and asked if she could be of help. I told her who I was and how Mary Burns had been my social worker. She seemed to know my case without checking the files. Then I said, "I would like to know who my foster family was."

There was pause, and then I heard a patronizing tone of voice. "Oh, Margaret, you know we can't give you that information," as if I had requested the crown jewels.

"I know you can't give me my birth parents' names, but I don't believe the law protects foster families. Foster families' names are not considered confidential," I said.

The director seemed startled and told me to hold. In a few minutes, I heard the director's voice again. Her pleasant, social worker tone had been replaced by a businesslike one. "You were in the care of Mrs. Dorothy Shea and her husband. They lived in Belmont. I hope this is helpful to you." I was immensely grateful for the information, but I wished she really meant the part about being helpful.

"Dorothy Shea…Dorothy Shea," I repeated as I scrounged for a pencil and paper to write it on. I had only thought of the foster home in a matter-of-fact way, but now I was letting myself feel excited. No one in my adoptive family ever talked about what good care I had received or how grateful they were. In my home, my birth mother had no status. My foster mother had even less. She was simply referred to as "the foster family."

"Yes, I was in a foster home before I was adopted," I'd tell people when someone asked where I lived before I was adopted. Sadly, most people looked at me as if they were sorry. Now I had a name to attach to this foster mother. The most important people in the world for the first seven months of my life were Dorothy Shea and her family, and I was only now thinking about them. I felt as if I had let them down.

I hung up the receiver and grabbed for the same phone books in which I had found my biological aunt—Boston, North, Belmont. I flipped through to the S pages, but there were no Sheas. I reassured myself that it had been a while, but I was more disappointed than I had expected. I decided to drive down to Belmont. Maybe there was some information about them in the library.

I walked up to the librarian seated at the front desk. "Hi, I'm looking for a family that lived in Belmont in 1949."

"Well, you could try the city directory for that year," she said and pointed me toward the old copies.

I opened up 1949, and right there among the S's was the name Shea, Dorothy and Edward. He was a furniture representative. The street name and number were there, too. I sat back in the chair enjoying the moment— my foster family was real and included real people. I was elated.

The Sheas showed up in those city directories continually until the latter part of the 1950s, when their names disappeared. Did they die or just move away? If they moved, this library wouldn't be any help. If they had died, I might find an obituary. The librarian retrieved old copies of the local newspaper.

Dorothy and Edward had both died in the mid-1950s. They were young, only in their fifties. Sadness came over me as I thought they deserved a longer life. I read Dorothy's obituary. Three daughters were listed as family. Each had a married name and hometown. I felt my body getting heavier, and I gathered up the information I had found. As I climbed in my car, a voice in my head kept repeating that the Sheas had died. They were no longer around, and I wouldn't have a chance to thank them.

I started the engine and pulled out onto the main street. Within another moment I was weeping harder than I had wept since my father died. I was completely inconsolable. Tears poured and poured. As I turned west onto Route 2, the thought occurred to me that I really shouldn't be driving. I could hardly see, and controlling the car through my sobbing was almost impossible. I hoped a policeman didn't pull me over. He'd have to cite me for driving under the influence of grief.

As I drove north on Route 128, half my brain was absorbed with sadness, while the other half was trying to make sense of this sorrowful reaction. I challenged myself—*you only knew that woman for a few months. You wouldn't recognize her if you tripped over her, and yet you have all this emotion. Where did this come from?* I really didn't know. I just felt so desperately sad.

The tears came in torrents for a woman I never knew. I really must be a nut, I thought to myself. How could I be so emotional about people I had never met? My foster care experience was never depicted with actual humans in it. As a child, as far as I was concerned, I had lived in the foster home all by myself. I never thought of a mother, father, and kids caring for me. I knew nothing about Mrs. Shea, but I cried for her as if I had known her all my life. I couldn't stop. I didn't want to stop. I had no idea how this had been walled up inside me for so long.

The next morning I took out the obituary and read it a few more times. Dorothy Shea had been a homemaker. The three names at the bottom were the daughters Mary Burns had told me about. They had been teenagers when I lived in the home. I called information and asked for the phone number of what appeared to be the name of the oldest girl. I was surprised when the operator immediately had a number for me. I dialed it without hesitation. A woman answered, and I introduced myself. She was genuinely happy to hear from me and wanted to tell me all about that time I lived with them.

"We actually hoped the agency would let us adopt you. I was eighteen, and my boyfriend and I were getting married right after graduation, but the agency wouldn't consider it. We loved having you so much. You were such a beautiful baby. We wanted so much to keep you. You were the cutest thing! We took you everywhere. Even if we were going into Boston, we took you. We never put you down."

"My father loved you, too. He usually came home after your bedtime, but he always went into your room to check on you and give you a little kiss. He adored you."

"You were *really* attached to my mother. That's who you wanted to be with, but you came to all of us. When we came home from school, the first thing we did was play with you. You were the most beautiful baby." She seemed to be overwhelmed at recovering these memories, so she paused and asked me how Ann was.

"She is fine," I said and told her that life had been good to her.

"We always thought she would do fine. She used to visit us all the time, you know. My mother let her come whenever she could get away from her job. She would walk you up and down the street in your carriage. She loved you very much."

"Did you know you were our only foster baby? My mother loved babies, and when we were all grown, she thought it would be nice to take in a baby, but we didn't understand how it worked. We found out foster families couldn't adopt the children. After we took you in, we all fell in love with you, and we really wanted to keep you. The agency wouldn't let us."

"We never knew how hard your leaving was going to be. I guess we didn't think about it because we were having so much fun. The day you left was the worst day of our lives. After the social worker took you away, the whole family sat in the living room and cried. We were completely devastated."

Her tone of voice became somber as she recalled that painful day in her and her family's life. I didn't know what to say. I felt guilty for bringing back these memories, and I wasn't sure my calling benefited her in any way, but I was truly grateful for all this information. We talked some more about our current lives, and I think I agreed we should meet. In the end, I never made another overture. When I told Ann I had contacted the foster daughter, she seemed hurt. Midge wasn't happy either. I began feeling guilty that I had upset both mothers. I couldn't handle any more guilt.

Shortly after I talked to my foster sister, I called the agency and thanked them for giving me Dorothy Shea's name. I told them the daughter seemed to appreciate my calling and was happy to hear my life was going well. The director told me she was glad the connection was good for both of us, and then she asked how my birth mother and I were doing.

"Fine," I said. "Ann even gave me the name of my birth father."

"Really? That's nice," the director said.

"Yes, I thought it would be so easy to find him, but I haven't had much luck."

"Really, what name did she give you?"

"Charles Wilson."

"Oh," she said, as if she didn't know what to say. Then her voice became quiet, "I think you need to ask your mother again."

"Really? Why?" I knew why. I had the wrong name. "Thank you," I whispered.

"Let us know how things go. If I can be of any more help…"

I never did call the agency back. While they sounded as if they cared, it felt disingenuous. If they really wanted to help, they would have been rushing to the State House to say, "You remember those families we broke up in the 1950s and 1960s? Well, some of those adopted kids need more information. Maybe we should think about opening up the records." They didn't do that, so I must assume she was just being polite. I truly appreciated what she told me. She could have given me a few patronizing pauses, but instead she gave me information I didn't have—that my father's name was not correct.

I had no idea how I was going to ask Ann about this. How would I raise the topic with her? Then during one of our regular conversations, I told her I was having difficulty finding information on my birth father. "I'm surprised you are following up on him so soon." To me it didn't feel too soon, but that's all relative. I told her the name Charles Wilson had met with many dead ends.

Before I could say another word, she interrupted, "Your father's name isn't Charles Wilson. Your father's name is Charles Stueve." She said it just as clearly this time as I thought I had heard the name Wilson the first time. Maybe I was distracted or was anticipating a name that didn't need to be spelled, as Stueve did.

"I didn't know you would be looking him up so soon," she said. "Are you planning to contact him?" she asked in a tone that said she hoped I wasn't.

"I don't know. I'll wait and see." I tried to reassure her. I didn't have any immediate intention of contacting him. I hadn't even found him yet, and the whole idea frightened the heck out of me. It just seemed like another opportunity to cause someone else pain and me rejection.

Soon enough, I decided it wouldn't hurt to look up this new name at MIT. My anticipatory excitement was gone as I drove up Beacon Street and crossed the Charles River. Now I just had a job to do. I had no idea if the name my birth mother gave me this time would be the right one. I prepared myself for more disappointment.

As I entered the library, I saw the same books lined up in the same place. I pulled out the most recent one and turned to the *S* pages. My finger went down the column and stopped. There was only one person with the last name Stueve, and he was a Charles, class of 1949. My heart jumped. Charles Stueve was right there in the alumni book. Oh my goodness. I couldn't believe it! I found him. I had found my father. The search had finally ended. I looked at his name and then I looked over at the address—*Oklahoma*! I was not expecting that. I silently called out each syllable in disbelief, *Ok-la-ho-ma*.

How could my father come from a place that was so foreign to me? My eyes widened. I repeated the state to myself. They told me at the agency he was from the Midwest. To me, that meant Indiana or Illinois, not Oklahoma. Oklahoma never occurred to me, but I laughed because in a funny way, it was familiar. I had played the score of the musical *Oklahoma* in symphony. I also had dreamed of owning a ranch on the plains some day, although I had no idea where that dream came from. "Out West" was as unfamiliar to me as the rest of the world. "My father and his family came from Oklahoma," I repeated again to myself. Maybe that explained my love of cowgirl boots. Maybe I *was* an Indian after all? The end of my search was making me a little weird.

I copied everything, even his phone number, but I had no idea what I was going to do with it. I might have the right information but the wrong guy. At least that was sometimes the male consensus. I reached for the 1949 yearbook and turned to the "S" section, but there was no Charles. I looked at other pages, thinking his name might be out of order, but there was no sign of him. He may have graduated, but he didn't bother to put his picture in the book.

On my drive home, I thought again how I could not imagine contacting this man. But if the Belmont library had information on Mrs. Shea, maybe they'd have information on Charles Stueve. I called the library in Oklahoma City and asked if someone might look up a name in the city directories. A very nice woman told me his occupation was listed as an engineer and his wife's name was Mary. But somewhere between the first city directory and the later ones, the wife's name changed. The librarian also offered to look at the local census. The name of the second wife was in the census, along with two boys living at the house. Brothers, I immediately thought and got excited. I could have brothers. I quickly dismissed that idea because they could be from the second wife, and they were only in the eighth and tenth grades. That seemed young to be my siblings. I drove home with my new information, but I wasn't sure what I would do with it.

My husband and I talked periodically about how—if ever—we might contact the man in Oklahoma. As much as I was petrified to call him, my husband was not.

A week later, Jed and I sat down on the side of our bed, and he dialed Charles Stueve's number in Oklahoma. A man answered.

"Hello, are you Charles Stueve?" I heard my husband ask. The man apparently answered in the affirmative. Jed introduced himself as the husband of the baby who was born when this man was at MIT. There was no misunderstanding about to whom Jed was referring. Some more pleasant talk was made between the two of them. I was excited, but I didn't have the nerve to take the phone and talk with him. After a few minutes, my husband hung up and smiled at me.

"What was he like?" I asked.

"He sounded very nice.

"Was he upset that you called?"

"He wasn't upset at all," Jed said. "I think it went really well."

"You didn't give him a way to get in touch with us."

"Oh, I forgot. We'll write him and give him that information."

The next day I typed out a letter:

Dear Mr. Stueve: After our recent telephone conversation, I realized that I had failed to advise you of a way to contact us. Please feel free to either call or write to the number or address noted above. It was a pleasure speaking with you, and I shall greatly look forward to hearing from you.
Very truly, Jed

The letter was mailed the next day, and I anxiously awaited a response. He had sounded so agreeable. Maybe this was the beginning of a wonderful connection. I might have siblings, too. He could have hung up, told my husband to go away, but he didn't. Dave Meaney had been dead for almost ten years now. I missed having a father. I missed the things you talked to fathers about—football, house repairs, cars. I just missed him.

A few days later, letters flew through the mail slot on the front door and fell right at my feet. On top of the pile was a long, white envelope. I bent down and could see the postal cancelation mark was Oklahoma. My head felt light as I swooped down to grab it. I fumbled with the flap and pulled the letter out. I looked at it in confusion. This was the same letter that I had just sent. I turned the envelope over and looked at the front. It didn't say, "return to sender." The cancelation was Oklahoma. Then my eyes traveled down the familiar letter, past the typing to the bottom of the page, where someone had handwritten:

> *Sir, you have reopened a very sore subject. I have no information that would be of any use to you or your wife. I may not even be the person you are looking for. Please—do not contact me again. Thank you, CCS*

My body slumped back against the sofa. It was a blow I didn't want to take, but I was not surprised. I understood how he might feel. I had stepped into his life, unannounced and uninvited. He had concerns other than me. I was disappointed that while he had the courage to pay for my birth expenses and to participate with the agency, he didn't have the courage to talk with me. I had hoped he would. We might both have benefited from a relationship. Now it was time for me to let go. It was time for me to move on.

Chapter 24

SAND DUNES AND SALTY AIR

Our visits to Cape Cod did not stop after marriage and children. Midge opened up the Mild Bay cottage every June and closed it on Labor Day. Each summer she expected us to take our one-week vacation with her, but over the years, I had become less enthusiastic. Memories of my father's mental illness were triggered every time I stepped into that cottage living room.

After we arrived I'd settle in and enjoy the beach, take the kids out into the woods, go for walks around the circle, and meander down the right-of-way remembering some of the fun times I'd had as a child with our dog Teddy. Once, I took them past the building we all called the "cranberry factory," and I told them about the adventure I'd had with Teddy one summer.

I was never sure why we called it the "cranberry factory." I never saw it doing anything to a cranberry. It was usually just a locked-up building with high windows so we couldn't see inside, although we tried. It wasn't as scary as some of the other abandoned buildings in the area, which had broken windows and creepy leftover equipment. One summer day when Teddy and I were walking by the cranberry factory, it was open.

Teddy rushed ahead, climbed up on the loading dock, and I followed. We peeked inside the first room. There were towers and towers of stacked wooden boxes filled to the top with red ripe cranberries. Teddy pushed past me and ran inside. I didn't worry about him getting lost, because he always came home, but then a man yelled, "Iz that yah dog? You bettah get 'im outta heeyah!"

I began running after Teddy one room into the next, each one filled with ceiling-high stacks of cranberry boxes and the berries were spilling onto the factory's wide-planked wooden floor. I grabbed for Teddy's collar, but now he thought it was a game and dodged me. As we ran through more and more rooms, the spilled cranberries under my feet made loud popping noises that sounded like firecrackers. *Pop, pop, pop* echoed throughout the building. Men came scurrying to see what the commotion was. *Pop, pop, pop.* I couldn't get away from the floored berries. I finally grabbed Teddy by the collar and pulled him back out the door. We ran home and never looked back.

Those vacation visits were not relaxing. Each day was organized around my mother's beach requirements, which often conflicted with the boys' naps and feeding schedules. This summer, Matt and Mike were five and three, and we decided to make a change in our vacation plans—we would rent our own cottage. The boys loved their grandmother, and we all loved the Cape, the beaches, and the summer fun, but I couldn't stay in the Mild Bay cottage again. I called my mother.

"Margy," Mum greeted me on the phone. "I was just going to call you. I've been making my summer schedule, and I wanted to put you down for a week. I have Margaret and Edith and the Caseys coming. Which week will you and Jed be down?"

I took in a deep breath. "Mum, we are not coming to Mild Bay this summer. We're renting our own place off Old Wharf Road."

There was a long pause, and then I heard, "Well, that's ridiculous. Why on earth would you want to do that when you have a perfectly good place to stay right here?"

"Mum, I just thought it would be easier for you, because the boys get up so early. I don't want them waking you in the morning." That was a lie, but I couldn't tell her the real reason. I'd simply had enough of the old, rusted metal shower, the water-stained bathroom walls, and the asphalt tile floors all through the house, now warped, cracked, and in pieces. I was tired of checking for spiders every time I climbed into the lumpy pullout sofa.

"We're going to be staying near Longell Road," I said with the airiest voice I could muster. "There's a beach we can all walk to, which would make it easier for us. If Mike needs a nap, then Jed can take Matt to the beach. You can come to our beach this year, Mum."

"Well, I just don't understand why you'd spend money on a cottage when you have a perfectly good one right here," she said in her annoyed tone, and she spouted on about that for a while.

Our little rental cottage that year created a true vacation for us. I was pregnant, so with Jed at the beach with the boys, I put up my feet and watched Charles and Diana get married. It was working out well, and my mother even offered to babysit one night. I wasn't sure what brought that on. She had never done it before. I was thrilled with the offer, since Jed and I didn't get out much. Our two boys were adorable, but sometimes a handful. Two-year-old Michael didn't like babysitters and could be quite unpleasant to them. They would hardly have time to walk in the door, when he'd tell them to go home. I'd tell him if he couldn't be nice he should go to bed, and he usually turned and marched up the stairs.

On babysitting day Mum arrived early. Jed was still at the beach with the boys, so she and I sat outside under the trees on the pine needle lawn. She seemed unusually thoughtful. The romantic in me hoped she might want to talk about our relationship. I wanted to understand what we were all about. Our relationship confused me. I hoped she'd tell me how she viewed us, and we could talk about it.

Instead of a candid conversation, my mother began telling me how thrilled she was that my cousin Helen, Irene's daughter, had given birth to a baby girl. "There is nothing like having a daughter," she said. I was surprised to hear this. I wanted to ask her what about having a daughter she liked best, because she had never given me the impression she liked girls at all. She liked everything about boys and their activities.

"Since Helen had a girl, and if you don't have a girl this fall, then you will need to give the family ring back so Helen's daughter can have it when she turns twenty-one."

I shifted in my seat. The ring with three small sapphires and four diamond chips had been given to Midge, as the oldest daughter, when she turned twenty-one. I had received it on my twenty-first birthday. Now my mother was telling me if I didn't have a daughter in October, she wanted me to make sure I gave the ring back to Irene's side of the family. *Okay, I thought. I would keep that in mind. But why couldn't I just enjoy the ring for the next twenty-one years?* Sadly, this sounded like something her sister Irene would have put in her mind.

As the ocean breeze continued to create a lovely afternoon, we sat in the pine grove with our iced teas. The longer we lingered, the more immersed Mum seemed to be in her own thoughts. Maybe she'd had another disagreement with her sister, I thought. I was surprised when she told me a couple months ago about Irene becoming angry with her, because she never seemed to be bothered by the natural off-and-on of relationships. The problem began when my mother shared her honest thoughts about Irene's husband Bob. She told Irene that years ago she hadn't always liked Bob, but her views had changed and she now liked Bob very much. My mother never saw the attack coming.

"How could you *ever* think ill of my husband?" Irene roared.

My mother shared with me her sister's rage, but then her thoughts moved onto something else, and it was at that moment, I had a glimpse of how my mother processed problems. She just dropped them. It was this way of her dropping an argument that always made me feel dismissed.

I was pondering that important revelation when my mother turned to me and said, "You know...your father had his first nervous breakdown when Robbie was two years old."

I wasn't expecting this change in the conversation. As far as I knew, my father's first nervous breakdown was when I was in the tenth grade. For some reason, my mother now wanted to tell me that it was much earlier.

"It was dreadful," Mum continued. "Dave couldn't go to a hospital for his electroshock treatments, so he was given them on an outpatient basis and came home a shell of himself every night."

She didn't explain why he had to suffer the treatments without the support of a hospital. I didn't ask. Mum seemed far away, deep in her thoughts, even though she sat right in front of me.

I didn't want to say anything and interrupt her musings. So my nodding was the only way I could acknowledge what she was telling me. I didn't understand why she was sharing this all with me. Had she told Robbie about this?

"He was a ghost of himself," Mum continued. "Your father crawled up the stairs to our apartment each night on his hands and knees. Those treatments took everything out of Dave. He had no emotion, no memory. He was physically and mentally devastated. It was as if everything that was Dave had been ripped out of him."

Why was she telling me this now? My father had been dead twelve years. My brother was away in the army with his wife and three children.

My mother was still sitting comfortably in the lounge chair. She didn't seem to know I was even there. "Where was I, Mum, if Robbie was two?" I had not really thought out my question—I was just trying to interject myself. My mother looked up from her ruminating, but as I watched my question settle in her mind, she abruptly stopped talking. I tried one more time. "Mum, if Robbie was two, where was I?" She was done, though. She had nothing else to say.

That night I began my own calculations. Robbie turned two in January of the same year I was born in March. He was two during the year my parents were looking to adopt a girl. In June, my parents were offered a daughter, but they didn't take her. Then, in October I was placed with them. All that year Robbie was two. If my father had been having shock treatments any time that year, he and my mother should never have been looking for another child. Perhaps he only became sick after I was placed with them. In that case, they should have given me back to the agency.

Sadly, his shock treatments were likely on an outpatient basis so the adoption agency would never know he was sick. I began putting the pieces together and suddenly a large part of my life made more sense. My parents and the extended family had gone out of their way to hide my father's mental illness, to keep me from being taken back to the agency. When people go out of their way, they usually feel they are owed something in return. I could never have paid them back for the angst and anxiety they must have felt when hiding my father's illness. Only a perfect child could have rewarded them for their efforts. I was not even an exceptional child. I was a run-of-the-mill kid who did not make my parents' lives easy. So what I saw as impatience and anger toward me from family members was because they had concluded their sacrifice had not been worthwhile.

Chapter 25

MIDGE

Our beautiful daughter, Lauren, was born in October of 1981. My sweet Dr. Bettencourt who had delivered the boys, had died between Mike's birth and this pregnancy, so I went to a large Boston hospital for my third C-section. In the suburban hospital where I delivered the boys, I had been given a spinal tap to numb me from my toes to my teeth. It wasn't great, but it was what I was used to. In Boston, the anesthesia allowed me to feel everything but the pain—at least in theory. My doctor was a friendly, funny man who must have invited every medical student, intern, and nurse to watch the C-section, because when the announcement came—"It's a girl!"—a startlingly loud cheer erupted from inside the operating room.

We were so happy to have another healthy child. We had expected a boy because everyone told us after two boys, no one gets a girl. We would have been thrilled either way. I worried during the first two pregnancies that I would not be able to create a better relationship with a daughter than I had with my mother. By this third pregnancy, I felt I could confront the challenge.

When we brought Lauren home from the hospital, my mother Midge came to help us for a week. She had done this before when Matt and

Mike were born. She kept up with the cooking and laundry and was a great help.

At the end of a week Mum was ready to go home, and in spite of my large abdominal incision, I was ready to be on my own. A couple of weeks later, Mum called.

"I'm just calling to tell you I went to the doctor today."

"Oh, I didn't know you had an appointment. What'd you go for?"

"I had some tests last week. The doctor saw something he didn't like. He wanted me to come back today."

"What do you mean, something he didn't like?"

"I have cancer, Margy. It metastasized from my colon to my liver."

"Your liver!" I exclaimed. I knew that sounded serious.

I was listening to her, but I wasn't hearing her. I didn't know what to do with this information. Terminal cancer?

"It isn't as bad as it sounds," Mum said. "The doctor told me I could live another ten years. I will get some chemotherapy, but it won't cause my hair to fall out." She was glad to hear that. "I'll just be tired the next day."

As she talked, I felt more reassured. She had come to the conclusion that she would be around for a while. Over the years, she had always made light of her illnesses, which protected me from obsessing about them. When she had the polyps removed six years ago, she told me it wasn't a big deal, although it had been. When she had a blockage in her colon three years ago, the doctor said he got everything. Now she was telling me he didn't, and I was going to lose my mother in the nearer future.

My mind raced as I tried to make sense of what she was saying. Was she worried and holding back so I wouldn't fall apart? She didn't like anyone falling apart. Or was she taking this issue as she had most of her life, stoically? Even when my father was at his worst, she seemed calm more often than not. She handled this thing called life much better than I did. I wanted to say something reassuring, but nothing came out. All I could do was say I was sorry, but that seemed inadequate.

"I guess everyone has to go sometime," my mother said, "And this will just be the way I go." I didn't know whether I should agree or object to such talk. "I wish I were going to have more time," she added, "but you get what you get."

I ached for this woman. I didn't think she could be as resigned as she sounded. She was trying to have an intimate conversation with me, and I didn't know how to do it. We seldom did. I had never anticipated talking to her about when she was going to die. Even with all her illnesses, I somehow never expected that she would.

I wanted to stay on the phone and be a comfort to her, but I didn't know how. I had never been able to comfort her, even when I was really trying. Now my three little ones needed to be fed and put to bed. I felt so inadequate. "Mum, I'll call you in the morning," was all that came out.

I tried to grasp in small doses what she had told me, and then I didn't want to think about it. Life was already complicated. Our three-year-old had been hospitalized for asthma, and I was struggling to balance his medications. Our five-year-old had gone through two operations before he was three. And Lauren wasn't sleeping through the night. My body, mind, and soul were raw. I wanted to give my mother what she needed, but I had no idea what that was.

During her chemotherapy treatments, I drove down to Braintree to visit, and sometimes she'd drive up and visit me. She told me the chemo wasn't that bad. I convinced myself that she could live the ten years the doctor said was possible.

A full year passed before we were confronted with her diagnosis again. Mum decided to go to her sister Irene's for Thanksgiving. We went to New Jersey to visit Jed's brother. I called Irene just before we left New Jersey on our way home to say we'd be stopping by, but she said my mother had already left. She had not been herself all weekend, falling asleep and being drowsy most of the time, so Irene thought it best if she went home rather than upset the company Irene was expecting later that day.

Three hours later we pulled into my mother's driveway in Braintree. Her blue Chevy was parked in front of the garage. Jed walked around my mother's car and pointed out a dent in the front fender and scrapes down the side doors. I had never known my mother to have an accident. We hurried up the back steps.

As I walked through the kitchen, I could tell something was terribly wrong. While my mother was not the best housekeeper, she cleaned dishes and counters well. That day, dishes cluttered the sink, food was left on the table, and large burn marks were on the stove and even the floor. I walked into the dining room and heard a weak voice call from the sofa in the living room.

She acknowledged our arrival, but her eyes were half closed. Her head bobbed periodically as if she were trying to stay awake. She looked drunk, but she had never been a drinker. She wasn't upset about the condition of the house or her inability to stay awake. She was aware something was wrong, but it didn't seem to bother her.

Puzzled by all the disorder, I began a light conversation. She answered simple questions, but she didn't ask any. When I talked, she appeared to be listening, until she dozed off.

"Were you in an accident, Mum?"

"Oh, yes," she said with no change of affect. "I ran into one of those cement barriers on the highway on my way back from Irene's."

"Mum, I'm going to come back tomorrow and take you to your doctor." I expected that she'd disagree, but she did not protest.

First thing in the morning, I called her doctor, and we saw him in the afternoon. He didn't have an explanation for the bizarre symptoms, but he didn't think they came from either her chemo or her illness. His lack of curiosity surprised me. He said if she didn't get better in a week, he would put her in the hospital.

I drove the hour back and forth from our new home in Topsfield to Braintree every day. I had never visited my mother so often. I was worried about her, but I was also enjoying the visits. She was letting me be helpful. She was enjoying my humor. I entertained her with silly stories about the kids or something that had happened at the grocery store. She laughed and smiled. I loved making her laugh. She became delightful company, but she was still dozing off and sleeping a good part of each day.

Sunday afternoon I checked my mother into the Carney Hospital in Dorchester. The staff immediately made her comfortable, and I calmed down as doctors, nurses, and specialists came in and out. I sat next to her, made jokes, and she laughed. She looked distant and confused, like an Alzheimer's patient, as she lay back in the bright-white sheets, but her eyes were staying on me. There was love in them. There was gratefulness. She was enjoying my presence. I could never remember feeling so close to her. As much as I didn't want to leave her, it was getting late, and I had to get home.

The next morning a doctor called. They had operated on my mother last night to clear up a blockage they found, which was trapping toxins in her body and creating the strange behavior we had seen. I called Irene to relay the doctor's message. I knew she'd want to know. We had never been close, but I hoped with my mother's illness, we might develop a new relationship as we discussed Mum's treatments. Irene's voice was reassuring at first until I heard, "I just don't understand why Midge couldn't have gone to the hospital sooner. Why did it take a week?"

I didn't take her comment as criticism, although it probably was meant to be. "I was just following the doctor's orders," I said. I didn't understand why she had sent my mother driving up the interstate when she had difficulty staying awake, but I didn't say that. Instead I said, "Mum is recovering from a terrible operation, but they think she will be okay."

"Well, I just couldn't believe how bad she looked over Thanksgiving. She couldn't stay awake, and I couldn't have my son and his wife see her like that. It would have been terribly upsetting to them," she repeated.

I had heard that story one too many times now. I didn't understand her point. I wanted her to stop.

"Irene, I don't know why you keep telling me how awful my mother looked, but we have a long road ahead. My mother is dying. We need to work together."

The word "dying" came out of my mouth, and it even startled me. None of us had talked about my mother dying, but with this operation and her diagnosis, dying was now on my mind.

"Dying? How could you say that? It's like putting a knife in me. You don't know anything about your mother dying," Irene spit over the phone.

"Did you know your mother almost died when she had those polyps removed? No, you didn't even know how sick she was, did you?"

"I only knew what she told me," I said defensively.

"Well, that's because you and your mother aren't close. You have never been close to your mother, not like Helen and I are."

My mind was trying to understand these attacks. I didn't know what I had done to deserve them. I never criticized her for making my mother drive home—I was too insecure to do that. She must have known her comments would hurt me. She knew I had difficulties with my mother. Why did she want to hurt me? I had only one thing on my mind, and that was getting my mother the best care possible. I had hoped Irene could be my support, but now I knew I wouldn't be able to count on her.

"Irene, you and I are not going to talk again," I said. "I will not call you about my mother's progress. You will not call me. I will make sure you have updates. I have too much on my mind and too much work ahead to be distracted by this nonsense." The call ended. I was shocked by my boldness. I melted into a chair, chastising myself for throwing away one of the last family connections I had.

The next day I walked into my mother's hospital room. She was sitting up in bed, looking much more like herself. Her slow speech had disappeared. She was no longer having difficulty filling out the hospital forms. Also gone was the softness in her eyes, which I had seen when the toxins were attacking her brain. Gone was the confusion. Her attempt at a personal connection seemed formal and distant. I tried a bit of humor, the same kind she enjoyed two nights ago, but now it lingered in the room like an uninvited guest. When a couple of her friends arrived, she let me know it was time for me to go.

When I arrived home, my husband asked how my mother was doing. "She's good," I said. "She's back to her old self. She no longer laughs at my jokes, and she wanted me to leave when Margaret and Edith showed up. She's back to normal." I smiled and we both chuckled to keep me from crying.

$\mathcal{S}$ix months later, my mother called to say she was going into the hospital the next day. I checked her tone of voice for signs of illness, but I only heard a woman in charge of her health. She was going to the hospital for some minor procedure after she had lunch with friends. I called her the next day. She was still in the hospital and sounded normal. She discouraged me from coming down to visit since she expected to be out in a day or so.

The next night, as I was making spaghetti for the kids (sauce out of a jar—I have no shame and clearly no Italian), the phone rang. It was my mother's doctor.

"Are you coming to visit your mother tonight?" he asked.

"No, I hadn't planned to. She told me she'd be going home tomorrow."

"No, she's not going home tomorrow," he said firmly. "I think it would be a good idea if you came tonight."

"Okay, I'll get the kids to bed, and I'll be down in a bit," I said.

"No, you need to leave now. We are operating on her as soon as you get here."

I didn't understand how someone could be fine one day and the next day need immediate surgery until I entered my mother's hospital room. Mum was lying flat on her back, her whole body grossly disfigured from water retention. Her face was almost unrecognizable. The doctor told me they were on their way to the operating room. My mother looked at me woefully. Her face was full of resignation, and she told me weakly, "I don't want to live like this." Two nurses appeared and whisked her away. Another nurse came in and told me to leave my mother's room because it was being made up for the next patient. I wanted to stay in the place I last saw my mother, but I was shown to a chair in the corridor.

Hours later the doctor came out and found me in the same chair. "Your mother came through the operation. We had to put a tube directly into her kidney, which will now drain into a bag. I know she didn't want a bag, but it was our only choice. The cancer was completely blocking her ability to void. We are not out of the woods, though. The operation abused her one kidney pretty badly. It may not start working again."

"Really? Then what will happen?"

"Well, ordinarily we'd start someone on dialysis, but at her age there is nothing we can do."

Nothing? I couldn't believe what I was hearing. Were they just going to let her die? My mother was only seventy-three. Why would they do that? I stood in the middle of the hospital corridor shaking. I wanted to yell at them for thinking my mother's life was not worth saving, but I didn't.

"You should go home," the doctor said.

"I'd like to see her."

"Yes, if you insist." He warned me her appearance would be difficult to handle. I had seen my mother during a number of different illnesses, but nothing prepared me for this. She was still horribly swollen and as white as the sheet she was lying on. She was connected to tubes and beeping machines, and she looked more ready to die than live. I stayed for just the minute they allowed. I touched her hand, wrinkled and gnarly from arthritis. I didn't know what to think. I ached to my bones. I knew she didn't want her life to be prolonged like this, but I didn't want to lose her.

After a few worrisome days, the doctor announced her kidney had not given up. She was on the mend, as my mother would have said. The doctor told me that she would need a health aide to check in on her when she went home. A longtime neighbor of ours, Dottie Burke, wanted to be that aide. Dottie was wonderful. I used to babysit for her children when I was in high school. She would tease me sometimes about how the first time I introduced myself to her, I told her I was adopted, as if I had to get it out in the open to make sure it wasn't an issue.

As my mother settled back into her own home, with Dottie keeping a vigil from across the street, I was reassured that she was well cared for. I could now refocus on my own family again.

I still visited regularly, and we'd eat our tuna salad sandwiches while watching *All My Children*. During one of those visits, my mother turned to me and said, "You know, I really didn't need this last year of my life. I didn't need to live this long. We treat our animals much better than we treat humans. When a dog is suffering, we put him down. That would be better than living with this tube in my side."

I wasn't sure how to take what she was telling me. I felt hurt that she didn't mind leaving us all here. She saw life as something that simply began and ended. She didn't seem bothered by the finality of it, only by discomfort from illnesses. She was upset that she'd never see my father again in an afterlife. She knew other people believed they would see their loved ones in heaven, but she had no faith in that. She was not going to invent any beliefs, she told me, just to make missing my father less painful.

Dottie took Mum food shopping and to doctor appointments when necessary. Jed and I were lulled into a rhythm of normalcy. The summer, fall, and winter came with no emergencies. Toward the end of March, Dottie called to say the tube in my mother's side had come out, but there was nothing to worry about. "These things happen," she said. "No need to rush down. I've taken your mother over to the Carney. They'll put it back in…no big deal."

The next morning I received a call from my mother's doctor. I was surprised to hear him say, "We have to get hospice involved." I didn't know who had been more in denial—my mother or me. I had been enjoying how each day turned into the next in spite of her diagnosis of terminal cancer.

"You can't talk hospice to a woman who doesn't think she's going to die," I said.

"Well, I'm going to sit down with her today and tell her she has two weeks to two months to live. She needs to know that," he said.

"Two weeks to two months," I repeated to myself as I hung up the phone. I kept it from settling in so it wouldn't overwhelm me. I knew the medical profession liked being direct, and I'm sure many people preferred it that way, but I had been enjoying my ignorance, as I floated along in denial every day.

Chapter 26

DEATH AND REBIRTH

I placed the receiver back on the wall and took a deep breath. I had to go to the hospital immediately. I had to see my mother. I couldn't let her sit alone while she heard her life was ending. My mind went into overdrive as I scrambled to find people to watch the kids after school.

Mum was sitting up in a straight chair next to her bed when I walked into her hospital room.

"How are you doing?" I asked.

"I'm okay," she said.

"Did the doctor come in?"

"Yes. He just left."

"What'd he say?"

"We went over some things. He told me I have two weeks to two months left, and he wanted me to decide where I'd be staying when I left the hospital." Even as she discussed the end of her life, there was no particular emotion on her face. The end of her life was being lived the way she had lived the rest of it, keeping thoughts and emotions to herself. I watched as she seemed to be going over some things in her mind, but she wasn't letting me in on any of it. Then she sat up straight and said, "I have decided to go live with Irene in Connecticut."

Connecticut? I yelled to myself. *Why in heavens did she want to go to Connecticut?*

"Irene has that guest room with the separate bath. I think that would be a good place for me. Don't you think?"

I knew she didn't want to die in a hospital, but I was a bit shocked at her decision. I couldn't imagine anyone but a professional taking care of a dying person. Irene had never made herself available during any of my mother's crises. She'd only come by after the healing had begun. I didn't blame her. I'm not sure I would have hung around either, except I often seemed to be the last person standing.

"Mum, I don't know about that. I don't think it's a good idea to go to Connecticut. Irene doesn't do things unless they're fun, and this won't be fun." My directness even surprised me.

My mother wasn't budging from her decision. "Well, I can't stay up in New Hampshire with Robbie and his family, and I can't stay with you and the kids." She said this as if she had put some thought into it. I didn't understand why she couldn't stay with my brother. Their kids were older, and his wife was a kind, thoughtful person. I never asked where all her unmarried friends were and why they didn't offer their spare bedrooms.

I hated to admit I relaxed a bit when I heard she didn't want to come to our house again. She had stayed with us after the drainage tube was put in and before Dottie Burke took over her care. For three weeks, I changed the dressing around the tube and gagged each time I looked at the rubber tube waggling loosely around in her flesh. Nothing I did made her comfortable or seemed to be enough. That inner, intrusive voice coming from our convoluted relationship said, "Margy, I never worry about you." And now, even though I resented it, I worried about her all the time.

I tried to make sense of her plan to die at her sister's in Connecticut, but I couldn't. She was taking herself at least four hours away from me, and more than six from Robbie. I didn't understand her decision, because Robbie and I had been there for her every time she had become sick over the last two years. We talked to doctors, held her hand, and sat waiting in hospitals. A thought suddenly came to me—my mother was going *home*.

She was going home to her "real family." After all these years, she now wanted to be near her sister. Robbie and I had filled up her life with children and grandchildren, but she didn't need her life filled up any longer. She wanted her "real family," her blood relations. No other explanation made sense. I was hurt, but I told myself I had no right to be. My mother was dying. This was her time to have it her way.

"Irene and I aren't talking, you know," I said.

As soon as my words came out, I knew how petty they sounded. My mother was trying to find her last resting place, and I was worried about some stupid issue I had with her sister. I immediately reassured my mother that I would visit her in Connecticut. It was a distance away, but I'd do everything I could to make her decision work.

My eyes stayed on Mum. I watched her contemplate another thought. She sat up straight and looked directly at me and said, "You were a... *good*...daughter."

The long pauses and blank facial expression were disconcerting, and it took me a moment before I figured out what she was doing. The former teacher was assigning me a grade! She hadn't said, "You were such a good daughter," with rising tones and positive emphasis. It was as if she had contemplated giving me a higher grade, but then she couldn't ignore certain things, and in the end, I just passed.

My mother's honesty and spontaneity caught me off guard. I didn't know what to think or say. I was hurt, but she was dying. I had no right to be hurt or offended, and yet, after all these years, I had only received a passing grade. I didn't know what to say. I couldn't say to a dying woman, "Well, you're pretty average yourself." I bounced out of my chair and did the only thing I knew how. I leaned over her frail body, wrapped my arms around her shoulders, and said a variation of what I would have hoped to hear from her—"You were a terrific mother." I didn't know if I were being truthful or not; our relationship was so complicated. She must have known that I didn't think she was terrific, but I honestly had no idea what I thought. I wasn't about to analyze it here in her hospital room, where her life was ready to be over in less than two months.

I knew why I had received the lower grade. I had never been the daughter she had in mind when the agency said they had a girl for her. I was never the blank slate she had been promised. I wasn't the child she wanted to fall in love with—the bookworm, the quiet, unchallenging, petite, polite— and so she never did. I had been difficult to raise. I bounced around rooms with undisciplined enthusiasm. I was a "contrary Jane,"—questioning, full of energy, and full of myself. My thoughts were seldom filtered before they ran from my mouth. She did the best she could. She tolerated me most of the time. In truth, while I was trying to make her love me, my mother was trying to make me loveable.

After a few days, I heard that my mother was settled into the upstairs guest bedroom of my aunt's lovely colonial style home in southern Connecticut. I felt a strange sense of relief, thinking I was no longer the point man. Irene had made her very comfortable, and her daughter Helen had already visited. I let the calm wash over me for the first time in a few years.

When I envisioned my first visit to Connecticut, standing face-to-face with my aunt, the idea scared me. I knew I had made the right decision in not keeping in close contact with her over these last couple years. She was a formidable character—you would never want to be on her bad side, but there I was.

For the first weekend in a long time, I didn't feel the burden of responsibility for my mother's well-being. While we drove home from church, I pictured my mother in Irene's lovely, quiet house in that pastoral setting. We walked in the door and I sent the kids upstairs to change their clothes, while I walked ahead into the kitchen. On the counter was the telephone answering machine and the light was blinking. I pressed the play button and my aunt's voice came on. "Bob is driving your mother back to Braintree this morning," she said. "Your mother needs much more care than I realized. All my friends agree that taking care of your mother is too much for me. Bob is bringing her back."

I stepped away from the phone, trying to understand the message. Bob was bringing my mother to her empty house in Braintree. Why there? What had happened? I called Robbie. He had received the same message.

I hesitated to call Irene, but I dialed her number. She was happy to repeat the same things she had said on the answering machine.

"Your mother cannot even make it to the bathroom without help. I have consulted with our doctor friend, and he agrees that Midge needs to go home."

I told her I couldn't be in Braintree to meet Uncle Bob. Jed was in Chicago, and I needed time to line up sitters for my three children. None of that mattered to Irene. Bob was going to drop Mum off and return quickly to Connecticut.

Without even a half-day notice, Aunt Irene expected my brother and me to drop our jobs and families and come to care for our dying mother, her dying sister. Who treated people like that? Had she been angry with my mother all these years? Was this a big sister–little sister thing? Was Irene getting back at a bullying sibling? Why treat my brother and me as if we were the hired help who deserved no notice or support? Was she sending Mum back because we were the "bought" children, and she felt we still owed our mother something? If it weren't an adoption issue, wouldn't she have said, "I'm so sorry, kids, I just can't do this. I hate to put it all on you. I know you have young families, and neither of you live close to Braintree, but this is much more than I could have imagined." No, she didn't say that.

Although it took some work to find last-minute care for the kids, I finally pulled into the Braintree driveway. I stepped into that tiny back hall with winter boots still underfoot. The whole house was silent. I looked ahead into my parents' bedroom. A pile of blankets was on the bed. I hoped I'd find her underneath. As I moved closer, I was grateful to see the pile stir. My mother's face emerged and looked up at me. Then I heard soft, soulful, grateful sounding tone, "Oh, Margy." Her voice and facial expression showed an intimate connection I hadn't expected. She said no more, but her groans told me she was in tremendous pain. I looked around and realized my uncle had left no medications.

I called her doctors. One finally responded and prescribed some pain medication. I went on a wild goose chase for the heavy narcotic, Dilaudid, which no pharmacy stocked because it was so powerful. I was surviving on frustration and annoyance, which was much better than facing my fears and sadness.

Robbie's wife and her mother came by later that day to relieve me so I could go home and line up care for the kids in the morning. After getting the boys off to school, I drove back to Braintree with two-year-old Lauren. My mother was sitting on the sofa wearing a blank expression when we walked in. Lauren, excited to see her grandmother, ran forward yelling, "Mimi Meaney!" and then stopped short in the middle of the room. My mother sat like a rock. She was in another world, and there was no place for Lauren in it. Before this illness, my mother would have put out her arms and with a big smile said, "How is my girl, my Lauren?" Now my mother was silent, and the blank stare began to frighten my towheaded toddler. Tears appeared on Lauren's sweet face before I could scoop her up and rush her out the front door to Dottie Burke, who was delighted to see her and kept her for the night.

Robbie arrived again later that day, and the two of us found a rhythm of caring for our mother. I handled certain things and he handled others. I was in charge of giving Mum her pain medication. She could no longer take food or drugs by mouth, so I unwrapped the suppository containing Dilaudid, found a dissociative place in my mind from which I could cross all personal boundaries to insert the drug.

The remainder of that afternoon, my mother sat in a chair quietly for a few moments, and then like a toddler, her body moved upward, telling me she wanted to stand. I wrapped my arms around Mum's waist and assisted her as she pulled herself up. I held her in that position until her body let go, and then I lowered her back into the chair. We repeated this all afternoon and into the evening—up and then back down. I never had so much physical contact with my mother as I did that afternoon.

Later that evening my mother's doctor surprised us with a home visit. He made himself comfortable in a living room chair across from where my mother was sitting in her silence. We told him what and how she was doing.

He interrupted, "She needs to be in a hospital. We need to get her back in the Carney."

Relief! Such relief flowed through me. To just go and visit my mother, hold her hand, talk to her, and then go home to my family for a good night's sleep, sounded wonderful. Out of the corner of my eye, I saw Mum move just before she yelled a loud, definitive "No!" She hadn't spoken since she called my name that first day, and now she spoke again—she did not want to go to the hospital.

The doctor was startled, but any questions had been answered definitively. She had always said she didn't want to die in a hospital, and now she affirmed that. Our orders were clear. I was trained to please, not to disappoint. The doctor was disapproving, but I told him we had no choice.

"Please, just give us as much support as you can," I begged, and Robbie agreed.

The doctor said he'd call hospice and a visiting nurse. Great, I thought. We'd be handing over our mother's care to knowledgeable people. Unfortunately, things never happen as you expect. The visiting nurse only came to give her a bath, and hospice stopped by to see where she was in the dying process. I had no idea what I was doing, and I was scared.

Our nighttime schedule put me in bed at ten o'clock and up again four hours later. My brother then went to bed and got up four hours later. The days felt full, and by night, I was exhausted. Robbie woke me up this night at two, just as we had agreed. I stumbled out of my bedroom. I had that sick feeling like when you're forced to stay awake for infant feedings. I couldn't help think, as I looked over at my mother's quiet body, how the process of dying was so much like the process of birthing. She had been struggling, and now she was peaceful, but tomorrow would bring a new stage. Coming into this world and leaving it seemed to be just reverse processes.

As I sat in the nighttime glow from the streetlight outside, I watched the same silly shadows dance on the walls that had scared me when I was little. That streetlight was now giving me a dim glow that allowed me to peek into the dining room and watch my mother's shallow breathing.

I began to worry she might die right here, right in front of me. "Oh, please, Lord, if you are listening, don't let her die while I'm alone." I knew Robbie would come if I called, but the idea scared me that she might cease to exist right there and then. I twisted and turned in my seat and then walked over to check if she were still breathing. I turned on the TV so I could stop feeding my fears.

In the morning I was grateful that we all made it through another night. I hadn't felt close to Robbie for a number of years. I knew I annoyed him. For most of our lives, we had been like oil and water, but this week we were a finely tuned machine. I appreciated his take-charge manner, which he must have developed during his Army officer training.

As the next evening turned into night, hospice arrived to evaluate how close Mum was to dying. The worker was pleasant but only stayed a few minutes. Robbie and I kept our mother's pain under control, moved her around in the bed, talked to her, cleaned her, tried to understand her needs, and gave each other support.

The evening progressed, but our mother was not settling down. She was highly agitated and showing fear. She was gasping for each breath. A distinct sound of fluid was in her throat. I never expected my mother to struggle like this. I couldn't stand the idea of her suffering or being scared of choking during her last moments on earth.

I paced around the house, not able to sit still. I felt like I was letting her down—completely incompetent to be one of those in charge of her dying. This wasn't fair to my mother. She deserved to die peacefully.

Rob was calmer. He sat next to my mother's head, stroking her arms and holding her hand. I walked around. My mother would have understood. She used to ask, "Margy, why can't you just sit still for a minute?"

By midnight I was in full panic mode. Nothing we did made her comfortable. Real fear appeared on Mum's face as she struggled for each breath. I called hospice and told them someone needed to open up her trachea so that she could breathe more easily. "This is not fair!" I raised my voice.

When the worker came, she checked my mother, opened her medical case, and took out eight syringes of morphine. This was not what I had in mind. I didn't know what we were going to do with one needle, let alone eight. I didn't know how to give a shot, but Robbie did. The hospice worker said the morphine would make her more comfortable and slow down her breathing. She warned me it might even hasten her death. My mother would have agreed with that. So hospice gave one shot and left seven for us, which we never had to use.

Before the hospice worker left, she encouraged us to talk to our mother. "Tell her she can let go—that it's time to move on." Never in my life had I imagined saying those words to anyone, but with those specific instructions, I became more comfortable sitting at my mother's side. She began to relax, and I began to stroke her hands, arms, and head.

"Mum, you can let go now. It's time to move on. You've had a good life. Be good to yourself. You can pass on now," I said to her.

I watched as her mind moved into another place, and the fear drifted away. Within a short period of time, her body stirred, relaxed, and fluid ran from the corner of her mouth. I felt her neck for a pulse—she was gone.

I looked at my brother, and he looked at me. We said nothing. It was over. I was surprised it came so quickly, just like a baby popping out of its mother when everyone was waiting for the next contraction. Had my mother found peace? People liked to say there were no non-believers in foxholes, but I watched my mother in her foxhole of life, and I never sensed she suddenly believed. She was happy for those of us who did, but she was not going to be one of them.

My first thought as I looked down at her limp body was, "Did I do a good job, Mum?" How very sad, I thought—I had never really grown up. I was still looking for approval.

My tears came and went regularly the next day. I wanted the whole world around me, and I wanted no one around me. My brother and I did not discuss my mother's leaving us. We only talked about what needed to be done—a funeral, a wake? We decided not to have a wake and simply bury her one day later with a small ceremony. Wakes were for the surviving people to receive company and comfort. Robbie and I could have used some of that while our mother was dying in her dining room, but only

Dottie Burke came. We didn't need anyone anymore. We wanted to get back to our own families.

We organized a nice memorial service to be held a week later. The same people who had no interest in saying goodbye to my mother during her last days were quick to criticize us for not having a wake. Some thought our not having a wake was because we were the adopted kids who didn't care about doing the right thing for our mother.

Grief came in waves, but it was not the same debilitating sorrow I had felt for my father. Thoughts of Dad could still reduce me to tears. My mother's death brought sadness only when I thought of a life that had moved on, what my children were missing, and how I never had the relationship with her that I had hoped for. How did you miss someone who had not made herself "missable?" Maybe in her eyes, I had never allowed myself to be the daughter she wanted.

The memorial service was held at St. Chrysostom's in Wollaston, my mother's childhood church. My brother gave a nice eulogy while standing in front of the stained-glass window that Mum's father, Hastings Masfen Moles, a professional stained-glass-window maker, had made and donated many years earlier. After the service, Robbie's wife and her mother organized a luncheon in the gathering room.

Aunt Irene came up to me and commented on how sometimes terrible things like death bring people together. I didn't disagree. I had no fight with her. We smiled and then she went on about the room to chat with other mourners. Some of the people there were kind and connecting; others inexplicably kept their distance. I walked over to a group of my parents' friends that I had known since childhood. Some of them acknowledged me pleasantly, and some reluctantly.

My mother's friend Margaret, my namesake, stood inches from my face to tell me how much she missed my mother. She didn't seem to know whether I missed my mother as much as she thought I should. Margaret told me how much my mother's life changed after they adopted me. "We used to do lots of things together...play bridge, go to the theater...before you came along," she said. I tried to reassure her that I missed my mother, too.

As I stood in the reception room, I felt as if my mother were being taken away from me a second time—first in death, and again now, as some no longer saw me as Midge's daughter, just like some stopped seeing me as Dave's daughter after he died.

The son of my father's friend came over to chat. "Oh, Margaret, I remember your father. Dave Meaney, he was such a great guy. I miss him so much. Gosh, he was terrific," the young man said warmly. Then he stammered and shifted from one foot to the other looking uncomfortable. "Ah…he is your father, isn't he? Um…you still think of him as your father, right?"

I nodded and reassured him that the man he was talking about was, in fact, my father. I didn't have another one, and I agreed Dad was a prince of a person.

This man and most of my mother's friends knew I had found my birth mother eight years earlier. Some had judged me harshly, viewing the search as a lack of loyalty. Although I had continued a reasonable relationship with my mother Midge right up until her death, for some that wasn't enough. Convincing them Midge was still my only "real" mother was no longer possible. They had made up their minds, so I expected to have little contact with them again. Although my brother had not looked up his birth family, he and I seemed only to belong to our mother and father and their extended family, while our parents were alive. Now that our parents were gone, Robbie and I belonged to no one.

Chapter 27

COURT

During Midge's illnesses, I had limited contact with my birth mother, Ann. I did not seek her out, and she respected that. I found juggling the emotional pulls of two mothers overwhelming. No books had been written about how to handle the dueling loyalties between birth and adoptive mothers, so I just avoided it. I focused on Midge, the one who needed me most.

After my mother Midge's death, my brother bought my ownership in the Mild Bay cottage. Staying there had become increasingly uncomfortable. Too many memories revisited me each time I walked in that front door. I still loved Cape Cod though, so Jed and I began looking for a place that didn't have the emotional burden of Mild Bay. After a few years, we bought a summer place in Harwich Port.

In June, as we all settled in for our summer vacation, I went around town locating grocery stores, pizza parlors, and all the other businesses necessary to make our stay comfortable. This canvassing of the town also included a trip to the library so I could collect my "beach books." I had heard the library was newly renovated, and the old district courthouse had been incorporated into it. I wanted to see what the renovation looked like and if I could still recognize the courthouse building.

As I drove into the enlarged parking lot, the courthouse was still discernable. I stared at the white clapboards and columns across its front, and then unexpectedly, vivid memories came rushing back. The episode that created those memories had begun in Mild Bay when I was nine years old. That summer I learned, when someone had bad intentions, he would find a victim. A little girl with too much time, too little supervision, and an independent spirit made for a good mark. The family whistle calling me home for dinner on that late-July afternoon probably saved me from a more disastrous consequence.

"I have to go home," I yelled to the man. My words came out before I formed the thought. "My mother is calling me." I only hesitated because I thought I needed the adult's permission, but I really didn't want to stay any longer. Everything changed when the man used a bad word. Only bad people used that word. I had to go.

"You don't have to go," the man said pleasantly.

"No, I have to go home," I responded with increased agitation. "The whistle means my mother is calling me home for supper."

My brother's voice startled both of us. "Margaret! Mum's looking for you." He was right outside.

"I have to go!" I insisted. "My brother's here!"

I didn't wait for the permission I still thought I needed. The man was scaring me now. I didn't want to help him anymore. He had tricked me. The man became distracted for a moment, giving me a chance to roll onto my stomach and push off hard with my knees. I dug into the deep sand with my toes, and reached out as far as I could in front. My progress was slowed by the sand and low ceiling of the basement crawl space. A sudden fear that the man might grab me triggered a burst of energy. As I pulled myself through the opening in the basement wall, I heard the man say, "Now, don't tell anyone."

His voice coming from a distance told me I was safe from his grasp, and for one brief moment, I felt sorry for him. He had chosen the wrong girl. I could never keep a secret. I looked back and said, "Okay," but I knew I didn't mean it. I'd have to tell someone.

I pulled myself out into the late-afternoon sunlight. My brother was standing on the pile of dirt dug out from the new foundation. "Come on, where yah been? Ma's gonna be angry," he yelled. "What were you doing down there?" he added, but he didn't want to know. His back was already facing me as he began walking toward our cottage.

His question hit me hard. That man had tricked me. I had gone down into the crawl space because he wanted my help. When the spell of the man's charm broke, I was left with swelling shame. He told me how helpful I had been in that unfinished cottage, but I now realized he wasn't the new friend I hoped for. He wasn't nice. When he said that bad word, he frightened me.

My mother was standing at the kitchen sink when I walked in the door.

"Margy, where have you been? It's your week to set the table. Go wash your hands."

We all sat down to dinner. Aunt Dot was in the middle of her vacation with us. I ate only a little before I asked to be excused. I went to my bedroom, sat on the edge of my bed, and tried to make the afternoon memories go away, but I knew I couldn't do it on my own. I called my mother. I didn't care if she got mad at me—I just needed to tell someone.

Mum came into the room. When she realized what I was telling her, she sat down. After I finished, she asked if I could tell Aunt Dot. I began the story again. When I had laid out all the details, my mother looked as if she had a job to do. My aunt, the Army nurse, held back tears. My father walked over to a neighbor's house to call the Dennis Police, and then my parents drove me to the police station. I told my story a few times to the nice policemen there, but the bad man claimed he didn't do anything wrong, so a court date was set.

As I sat in my car looking over at the new library and what was left of the old courthouse, the memories continued to flood back, and they were painful. I didn't understand—I was a grown-up with children now. Why was this still haunting me?

The morning of our court date, my mother told me to put on my Sunday-go-to-meeting dress. It was lavender with puffy sleeves. I put on my black patent-leather shoes with white, lace-trim ankle socks. "There is nothing to be nervous about today," Mum told me. "You have to tell your story again, just like you did at the police station, but this time you'll tell it to a judge."

Okay, I thought. The men at the Dennis Police Station had been very nice to me. They kept telling me everything was going to be fine and made sure I wasn't scared even when I had to look into a special room and point out the man who had tricked me. If the police were that nice, I decided, the judge would be even nicer.

My parents, Robbie, and I arrived at the courthouse later that morning. We were taken into a room with a long, highly polished wood table that was surrounded by a dozen wooden armchairs. The windows were tall, curved at the top with multiple panes, and the ceilings were high. One wall was covered with floor-to-ceiling bookcases that housed leather-bound books behind glass doors. Time passed slowly. Eventually, a man came into the room and walked us all down a corridor. As we approached another door, my mother told me I had to go in by myself. She told me that was where I would see the judge.

A man inside the door pointed to a large, wooden-armed chair for me to sit in. I climbed up and scooted myself back and then forward so my feet were dangling. Out in front of me was the beautiful courtroom. It was two stories high with thick white columns, fancy moldings, and more tall, multi-paned windows. At the back of the room, my parents were sitting on a bench with my brother, who had already talked to the judge. They seemed too far away. My eyes continued around the room past the empty jury box and then rested on some men in suits down in front. I startled when I realized one of them was the bad man. Nobody told me he was going to be here. I began shaking, but before a second wave of fear struck, I heard a voice call my name from up behind me.

I looked up over my shoulder and saw a man in a black robe. He began talking to me, so my eyes fixed in his direction. He started asking me pleasant questions about things I wanted to talk about—my pets, my school, what I liked to play, who my friends were. I told him all about our dog, Teddy, who went everywhere with me. He asked what grade I was in, who my teacher was, and what my favorite subject was. I was enjoying our conversation, but I wondered when the judge was going to ask me to tell my story like the policemen did. Instead he asked me, "Do you know the difference between telling the truth and telling a lie?"

I sat up straight and thought, *well, of course I know the difference.* "Yes," I said. *Didn't good people always tell the truth to a judge? That was how it was on TV.*

A Bible was brought over to me. I was told to put a hand on it, and my other one went up in the air. I promised to tell the truth.

As I continued to tell the judge about school, I began to think he wasn't listening. He was talking to someone else—something about, "She looks well cared for." I didn't know why that was important, so I pretended we weren't changing the subject, and kept talking.

"Tell me what you were doing before you went to the house," the judge said.

I told him how Teddy and I had been walking around the circle that day. I decided we'd go look at the new cottages being built. They were the first new houses on Mild Bay and everyone hoped a girl might move in for me to play with, but the judge stopped me and asked another question.

"Tell me, what you were wearing that day?" This question scared me because I knew adults could be critical of how people dressed. The Dennis Police never asked me that question.

"A pink and white checked sunsuit," I said in a halting voice. "The shorts are connected to the top, and it zippers up the front." Fear took over. I didn't understand why he kept asking questions.

"What happened under the house?" the judge asked, interrupting my panic.

Finally, a question I expected.

"The man wanted me to go down into the crawl space to help him straighten out the chimney, because he said it was crooked and I had been so helpful upstairs. He told me this was a very important job and he really needed me. He told me how proud he was of me and that he was sure he could count on me. He said I needed to push the base of the chimney while lying down. He said that was the best position, but it was very uncomfortable, and I had to squirm out from under him."

"Did he *say* anything to you?" the judge asked.

I hated this part.

"Yes, he asked if he could teach me how to…. I can't say the word." *The Dennis Police never made me say it.*

"Tell me what he said to you." The judge used a very firm tone.

I had never said that word in my life. No one in my family ever used that word. The judge was determined and repeated his demand.

Reluctantly, I whispered, "F***… The man said, 'f***'." I was horrified that the word came out of my mouth.

My body then relaxed. I had given the judge what he wanted. I was done. I sat back in the big chair. *The judge now knew what a bad man he was. Surely he would be punished.*

Then I sensed some movement above me, and I looked back up at the judge who was now leaning over his bench, looking down on me. He said, "Do you know what that word means?"

Oh… I hadn't expected that. I thought we were done. My mind began racing. Even at nine years old, I knew I was in trouble. If I told the judge I knew what the word meant, he'd think I was one of those bad kids who knew bad words. I thought I might know what it meant, so if I said, "no," I'd be lying. I'd be lying right after I said I would tell the truth.

The judge repeated the question. "Do you know what that word means?"

I was devastated as I let the words squeak out of me. "No…no, I don't." I couldn't believe what I had done. I was sure I was lying right there under oath on the witness stand.

I rolled down the car window and continued to gaze at what was left of the courthouse, when one last memory exploded.

I was on the witness stand, upset that I had told the judge I didn't know what the word meant, when my father suddenly stood up in the back of the courtroom and yelled so loudly he startled everyone. "Your Honor, if

I hadn't had three heart attacks, I would have gone over to that house and beaten that man to within an inch of his life."

Oh my God, if he kept yelling like that, he might have a heart attack right there.

The judge exploded in anger. "You will sit down, sir, and not say another word, or I will hold you in contempt."

Why did my father do that? Even I knew it wasn't a good idea to yell at the judge.

"I had better not hear another outburst from you!" the judge yelled so loudly his voice echoed throughout the great hall.

I didn't understand why my father couldn't keep his feelings to himself. He had not said a word to me about the man since it happened. Why hadn't he told me at home instead of upsetting the judge? This was the most emotion I had seen from my father since I met the bad man, and it all came out at the wrong time in the wrong place.

My father never talked to me about any of it, which confused me. He and I chatted about all kinds of important things. My mother told me that I had done nothing wrong, but I was afraid my father thought I had. This thing that happened to me affected him too, but I didn't understand why.

I walked over toward the new library and wondered if that man had ever been punished. The more I thought about it, I doubted he had. When I was young I kept telling myself he was in jail, because it was the only thing that calmed me down. I thought I saw him everywhere I went. When the judge heard a nine-year-old girl wearing a skimpy outfit was playing without supervision and was not shy with a strange man, I guess he felt he couldn't punish him.

In the end, my father survived the stress of it. My mother avoided the shame of it. My poor brother was blamed for it, although I never thought he was responsible. The episode was never discussed again. I was ordered not to tell a soul, so every detail was trapped in my mind.

Chapter 28

A MASTER'S

When we returned from the Cape that summer, Lauren was going into junior high, Mike was finishing junior high, and Matt was starting high school. I anticipated the winter months ahead with trepidation. With the kids growing up, I could see an empty nest in my future, and I was not happy about it. Our children were wonderful—the most interesting human beings I had ever met. I worried about becoming the hovering mother, so I tried to stay busy. I joined organizations and coached sports. After working as a substitute teacher at the local high school, I learned that I loved working in a school, and I enjoyed coaching town soccer and softball. Someone suggested I should be a teacher, but my parents' warning still echoed in my head—teaching wouldn't be a good profession for me. A woman I knew was juggling a master's program in psychology while keeping up with two teenage boys, and it prompted me to consider getting a master's.

My application to Lesley College in Cambridge was accepted, and I began their graduate program in clinical mental health. I worried at first that I was too old. I would be forty-six when I graduated. A friend reminded me I was going to be forty-six with or without the degree. My drive home from orientation was full of satisfaction. I was going to get my master's degree! I was going to do what I didn't imagine possible. More importantly, I would get a job and not annoy my children with my empty nest anxiety.

I loved being back in school and challenged by my classes. One day, my emotional defense system was pierced by an expressive therapy presentation. The expressive therapy teacher passed out a piece of paper with two crayons. She instructed us to close our eyes and put a crayon in each hand and begin drawing on the paper. It seemed silly and my brain fought me. "What are you doing? I don't know. This is lame. Stop complaining."

A melody popped into my head, and I was grateful for the rhythm. I could move my crayons to a waltz, three-quarter time. My whole mind and body joined with the music. I swayed as the two crayons stayed on the paper, making large swirls. I began to enjoy it. It was soothing, and at the end of the exercise, I had a paper with a bunch of circles and a lovely, calm feeling.

As I drove home that night, I tried to remember where I had heard that song. I hummed along, hoping the melody's name would come to me, and then it did. The song was the waltz from *Cinderella*, a story about a girl who had no parents and lived a less-than-ideal life with unrelated people. I couldn't understand how my issues could be so obvious to my subconscious, but so oblique to my conscious. That simple crayon exercise brought up something my therapy never had. I suddenly had a new respect for expressive therapy.

While attending classes at night, I worked at internships during the day. One of those internships was at an agency that treated troubled adoptive families. The identified child usually had severe emotional issues and was either expected to be hospitalized or was coming home from treatment.

The parental commitment to these adopted children inspired me. Everyone was working hard to fix whatever was causing the child's emotional problems. I felt completely inadequate working with these families. Nothing in my graduate school training mentioned adoption or how to work with adoptive families.

I checked other graduate school curricula, and none of them offered courses on adoption either, or mentioned the topic as part of bonding and attachment. I knew a number of adoptive families who had used a thera-pist, but I had no idea where they were trained.

Graduate school was ending after nearly three years of classes. I was fin-ishing up my last internship on a lovely day in April. I climbed into my car in the school parking lot. I leaned over and turned on the car radio. All sta-tions were reporting breaking news—a terrible explosion had occurred in Oklahoma City. Someone had bombed a building, and many people were killed. Needles of nerves shot through my body. *Oklahoma City.* What if I lost siblings, cousins or a father, before I even had a chance to meet them? The TV was broadcasting graphic pictures of horror and bravery. I wanted to go there, but I didn't know who I'd be looking for. "No one would be sending out a welcoming party," Jed said, and of course, he was right. I squelched my fantasy of relatives lining up on the airport tarmac waving at me, as I disembarked from a 737.

Right before graduation, just as I thought I had addressed all my adop-tive issues, one of my classes presented an old black-and-white British film. It depicted a mother who was going away to have a baby and needed to stay in the hospital for an extended length of time. The film focused on her three-year-old daughter, who would be separated from the mother. The filming crew caught the girl's reactions to her mother's absence, showing us multiple stages of separation grief. The stages were painful to watch—from sorrow, to anger, to submission, and then finally rejection of the mother when she came home.

As I watched the movie, I began having a much stronger reaction to the little girl's experience than I had expected. I could feel myself joined with her in the parallel experience we shared. A vision came into my mind of being taken away from my foster family. I had never really thought of that moment before. Even when I found my foster sister a few years ago, I was thinking more about thanking her than I was about being taken away. Now my separation experience was being triggered by the little girl's strong emotions and it was very real. I was feeling my loss for the first time.

The movie showed the little girl waiting for her mother to return. I wondered how long I waited for my foster mother after I was placed in

Against the Tides

my adoptive home. Maybe I never did give up. All the crying I did when I learned my foster mother had died seemed to relate to my having waited for her. Maybe the sadness I lived with as a child was because I was waiting for my "mother figure" to come back for me.

Now I wondered if waiting for my first family had kept me from making a solid attachment to my adoptive family. Midge and I had always seemed at odds. Was that because I wouldn't allow myself to bond with her? Was the attachment disorder, with which we adoptees were so often labeled, simply a normal reaction to our grief? But how could we therapists treat this grief and lack of bonding effectively if no one recognized the symptoms, and no one was trained to treat it?

I graduated a month later with a sixty-credit master's degree in clinical mental health. After passing the licensing exam, I would be a therapist. What would Midge think? I doubted she would have said much of anything…except that Lesley wasn't Harvard, perhaps. I convinced myself she would be happy. It wasn't that important anymore.

193

Chapter 29

JOB SEARCHING

*W*ith the painful reactions I experienced in graduate school still fresh in my mind, I knew I had more personal work to do before I could begin treating other people. I tried to think of ways to work out my unprocessed experiences. I wondered, if I were able to see my original adoption records, maybe my emotional issues would lessen?

At the Norfolk County Courthouse, I asked the judge's clerk if I could petition the court to see my sealed records. The clerk had no interest in my bothering the judge, so he sent me directly to the Registrar of Probate. This was great, I thought—no special petition, no judge's decree. Perhaps looking at records had become so common that judges no longer handled these cases.

Registrar of Probate was written in black letters on the door. The office was a large room with multiple long tables for inspecting records. Along the side was shelving to hold record books. I told someone why I was there, and the actual registrar came over and greeted me pleasantly.

When he heard what I came for, his demeanor changed. He raised himself up with taller, stiffer posture—as people did when trying to show their importance—and told me he did not understand why I was there.

"What do you want with that old information?" he demanded. "Didn't you have a good life?"

When I said it had its issues, it seemed he couldn't decide whether I was ungrateful or just hadn't worked hard enough. Either way, from his perspective, it had been my fault. He repeated every argument I had heard before. Something was wrong with me. I was being disloyal. I was wasting people's time. He threw every cliché at me.

Next, he tried the approach of how pursuing this information might upset my birth mother, but I told him I already knew her. Then he mentioned I was being disloyal to my adoptive parents, but I explained that my parents were dead. I managed not to react to his barrage of childish berating by reminding myself that I was a grown woman who had raised three children, and I was not a child who needed scolding.

"My children are both adopted," he snarled at me. "They're teenagers now, and they have absolutely no interest in the people who came before them."

Okay, to each his own, I thought, but why was he so upset?

"In fact, we went to Germany when they were sixteen to the place where they were born, but they didn't even want to visit it." He was yelling at me now. "What do you think about that?"

"Adoptees have many different needs. I can't speak for your children," I said, surprised that I wasn't sinking under his bullying. "I just want to see the records from the beginning of my life," I said.

At some point he abruptly stood up, turned his back to me, and walked away. I didn't know where he had gone or if he would be back. I had no place to go, so I decided to sit and wait, hoping my abandonment issues wouldn't be triggered. I found a chair at the end of one of the long tables. After some time, the registrar came out of the door marked "Private." He walked back in my direction carrying a manila folder. He stopped at the opposite end of the long, eight-foot table and threw the folder frisbee-style up the length of the tabletop right at me. By chance, the folder landed close to my hands. The man then turned and walked away.

Unnerved by his anger, I opened the folder quickly, just in case he changed his mind. I turned the pages over and over. Nothing seemed exceptional. Maybe he had taken out the important papers, but I didn't actually know what I was looking for. I just wanted to touch the official documents and see all the familiar names.

I came upon my birth mother's signature, but it was unrecognizable. Each letter was formed with jagged lines connected with other unsmooth lines. I knew my birth mother's signature well, and this didn't look anything like it. If that signature had been challenged in court, no one could have said it was her "free act and deed." I closed the folder and sat still for a moment with the realization. *Ann had been devastated by losing me.* I guess I knew it, but until now, I really hadn't focused on her feelings. In my need to fill up my identity, I hoped I wasn't as callous as I felt at that moment. I rose out of my chair, picked up the folder, and moved slowly toward the front of the room. The registrar was nowhere to be seen. I placed the folder on the front desk and walked out the door.

⸻⸱⸻

I refocused on my job hunting. I was hoping to become a guidance counselor in a high school, but when an international adoption agency asked me to come in for an interview, I gladly accepted. My life experience and my internship with troubled adoptees might make me a good candidate. I looked forward to this agency being my next employer.

The first interviewer seemed delighted with me. My experiences both as an adoptee and working at the intervention agency impressed her. The more she heard about me, the more she showed her excitement. At some point in the interview, I told her I had found my birth mother, but that my adoptive family was mostly dead. I had learned people were more tolerant of my searching when they heard my adoptive family was no longer alive. I protected myself that way. Even with my searching, this woman couldn't wait for me to meet her supervisor, so another interview was arranged.

The second woman was not as happy to see me. The moment I walked into her office, a cartoon came to mind that showed a salesman being tossed out onto the sidewalk with his hat and briefcase flying out after him. This woman didn't just not want to hire me—she didn't even want to speak with me. While reading notes from the first interview, she expressed her displeasure that I knew my birth mother, that I had even searched, and that I was adopted. Above all, she seemed truly bothered that I had been home raising children for fifteen years.

"You know that you would be working full time," she said, "five days a week, don't you? You haven't done that in a while," she added snidely. "How do we know that you are organized enough to handle a full workload?"

She was not impressed that I had been working at internships twenty or more hours per week while managing a full graduate course load, in addition to all the other responsibilities in my family life. Yet she wasn't the first female interviewer who expressed displeasure at my having stayed home to raise children. Men didn't seem to be as bothered by it.

I didn't understand how she expected the children they were offering for adoption to bond with their new parents if the parents were working fifteen-hour days. The child needed to fall in love with their new parents, and they couldn't do that if the parent wasn't around. The adoptive relationship was different from the birth relationship in that it was more like a marriage, bringing strangers together in love.

When the interviewer expressed discomfort that I had found my birth mother, I tried to explain that I needed some medical information. She wasn't swayed—she was thinking only of her clients. She knew they could not be expected to pay exorbitant prices for a child without being reassured that the child belonged to them, and the only way to do that would be by limiting the child's access to their birth records. It reminded me of an international adoptive parent once saying to me, "Well, at least my foreign-born child won't be able to search for her biological mother." I was this agency's most dreaded nightmare.

So I was out on the sidewalk without a job—and not sure I would ever find one—when I was introduced to a retired friend of my husband. He was doing volunteer work for an inner-city elementary school. He told me the principal was always looking for a counselor.

"Is it a paying job?" I asked.

"Well, of course not," he said in that noblesse oblige tone of voice. I wanted to remind him that I might look a little privileged now, but that was not always the case. Salary or not, I wanted to work.

The principal welcomed my call and gave me directions to the school. The roads were in an unfamiliar part of Boston. The school was down the street from some boarded-up buildings and empty storefronts. I met with the principal and two other staff members at the school, who all wanted to make sure I would take this job seriously. They needed someone to provide counseling for nine hundred children, and if I could come three days a week—for free—that would be great.

I loved my job. By the end of the first semester, I had been officially hired into a paid part-time position. That school morphed into my spiritual center, even better than going to church. Hundreds of fascinating little souls came to school every day. Some had difficult lives, yet they were surviving, most with cheery faces, having no idea that other people might find their stories difficult. I loved all those little people—their openness, their humanity, their strength, and their survival skills. For ten years, they taught me more than I ever helped them.

Chapter 30

DNA

Since I was working in the Boston Public Schools and Jed's law office was in downtown Boston, we decided to move into the city and leave our comfortable country life behind. The kids had already moved out, so we began our empty nest experience in a townhouse in the South End of Boston with two dogs and three cats. We created our own rhythm at night, no longer dictated by our children's activities. After walking the dogs, we made ourselves comfortable in front of the TV in the downstairs den. We had a few shows we watched regularly and were particularly loyal to the CSI shows. One night while watching the execution of a crime and the solving of a mystery, one actor turned to the other and said, "We can get the DNA off the envelope." The words had hardly left the actor's mouth when Jed's head and mine turned simultaneously. We stared at each other with our mouths open in disbelief.

"What happened to that letter from the guy in Oklahoma you thought might be your father?" Jed blurted out. "Do you still have it?"

"I don't know," I said. "I haven't seen it in years. I put it in a dresser drawer way back when we lived in Reading. Lauren wasn't even born. We've moved a few times since then."

I stood up and began running up the stairs to the top floor where our old bureau now offered storage in the guest room. Looking for a forgotten envelope seemed like a fool's errand, but the letter had to be there because each time we moved, the contents stayed in the drawers. Maybe one of those times, we packed some drawers in boxes. If that were the case, I had no idea where the letter was.

I pulled out the left-hand drawer, the place I last remembered seeing the letter. It wasn't on the top, so I began pushing through old scarves, letters, receipts, and forgotten makeup. When I reached the bottom of the drawer, I still didn't see the letter. My heart sank. I tried the right-hand drawer with no success. Another drawer was full of silly saves and a few forgotten papers, but I didn't see the envelope until I pulled away an old pair of gloves, and there it was on the bottom at the back. The long white envelope, which had been such a sad communication so many years ago, was staring up at me. I opened the envelope and unfolded the letter. My eyes followed the typed correspondence down to the handwritten rejection note at the bottom. I hurried back down the staircase, yelling, "I got it. I got it!" But I really wasn't sure what I had. I didn't know anything about DNA testing.

"I wonder if we can get that letter tested," Jed mused as I arrived back in the den.

"I have no idea how you'd get DNA testing done," I said. "I'll try to find out tomorrow, but the TV show might be wrong. I don't know if there really is any DNA left on that envelope. Maybe you can't test DNA that old."

The next morning, I googled "DNA testing." More choices came up than I had expected, but they all referred to law enforcement. I called up one company and asked if they could help me test the DNA on an old envelope. They couldn't. They said I needed a scientific approach to study this man's DNA, and they gave me the name of a second company. This one was in California.

"Do you do DNA testing?" I asked the person who answered the phone.

"Yes, we do DNA testing for a variety of agencies, mostly law enforcement."

"I have a letter that was sent to me by a person I think might be my biological father, and I would like to have it tested."

A sudden panic shot through me. *What if this person is an adoptive parent like the registrar? What if she refuses to test it? What if I came this far, and no one will test it?* I braced myself for her response.

"What do you have?" I started to relax.

"I have a letter and the envelope that was probably licked by this man, but it was sent to me in 1979. It may be too old to get the DNA from it."

"Oh, no," the woman said. "DNA never gets too old. It lasts a long time. We should have no problem getting a sample to test."

I didn't know what to think. Could this really be the answer I had hoped for all these years? Could it be this easy? The woman at the company said a kit would be sent to me, and when it arrived I was to use their Q-tip to retrieve my saliva. She warned me that they only worked on non-police matters when they had time. Since I never thought I could confirm my father's identity, I told her I had plenty of time.

I hung up the phone. As I thought more about it, I suddenly became unsure I wanted the DNA to be tested. The woman had convinced me they could confirm whether this man was my father. If the test results were negative, it would confirm that he was not. For years now, I had lived pleasantly with the thought I might be connected to people in the state of Oklahoma. I let Oklahoma become part of my identity foundation the way my husband used Holland until he found out he was Irish. Thinking I was from Oklahoma gave me a sense I belonged to something even if it weren't true. I had done that for years when I used my adoptive parents' nationalities of Irish and English as my identity foundation. With them both dead, Oklahoma became that comforting connection. If this DNA test didn't confirm the man in Oklahoma as my father, then I'd have to accept that the state and its people meant nothing to me and I would be connected to nothing. Maybe I shouldn't let them test the DNA on the envelope and just go on pretending.

Within a day or so, a small package arrived. By then, I had made peace with my decision. I could handle whatever the results were. I had lived without knowing anything about my father's side of the family before. I could continue to do that if the test said Charles Stueve was not my father.

I laughed as I took the long stick swab and retrieved saliva from my mouth, just like they did on TV. I put the original letter and envelope in the plastic bags provided. It felt strange sending off that letter and thinking it might get lost—then I'd never know anything. It wasn't as if I had treated it well, stuffed in a drawer, but I never thought it would be important. This letter was now the only thing that could connect me to a biological father. What if it never arrived? I tried to suppress the panic. I called the company and had a calming chat with the woman. She reassured me as best she could that the package would arrive safely, and she promised to call when it did.

I was surprised at how important confirming my father suddenly was to me. After his rejection letter years ago, some people urged me to put the issue aside. They told me to let it go and live with what I had. "Be grateful," they said. I tried to, but my lack of knowing must have been gnawing at me deep down, because as soon as I thought there might be a chance to find out who he was, I jumped for it.

Over the next few months, I put the matter out of my mind. It was now in someone else's hands, and I knew it would take a long time. I refused to think about it. If the man were not my father, I would not pursue it further. I'd have to accept that I'd never get back what had been taken from me by adoption.

A year might have come and gone when a call came one day. I jumped when I realized who was on the phone. The technician from the DNA company told me that retrieving DNA from my sample was more complicated than they had expected. They had to cut another sample from the envelope and administer a second test. This procedure was going to take more time, but I told them I had the time, and I sent them more money.

Some months went by and I got up the courage to call them. The woman was very friendly.

"Yes, I'm actually finishing up with your case right now."

My eyes widened.

"The DNA you gave us is a match for your father," she said.

My head dropped down. Relief swept over me. It was finally over. I was suddenly released from something that had gripped me for decades. I felt the layers of uncertainty peeling away. I was free. I was now just like everyone else. The amount of relief surprised me. I had no idea how heavy a burden it had been to carry the emptiness of no information all those years.

"Are you absolutely sure?" I asked.

"Yes, very sure. You will be receiving back your samples and a courtroom-quality report stating that the DNA on the envelope is from your father."

I didn't jump for joy—I sat down. I was simply content. This was the end. I was complete. I was no longer the person to whom no one could give information, have a folder thrown at, or be shown the door because I broke society's unwritten rules. I was now like everyone else, and more importantly my children were like everyone else. No one could take away our roots or ancestors. We belonged to something bigger than ourselves.

Chapter 31

SOUTHERN RELATIONS

*M*y Oklahoma identity began to settle in. A feeling of normalcy, of connection, and peace overtook me. I had decided even before the DNA testing that I would not contact my father Charles in Oklahoma. Perhaps I was protecting myself, or simply wanted to respect his wishes. Either way, he was safe from me.

My desire to know something about possible siblings or ancestors was strong, but what if I did find a sister or a brother? How could I call them up and say, "Oh, by the way, your father doesn't want to have anything to do with me, but I am your bastard sister from Boston." It was all a little bizarre when I thought about it. I didn't even know if he had any children.

Of course, if he did have children, they would probably support their father's wishes and not want anything to do with me. I didn't want an additional rejection from them, so I quickly put aside thoughts of brothers and sisters. However, deceased ancestors couldn't reject you, and they were an important part of my identity. I wanted to know what brought them to Oklahoma. Did they come in covered wagons and live in sod huts? I had heard that most families in Oklahoma came from somewhere else.

I wrote to a records office in Oklahoma to request a copy of my father's birth certificate. In my past searches, I found that birth certificates usually listed the parents. If I found out who his parents were, I might be able to go back and find earlier generations. A copy of my biological father's birth certificate arrived in the mail. Charles Stueve was born in Muskogee, Oklahoma. I hadn't expected that he was actually from Oklahoma. His parents were listed as Eleanor Eberle and Winfred Stueve. Winfred was born in Wapakoneta, Ohio, and Eleanor was born in Fort Smith, Arkansas. Arkansas! The state's name jumped right off the page at me. I had never heard of Fort Smith, and Arkansas was in the South. I wasn't ready for my identity to have any Southern in it. I was born and bred in Massachusetts, in New England. I was not prepared for any remarkable difference between who I thought I was and what this information was telling me.

A Southern grandmother, I mused. I had assumed my Oklahoma relatives came down from Kansas or Missouri, not from the South. In Boston, if Southerners or the South were mentioned at all, it was usually in a negative context with demeaning comments. My high school history classes made me feel lucky to be a Northerner. Yet, here I had a grandmother who was born in the South. I didn't know what to make of it.

I wrote to a records office in Oklahoma for a copy of this grandmother's death certificate to see if I could find out who her parents were. After some back and forth—not the correct form, not the right amount of money—I had almost given up when an envelope arrived. Inside was Eleanor Eberle Stueve's death certificate. Eleanor was born in October of 1894 in Fort Smith, Arkansas. She died in September of 1973 in Oklahoma City. My heart skipped and then sunk sadly. My grandmother died right after I got married. If we had known each other, she could have come to my wedding in 1972. All those years when I was in high school and college, she was alive. I wish I had known her. I never had a grandparent. All my adoptive grandparents had died before I was placed with the Meaneys. To think I actually had a grandmother while I was growing up was unsettling. I wondered if she had ever thought of me. Had she even known about me? Then I looked at the birthplace again. There it was—Fort Smith, Arkansas.

I looked up Fort Smith on a map. It was on the Arkansas River across from Oklahoma, and then I saw how it connected to the Mississippi River. I could see why people might go to Fort Smith, but I still had never heard of it. I had never come across the name Eberle either. What kind of name was that? How could I have never heard of the place my grandmother was born? It was all very different from what I had expected. Adoptees I knew in Boston were born around there, and their birth relatives, if they found them, were from there, too.

Eleanor's parents were listed on the death certificate. Her father was Charles Eberle, who was also born in Fort Smith, Arkansas. Eleanor's mother was listed as Lucile Wisdom. Wisdom—that was an unusual name. I had never heard of it. Lucile Wisdom's birthplace was Jackson, Tennessee. Oh, my goodness… another Southerner! My great-grandmother was born somewhere in Tennessee! I couldn't even remember if Tennessee was above Kentucky or below it. This meant the Southern connection was no accident. But I was *Boston* and *Northern*, not Tennessee and Southern. Or maybe I was Southern, and I just didn't know it. I felt like someone who had been raised Catholic and found out she was Jewish. Or thinking she was Swedish and discovering she was Italian. The South was a very separate culture as far as I was concerned, and I knew nothing about it.

We never really studied the South in school. When we studied history, it was all about the Pilgrims or Lexington and Concord. I never remembered studying the Civil War, and now I had ancestors who might have fought in it. I might have an ancestor who not only fought in that war, but was on the "wrong side." This identity thing I wanted so badly was becoming a bit of a burden, but at that moment, I resolved not to pick and choose who I was.

Chapter 32

Siblings

The New England Historic Genealogical Society was a resource in Boston I had used when I researched Jed's ancestors several years ago. I wanted our children to know at least one side of their family history, since I expected my side would be blank. At that time, one of their researchers was very helpful, even finding the village in Ireland from which Jed's family had emigrated. I hadn't been back to the Society since then, but I had heard some people were posting their family trees on the internet. I wondered if my father's family had been posted, and maybe New England Genealogical could help me.

The elevator door opened on the fourth floor. A young man was sitting right in front of me behind a tall counter.

"Hi, my name is Margaret Hendrick. I recently confirmed my biological father by DNA testing. I've heard that some people have posted their family trees on the internet and maybe his has been posted. I'd like to see if he has any children, but I don't have any idea how to go about looking for it. Could you help me?"

"Sure, what's his name?" the young man said, whose name was Chris Child.

I gave him the information. Chris began typing and looked up at the screen periodically. Within a few moments he said, "I think I found your father." He confirmed the birth date and place and then said, "The tree information seems to be on his wife's side. Someone in her family has been posting the information." Then I heard, "He has six children." Shock hit me hard as I watched Chris turn the screen around. There it was, right under my birth father's name, "six children—living." The children were born during the marriage of Charles Stueve to a Mary. The chart didn't say if the children were male or female or how old, just "six children."

I wasn't prepared to hear this information. It came so quickly. I thought I would have had years of searching before such a major discovery. Still stunned by this new information, I thanked Chris and walked back to the elevator. I didn't know what to think. I had siblings! Six of them… but I couldn't absorb what it meant. All I could think of were six ten-year-olds, since they were labeled "children." Having siblings was exciting, but "children" were not people you could approach. There were no names, so how could I ever search for them? Maybe the actual names weren't posted because they were, in fact, children. It was confusing but exciting. I was suddenly related to a big family, and yet it felt so foreign that I had to keep repeating the information over and over, hoping it might sink in.

Many months came and went—maybe a year. In the back of my mind, I thought of stopping by New England Genealogical again to see if any more information had been added to my father's family tree, but life was distracting. I wasn't sure I was ready to take the next step, and I didn't want to upset my birth mother Ann.

The next fall, I was back at my counseling job, and I had set up a private practice on the first floor of our townhouse. Christmas break arrived and my husband and I went out to California to visit our son Matthew. On the train ride back, I realized I had misjudged my arrival in Boston. I was coming back to town with one more day before I had to report to school. One extra day with nothing planned. I decided to walk over to New England Genealogical and see if Charles's family tree had been expanded.

I checked in at the front desk and rode the elevator up to the fourth floor again. As the door opened, I could see the same young man, Chris Child, sitting at the same desk. I stepped forward and said, "I don't know if you remember me. I was here quite a while ago and you looked up a family tree for me."

He looked up at me and smiled. Then he raised a finger as if to stir his memory and said, "Oklahoma? Right?"

"Yes, right," I said laughing. "You have quite a memory. I was wondering if you could check that tree again and see if anything else has been added."

"Sure, what was your father's name again and his birth date?" He began punching keys.

Finally, he moved the screen around so I could see it. Where the words "six children—living" had been the last time, now there was a list of six adult names, beginning with four females and ending with two males. The person in charge of this family tree site had listed everyone's full name with birthdays and in the case of the women, their married names. It was no longer "six children." I had six half-siblings. I had real siblings, and they weren't ten-year-olds. The oldest was only three years younger than I, and according to this data, they were all still living. I was shocked. I really had a family out there somewhere. I had a large family.

I stood there looking at the computer screen. Sisters—my heavens! Sisters—four of them! I'd never thought of myself as having sisters. Growing up, almost everyone I knew had sisters, and I always wished for one. The two younger brothers were the same age as the two boys who had been living in the house when I first contacted Charles in 1979, so they were not the second wife's children. They were *my* brothers, and I felt immediate regret that I hadn't known it then. Even with all this new information, I had no plans to contact any of them. They had lives, and they probably didn't know about me. How upsetting it might be for them to hear their father had left a child in Boston.

I thanked Chris for all his help. I still marveled that he remembered me as I stepped out onto the Newbury Street sidewalk. As I turned onto

Clarendon Street, I pulled my hat down over my ears and tightened my scarf as the January wind whipped off the Charles River, piercing my back. I was excited, but not sure what to do with the information. Maybe someday I would go out to Oklahoma, walk on the land of my ancestors, and just look around. I didn't want to disrupt people's lives. The DNA had confirmed my father's identity, so I now knew my people. Maybe that was all I needed.

My husband was already home when I walked in the door. He was shocked by the news that I had six real adult siblings. He had always known me as practically an only child, since Robbie had moved halfway around the world.

"Are you going to contact them?" he asked.

"No, I don't think so. I'm happy just to know about them. I don't need to put myself out there for rejection, and I don't want to upset any of them. I'm sure they don't know about me."

"Aren't we all adults now?" Jed interjected. "Adult things have happened to all of us. They're not going to be shocked that their father had a relationship years ago. It was before he even married their mother. If they get upset, well, that's life, isn't it?"

I began to think my husband was right. Looking at the situation from his point of view, my siblings deserved to know they had a sister living in Boston. Perhaps it wasn't fair to keep that information from them. Everyone seemed to worry about the biological parents, but what about the siblings? Why shouldn't siblings know about each other? Their relationships could likely outlive any parents. By the time our conversation ended, I had convinced myself I actually had an obligation to inform the siblings about my existence.

I went upstairs, sat down at the computer, and typed the sisters' names into the White Pages website. I had become much more proficient on the internet in the last year or so. The same message came up every time: "none found." I keyed in the boys' names. A man with the same name as my youngest brother was living in Oklahoma City, but I decided that he could be anyone. I had to know for sure it was a sibling. The other brother's name showed up in three different parts of the country, so I couldn't tell if he was the right person. I really thought contacting a sister was the best idea, and the older the better, but I couldn't find any of them. I put the search out of my mind and went back to work the next day.

A week later, I returned to the White Pages website. None of the siblings were appearing. Then I noticed one of the married names showed up with an Oklahoma City address. Then the maiden name associated with that married name showed up at the same address. The same first name, the same age at the same address—that must be the oldest sister! She must have divorced and then changed back to her maiden name. I couldn't believe it! I jumped up from the computer and ran downstairs.

"I think I have it," I yelled to Jed. "I think I found a sister."

"Really? Why? What'd you find?"

I showed him the married name and the maiden name, both with the same first name, both living at the same address, and both the same age.

"What are you going to do?"

"I have to write to her," I said. "I have to write." I was out of breath with anxiety and anticipation. I had made my decision without even being aware of it.

"It's eleven-thirty. Can't it wait until tomorrow?" he said.

"You know it can't." We both laughed.

I sat at the desk. I wanted to put enough information in the letter, but not too much. How awful if I turned her off before we even got to know each other.

Dear Barbee,

My name is Margaret Hendrick. I do not want to interfere or disturb your life, but as we both move into middle age, I wanted to contact you. I believe I am your half-sister. My biological mother had a relationship with your father when he was a student at MIT in Cambridge, Massachusetts in 1948. I was born in March 1949.

One of the difficult things about being adopted is not being able to pass along to one's children health and ancestral histories. I am hoping you will be able to help me in this area.

I have been married for thirty-five years, and we have three chil-dren, all grown. I am a licensed psychotherapist and work in a Boston public school.

I hope this letter is not coming at a bad time, although I don't know of a truly good time. I felt you should know about our biological connection, which I have recently confirmed.

Yours truly, Margaret Hendrick

I wrote my phone number, email, and return address on the bottom. My husband read over the letter and made a couple additions that were more humorous than helpful, so I inked them out and proceeded to the final draft. I folded the letter gently and slipped it into the envelope. How strange, how wonderfully strange, I thought. I had just written a letter to a sister. A sister! It still didn't feel real. The letter went in the mail the next day and had a weekend to be delivered.

I tried to put it out of my thoughts. I had no idea when it was going to be read or responded to. After mailing the letter, any wishful thoughts of a connection with my Oklahoma family vanished just as quickly as they came. I let them go. The possibility of rejection was too powerful. It was easier just not to think about it. When I got home after work, my husband asked me if I thought the sister had received my letter.

"Today would be the first day she could because there was no mail yes-terday," I said. "But I don't really expect to hear from her."

We watched that night's *CSI* show, walked the dogs, and climbed into bed after eleven o'clock. I was sound asleep when the phone rang. The clock said eleven-thirty. I jumped out of bed and leapt across the room, try-ing to keep the ringing from waking Jed. My mind was racing. Something must be wrong with one of our kids. Matt was in California. Mike was in New York. Lauren had just moved into her own condo. I could make a ca-tastrophe out of anything! I glanced at the clock. Who calls at eleven-thirty? I picked up the receiver and waited to hear the voice of one of my children.

"Hello?" I said.

Then I heard what sounded to me like a Southern accent say, "Hi, this is Barbee Stueve."

Every one of my muscles stiffened. But then again, I had heard that voice before—words spoken in tones. It was just like my voice.

"That was some letter you sent me," this Barbee Stueve said.

I was trying desperately to gauge the tone of her voice to sense any anger or animosity.

Then I heard, "Well, welcome to the family," spoken in that charming Oklahoma drawl, which was Southern with a little twang. As soon as I heard her light, friendly voice, my body relaxed, and I slid down the wall, landing comfortably on the floor. From then on, I just enjoyed the conversation with my new sister.

Barbee was a teacher at an Oklahoma City elementary school. She had three children, two boys and a girl, but her girl was in the middle. She was already a grandmother of two. We chatted as if I had been away at college, and she needed to fill me in on all the family's comings and goings. She found it interesting that her "old father" had been "naughty" up in Boston. She knew he went to MIT, but she knew nothing of me.

"I thought when I got your letter that you had sent one to each of us, so I called Joni, the next younger to me. She didn't get a letter, so I read your letter to her. She told me not to tell the next younger sister, Carolyn, because she might get emotional. But I called Carolyn anyway. She did cry, but it wasn't a bad cry. I called the next youngest, and she was surprised. I called the boys, Bill and Rick. Bill lives in Texas, and he told me he'd handle it and find out what you wanted from us. Rick, the youngest, just made a joke. Then Carolyn called me back because she really wanted to know about you. I had told her I was thinking of emailing you, but she thought I should just call, since you had given us your phone number. I told her I would and promised I'd call her back. She'll be real happy to hear all about you."

I laughed and asked questions. She wanted to know about my family. I wanted to know about hers. Our son Michael lived a twenty-minute walk from her oldest son in Brooklyn, New York. Mike could have been standing next to his first cousin in the grocery store and not even known it.

Barbee and I could have continued talking longer. She liked to chatter, as I do, and was teased by her siblings for it. Finally, we both decided we needed some sleep, but we promised to keep in touch. I hung up the phone and walked over to the bed. Jed, who had been in and out of sleep, congratulated me, smiled, and went back to his dream.

I crawled back into bed around one-thirty, and just as I began to doze off, the phone rang again. "Hi, this is Carolyn!" the woman said. "I'm the third oldest. But I guess I'm the fourth oldest now. Yes, I did cry when I heard about you, but I wasn't sad. Barbee always gets after me because I cry so easily. I can't wait for you to meet Rick and Joni. They're the funniest of us all. We are all pretty close, and I am so glad you are one of us."

Carolyn was a night owl and had decided to call. She wanted to talk to her "new" sister, too. She lived in Tulsa and had a son living a twenty-minute drive from our other son, Matt, in California. The world had suddenly expanded past my little Boston bubble. Carolyn did not have the singsong tone that Barbee had, but she did have a strong Oklahoma accent to my Boston ears. Carolyn said they hadn't seen much of their father over the last ten years. In fact, this past Christmas was the first time in a while. He had married again, and his new wife kept him pretty much to herself. We laughed and joked. She was a licensed mental health counselor like me. She had attended graduate school at the exact same time I did, although she was almost a decade younger.

I was overwhelmed when I finally crawled into bed at three in the morning, but I quickly fell into a blissful sleep. The next morning, after struggling a little to wake up, I felt my feet light on the ground as peace and calm accompanied me to work. I couldn't wait to tell someone at school about finding my family and that I had SISTERS.

The students came into school that morning in large groups, laughing and chatting, stopping for hugs—"Hi, Miss Hendrick!" When the groups thinned to one or two late ones, I usually chatted with the special education teacher who shared hall duty with me.

As the last student climbed the stairs, I began to tell my corridor companion about my late-night conversation with my newly found sister. By the end of the first sentence, my hall mate knew I had found my biological family, and immediately the look on her face changed from pleasant to stern. Without a word, she turned on one foot and walked away from me. I had been midsentence telling her how excited I was; she said nothing, but I heard her clearly.

I was hurt, but it wasn't the first time I had experienced that kind of reaction. When I found my birth mother years ago, people occasionally expressed their displeasure by not wanting to hear about it. While I didn't remember anyone walking away, some changed the subject. Reactions to my searching seemed to be either very positive or very negative. There was no middle ground.

Barbee arrived at her school that morning, and her news was greeted with excitement and congratulations. The difference between the reaction Barbee received and mine was startling but not unexpected. Barbee's colleagues celebrated her news, because she had done nothing wrong, while my colleague viewed me as a rule breaker. Searching for a birth family showed disloyalty to my adoptive family. The adoptive family was the one that society (through adoption laws) had given me. To some, searching was unforgivable unless sanctioned by an adoptive parent. Society expected adoptees to accept the parents given to them, be loyal, and not complain. I had broken all of society's rules.

Chapter 33

OKLAHOMA

*W*ithin a couple of days, I had spoken to each sibling at least once and several times with some. The calls always included laughter and chitchat. Carolyn sent me a packet of pictures from their last Christmas celebration. The photos included some children of my siblings and their children too. The family was very large with nieces and nephews and grandnieces and nephews.

When talking to my daughter a few weeks later I said, "I think I'm going to Oklahoma during my February vacation. Would you come with me?" Her positive answer surprised and delighted me.

Lauren and I changed planes in Chicago to the Southwest puddle jumper, which stopped in other southern and midwestern cities, places that never meant anything to me, but now I wanted to know all about them.

Flying over the Oklahoma landscape, the terrain looked flat with lots of rivers and lakes. I didn't expect to see so much water. It was so surreal I had to continually remind myself that Lauren's and my ancestors had arrived in this region when it had been either a young state or no state at all. I became overwhelmed thinking of those people who had walked on that land beneath me. Maybe they even rode horses, I laughed to myself. While Lauren and I were fixated on the view out the window, the plane began its descent into the Will Rogers World Airport in Oklahoma City (just for the record, Will Rogers died in a plane crash), and soon our Southwest jet was on the ground, taxiing to the gate.

People scurrying through the airport were openly friendly, offering their help and casual chatter, laced with a bit of humor. As we walked along the promenade, above us in the rafters were large pictures of famous Oklahomans. My favorite actor from childhood, James Garner, was there. I had known he was from Oklahoma, but I didn't know Mickey Mantle, Ron Howard, Brad Pitt, and Hopalong Cassidy were. My brother Robbie and I loved Hopalong Cassidy when we were little.

My mother Midge told me that one day, she and Dad took us to a grocery store opening where the actor who played Hopalong Cassidy was appearing as part of the celebration. We weren't there long when Mr. Cassidy surprised everyone by walking over to my parents, taking me out of my mother's arms and giving me a kiss on the cheek, while he declared that I was the cutest little thing he had ever seen.

I couldn't believe I was actually on the ground in Oklahoma. Lauren and I followed the baggage area signs. We didn't expect anyone to meet us, because they were all working. We had our directions and a car reservation. My brother Bill had arranged a hotel in downtown Oklahoma City near the newly restored Bricktown area. He was planning to fly up from Austin the next day.

Lauren and I found the stairs down to the baggage area and were halfway to the bottom when I saw a dark-haired woman looking up at us. Except for the hair color, her face was very familiar—narrow with small features. It was Barbee. She was standing to the side waving two little Oklahoma flags and wearing a red pea coat just like mine. We had hugs and warm, excited exclamations. We began talking and talking. We were the storytellers in the family, so between the flight and the last couple days, we had much to share. Lauren took my arm to direct me to the car rental, because Barbee and I couldn't find a pause.

As we drove out of the airport garage, a sculpture of four, two-story high feathered arrows were sticking in the ground at different angles, as if shot by a giant Native American miles away. We were certainly no longer in Boston. Lauren made me slow down just before the on-ramp to Route 44 so she could take a picture of an unfamiliar highway sign: Wichita and Tulsa.

We followed Barbee's car, a black version of my own little white SUV to the hotel. Lauren and I stepped out, and a smaller version of Barbee came up to us. It was Carolyn. Then a young woman carrying a toddler crossed the street and came over to us. It was Barbee's daughter Kristin. Barbee introduced her husband, Ray. Carolyn and I then sat down inside the hotel and caught up from the few days since we last talked. Plans were made to meet more siblings for dinner around the corner at Abuelo's. It was exciting, and yet felt so wonderfully normal.

As I stood in the reception area of the restaurant, I bumped into another sister before I realized we were even related. I shuddered to think of all the cousins and relatives I could have bumped into over the years and sadly had no idea we were even kin. This was Joni and her husband.

All the Stueve women carried a strong family resemblance, and everyone saw me as fitting into it, too. They had their mother's shorter stature, making me the moose in their midst. A long table was set up to accommodate those who could come. Lauren and I were sitting apart from each other, facing the entry door. A young man walked in and began talking to Kristin. Lauren and I immediately recognized his body language and turned simultaneously toward each other, mouthing "Matt!" My son Matthew was taller and fairer, but the body language was unmistakably the same. It was my youngest brother, Rick. He had been born when I was a junior in high school. Oh, I wished I had known them then.

I learned quickly that a gathering of the siblings was filled with laughter, warmth, and chatter. I always thought I had a pretty good sense of humor, but I couldn't compete with the quick and clever Rick and Joni. I just sat back and enjoyed the camaraderie.

The next morning, Lauren and I set off to Barbee's school. Everyone welcomed us and was excited to meet Barbee's new sister. After introductions to gerbils and ferrets also in the first grade classroom, Rick came by and took Lauren and me on a tour of the siblings' area of Oklahoma City.

He drove us by their old houses and schools. He showed us things that had been important to all of them growing up. I loved seeing these places, thinking about their activities and friends, while I had been separated from them.

Each of them at various times asked me when I planned to meet "our father," but I told them I had no plans. I didn't need to meet him. They had almost no contact with him anyway, so I didn't see how opening up the old wounds would be a good idea. I didn't hold it against him for sending me the rejecting letter in 1979, although some of them did. They all wished I had come years earlier.

The next day Jed arrived, as did Carolyn's husband. My brother Bill was grounded by an ice storm in Dallas, halfway to us and halfway home. He finally returned to Austin.

Lauren went home after a few more days. Jed and I drove up to Tulsa to see where Carolyn lived. Carolyn wanted to show me a large ancestral chart that our father had researched and presented to them at their last visit. As I looked over all the names, I could see he had done an enormous amount of work. I asked Carolyn about our grandparents.

Carolyn said our grandmother, Eleanor Eberle, was known as Mema Eleanor. "Mema" was a Southern title for grandmother. Carolyn remembered her well because she had moved in with the family after her husband died in 1957. Carolyn described her as a sweet, comforting, loving grandmother—a wonderful cook and talented seamstress. Only Barbee remembered our grandfather; he died when she was five.

Our grandparents, Winfred Stueve and Eleanor Eberle, were married in 1919. He was nine years older than she, but they were different in more ways than just age. Eleanor's family was Southern, Protestant, came to America in the time of Jamestown, and supported the Confederacy. Her uncle was head of Annapolis during World War I and then Chief of Naval Operations. Our grandfather's family was German, Northern, Catholic, supported the Union and had been immigrants in 1832. Our grandfather's uncle was a West Point graduate, cavalry officer and had been the commanding general at the Battle of the Marne in World War I. The only obvious commonality in the couple was their fathers were both attorneys.

Leaving Oklahoma was bittersweet. Lauren, Jed, and I had a wonderful time. My siblings were simply my siblings. I felt as if I had only been living away, and now I was home catching up with everyone. When they heard they had a sister from Boston, it had been a shock, and many of their early discussions were about how little in common they expected to have with me. As it turned out, we were remarkably alike in education, humor, attitudes, values and demeanors. I overheard a correction of a family friend who had labeled me a "half-sister." "No, she's my sister," was the definitive answer from my sibling.

Chapter 34

CHARLES

Back in Boston, I felt a new sense of ease and confidence as I went to work the next day. An emotional strength had woven its way into my psyche. I didn't know if this was the power of having siblings, or maybe just knowing where I came from.

My brother Bill never made it to Oklahoma while I was there, but within a month he had business in Boston, and we had a wonderful, warm meeting. We covered many topics during his visit. Since he was a scientist, he had wanted to view the DNA test results. After he met me, he had no doubt, he said. I sounded just like his other sisters.

As we caught up on other family topics, it was clear he wanted me to contact our father, so everything would be out in the open. I didn't want to annoy my newly discovered brother, but I had no intention of contacting Charles. I didn't want to upset him again, and I just didn't see the point. If the siblings felt our father should know about me, then I thought they could contact him.

Bill decided to do just that and emailed our father. He told Charles that the siblings had met me and were thrilled to have a new sister. Our father was not particularly happy. He had never told anyone about me, not even their mother. When Barbee heard about his response, she decided to contact him, too. He wasn't any happier to hear from her. After two siblings had told Charles about me, I decided to email him myself:

Dear Charles, After living many years without medical and ancestral information, and then growing into middle age, lack of this knowledge felt like a burden to me. I hoped that after all these years, my contacting your family would not be too much of a disruption in anyone's life. I am sorry if this is not the case. I have enjoyed a good life materially and it has been fulfilling in many ways, but lack of a family has been difficult. My adoptive parents were considerably older, and both died at fairly young ages.

Opening up this old chapter in your life may be painful, and I am sorry if that is so. Perhaps over time we might be able to correspond, but I will understand if that is not possible. Please understand that this letter is sent with sincerity and affection. Margaret

Fairly quickly I received this response:

Dear Margaret, Thanks for the e-mail. I can certainly appreciate your position. But having kept this secret for so many years, I find it is very difficult to deal with…I am glad you have been accepted by my other children. Charles

I wrote back:

Dear Charles, Thank you for replying. I will not bother you again if you wish. But if you would like copies of some of the ancestral information, which I have been collecting from New England Genealogical, I would be happy to send it to you. The family chart you created has been most valuable in getting this process going. I would be happy to send you one of the packets that I have sent to the siblings. Let me know. Margaret

Another quick response:

Dear Margaret, Yes, I would like to receive anything you have on the old ancestors. Perhaps we will meet some time. Thanks, Charles

Hearing that he was open to meeting didn't create a noticeable emotional response in me. I was happy that we had found the topic of genealogy to share, but I had long ago made peace with not meeting him in this lifetime. Since Jed and I were going back to Oklahoma for a family reunion on my siblings' mother's side in Paoli, I made plans to meet Charles while I was in town.

All my siblings were gathered at the Marriott Courtyard greeting all the out-of-towners for the next day's family reunion. They were also sending Jed and me off to meet their father the night before. Most of their instructions were funny and some had a little edge.

"I can't believe he hasn't canceled at the last minute. That's what he usually does with us."

"You're more like Daddy than any of us. You look like him, and you enjoy all the same things he's interested in. You'll get along great with him."

Jed and I pulled into the short driveway of a retirement cottage in southwest Oklahoma City. I took a deep breath. Jed and I walked up to the door and I rang the bell. A medium-height man, a little on the thin side with a thick crop of light-brown wavy hair came to the door. He gave us a warm welcome.

"Welllll, come on in!" he said in a thick Southern accent, tinged with strong Oklahoma twang and musical tones. His accent was more intense than those of my siblings. He invited us in as if we were old neighbors who had just stopped by. He introduced us to his wife and then showed us around his small two-bedroom retirement cottage. He seemed genuinely pleased to see me. We talked about the weather, the Army in which he had served, University of Oklahoma football, and generally about growing up in Oklahoma. He was the consummate teacher. He told me how he went to MIT on the GI Bill to finish up the degree he had started at the

University of Oklahoma before the war. Two of his high school friends had already graduated from MIT. They told him sailing in Boston was great.

He told me if anyone from the adoption agency had contacted him about meeting me, he would never have agreed to it, but now he was very happy to have a chance to meet me. We never talked about the letter he sent me years ago. The visit lasted longer than I had planned. He encouraged me to come back and have lunch with him and his wife later that week.

Jed went back to Boston a couple days later, and I drove back down to have lunch with Charles and his wife. As we sat at our table, people approached to meet the Stueves' guest. Without hesitation, Charles introduced me as his daughter Margaret from Boston. I didn't expect he'd show such a public acceptance of me. Before I arrived, I thought about whether he would or not. I kept telling myself it wasn't that important, but when he introduced me, I realized how much it really meant to me.

I followed Charles and his wife back to their cottage after lunch. Charles left the room for a minute and came back with containers of hanging file holders. "I want you to have these now that you are picking up the family genealogical work. These are all the things I have been working on, but it's time for the next generation to take it over. I don't think any of the other kids care so much about it. I'm so glad you do."

I was overwhelmed. Not only did he recognize me as his daughter, he was treating me as an equal to his other children. The boxes of multiple hanging files were neatly sorted, as expected of a retired engineer. I put them aside and sat down to continue our visit. I didn't know if I could get personal about our past, but I decided it was now or never.

"Did your parents know about me?" I asked.

"Oh, yes," he said with an enthusiasm I didn't expect.

"Were they upset?"

"When my mother heard about you, she wanted to go right up to Boston and bring you home to Oklahoma, but they didn't do things like that in those days."

I looked at him a little skeptically. "What was she going to do with me?"

"She was going to raise you, of course. You were her son's daughter."

His face looked sad as the memory of our separated lives settled in.

"I only heard my parents argue twice in my life. The first time was when my mother wanted her father to live with us. I really liked my grandfather Eberle a lot, but my father didn't want him staying with us. The other time was when my father didn't want my mother to bring you back to Oklahoma." Charles's expression became thoughtful. "I often thought of you over the years and wondered how you would have fit in with all those other kids of mine. They are quite a bunch, aren't they?" he said with a loving smile. "I'm really glad they have accepted you. I can't tell you how glad I am you found us."

Chapter 35

The South

*M*y life had become extraordinarily wonderful. Our sons had created fulfilling lives for themselves. Our daughter loved her job and was marrying her college sweetheart. I had been reunited with all the family I had lost. My family genealogy was demanding more of the research I loved. My tennis game was improving, and the horses I dreamed of all my life were now a part of it. Friends teased me, saying they wished they had my life, and I didn't disagree with them. Winning the lottery would even have been a setback.

The more information I gathered from New England Genealogical, the more I realized I needed to go down South to find out more about those ancestors. The South, with all its history and mysteries, had been beckoning me from the moment I heard my ancestors were born there. I needed to walk on the land where my ancestors had lived and learn more about that family history.

I received a year of unpaid sabbatical from the Boston Public Schools and packed up my Toyota RAV with the family information I had collected so far from Chris Child, some food, and my first laptop (which I had little idea how to use), and I began a two-month trip into the South. My husband and family were a little startled by my plans. Never had I really traveled alone, but the pull to find the story of my relatives was stronger than any traveling fears.

The Wisdom family was the main southern line from which I was descended. The Wisdoms first settled in the Tidewater area of Virginia near Williamsburg in the early seventeenth century. They moved up to Spotsylvania County near Fredericksburg in the early eighteenth century and then south into North Carolina during the Revolution. After the war, they began a migration west into Tennessee, Arkansas, and finally Oklahoma. My plan was to follow that migration route and find out all I could.

My husband understood my need to walk on the land of ancestors. We had gone to Ireland a few years back and did just that. My children were more surprised by my wanderlust. To travel to a strange place all by myself was not typical of the mother they knew. Their mother hesitated each time she stepped into a motel or vacation rental, not necessarily checking for cleanliness, but waiting to feel at ease in a strange place. They loved to imitate my circling rented rooms, then finally concluding, "This is nice"… even if it weren't.

I had been in the South twice in my life—once when my mother Midge and I flew to Fort Rucker in Alabama to visit Robbie and his family. The other time my husband and I drove down to Williamsburg, Virginia. We had heard it was very interesting. We loved it, and took in all the wonderful history it offered.

"You're going to think I'm crazy, but this town makes sense to me. I don't know why. I have grown up around Puritans and Mayflower people all my life. While I probably will never know where my ancestors came from, I'd want them to be from here," I declared to Jed as I stood in front of the House of Burgesses, ten years before I had ever heard the name Wisdom.

Starting my road trip, I exited Route 128 and merged onto Interstate 95 and began driving south. Later that day, as I continued south of the Washington, D.C. suburbs, I noticed signs commemorating Civil War battlefields—Manassas, Wilderness, Fredericksburg. I had never thought much about the Civil War. I didn't know anyone who fought in it. It was like every other war to me—fought on someone else's soil and studied in books. But these Civil War signs depicted a war not fought on foreign land. It was fought in people's front yards and backyards—right where everyone lived.

I tried to picture a war fought in front of my childhood home in Braintree, people dying next to the wooden rail fence with the red roses. The image was overwhelming. We Northerners pointed to Lexington and Concord for our close-to-home war experience. I suddenly realized that Massachusetts battle was really a small skirmish compared to the endless days of slaughter and bloodshed on these Southern battlefields.

The library in Fredericksburg, Virginia had a historical research room whose access was either down an awkward spiral staircase or through a warren of rooms. Despite its size, it was packed with an abundance of information about early Virginia. I loved the smallness of the space. I began pulling out index books and wrote down any references to the family names New England Genealogical had given me—Wisdom, Buford/Beaufort, and Lewis. There was a "Wisdom birth", in 1634, referred to in the *Virginia Magazine*, which meant the Wisdoms had come to Virginia even earlier than I originally thought.

After a couple of days in Fredericksburg, I drove farther south to Richmond. I heard the Virginia State Library was an important place for research. The next morning, as I walked from my hotel to the library, people on the street, both black and white, all greeted me warmly—nods, hellos, wishing me a good day. Everyone looked directly at me wanting an acknowledgment. "Good morning. How are you today?" This chatting, concern, and good wishes expressed between perfect strangers was lovely. Having grown up in the more reserved Northeast, I was distracted by all the polite stimulation. There was a joy in it all.

The State Library had the will of Francis Wisdom, who I already knew to be my sixth great-grandfather and a direct ancestor of Lucile Wisdom. At the beginning of Francis Wisdom's will, he wrote that he had given to his children all that he wanted them to have over his lifetime. The will was written when he was well into his 80s. The remainder of the will addressed the needs of what he called his "family." Francis's family was made up of his twenty-one slaves. Half of these slaves were over the age of sixteen, and half under. The names of his slaves were listed and grouped by families. The will stated that each of the five slave families were to be kept together and given to his children. None of his "families" were to be sold.

I leaned back in my chair in horror upon realizing I had uncovered what I had long feared—I was descended from at least one slave owner. I didn't know what to do with this information. I had hoped it would never be true. It was not an identity I ever thought would be mine. I wanted to reject it and pretend I hadn't seen the records, but that didn't seem fair. I decided to collect the names, and hope I'd have the opportunity to share the information of how these slaves were involved with helping Francis Wisdom supply the Revolution.

After a week, I left the State Library with more information on the Wisdoms and other intermarried relations than I ever expected. I was related to many ancestral lines of the early Virginia colonists. Within this information were records that included land owned by Francis Wisdom in southern Virginia, Pittsylvania County, where he had moved during the Revolution. I never realized the records could be so specific, but I was confident that if I were in the area, I could find his land. I was anxious to begin driving farther south.

I drove west and began looking for Route 15 south, knowing it would take me to Chatham, Virginia, the county seat of Pittsylvania. The pastoral scenes along this drive were beautiful. All the fall colors that I thought only New England produced were just as vibrant here in Virginia. Unexpectedly, I came upon Appomattox. The Civil War was not on my agenda, but I had to stop and see where Grant had treated Lee like a gentleman and the South became that defeated cousin.

I finally arrived after nightfall in Chatham, Virginia. It was a small, sweet, sleepy town, without a motel. I began to worry that I might be sleeping in my car until I saw a sign for a bed and breakfast named The Columns. I pulled up in front. It was a beautiful Queen Anne style Victorian with a large wraparound porch. I crossed the porch and pictured wicker chairs and swings for everyone to enjoy on warm summer evenings of days gone by. I rang the bell, and a pretty dark-haired young woman answered the door while holding back a small dog. She seemed a bit distracted.

"Do you have any rooms tonight?" I asked.

"Well…" I heard the beginning of the lovely smooth Virginia accent. "I hadn't really planned on having guests tonight. It is Halloween, you know." I had completely lost track of the days. "There will be a lot of children coming and going. They might be a bother," she explained with a sweet, worried look.

The image of sleeping in the tiny back seat of my RAV frightened me now, so I told her I had come from Boston and really needed a place to stay. Upon hearing that, she did not hesitate.

"Please, come on in. We will be happy to have you. Anne Meadors, would you show Miss Hendrick up to the front room?"

The daughter looked to be in the first grade. She was a beautiful little girl with short, straight hair pulled back on one side by a large bow and immediately answered her mother, "Yes, ma'am," and gave me a big smile. The mother, hostess Staci, warmed up quickly and mentioned that as soon as the night calmed, she and her husband Andrew would love to join me for a glass of wine in the living room.

As the number of trick-or-treaters slowed and the porch light was turned off. The owners came into the living room and served some lovely wine. When the two older sons came home, Andrew asked them to greet me, "Turner and Raines, would you please say hello to our guest, Miss Hendrick?"

Their "Yes, ma'am" came in unison, and I received two lovely, polite greetings.

I was sitting in the midst of what felt like the best of family life any-where, but now it happened to be in the South—beautiful manners, good conversation about families, life, death, love, hate, religion, North, and South. The Wall family was charming and loving. By the end of my two nights, I had a good flavor of what being a Southerner meant to many who lived here. I wondered if it resembled my ancestral family in any way.

The next day, I went down to the small county courthouse and looked up records pertaining to Francis Wisdom. The records included land transfers and the dispositions of his slaves, which had been recorded at the courthouse. I was told that was unusual. The slave families went to his daughters, his grandson and a granddaughter. No slaves went to the son from which I was descended, Thomas Wisdom. I wasn't sure what that meant.

The next day, with great difficulty, I left the warmth and graciousness of my hostess and her family. I was anxious to see the actual land of my slave-owning, Revolution-supporting, sixth great-grandfather, Francis Wisdom. I drove over miles of country roads before I found the one leading into the acreage Francis Wisdom owned from 1778 until he died in 1794. When I first learned that my ancestral land could be identified, I shuddered to think that a drug store could be on one corner and a gas station on the other, but the land I had been driving through was lovely with lots of tall trees and wide pastures. I began driving down the narrow dirt road that was supposed to be the opening to Francis Wisdom's land.

At the end of the dirt road was an antique Virginia farmhouse—two rooms on the first floor and two on the second. These types of houses were wide across the front, but only one room deep, and each had a small peak centered over the front door at the roofline. This antique style of house was seen all over the Virginia countryside.

As I walked into the yard, an older couple came out to see what their dogs were barking about. I introduced myself and told them I was looking for the property of Francis Wisdom. The man told me the house and land had been in his family since the Revolution, but he had never heard of the name Wisdom. I was disappointed—I had come this far, but finding Francis Wisdom's land didn't seem likely.

Since I was already there, the gracious couple wanted to show me around their small family cemetery. On one of the headstones, I recognized the name of an executor from Francis Wisdom's will, Matthew Clay. The owner of the cemetery told me his ancestor Matthew Clay was a first cousin of the great orator Henry Clay. Then I checked my notes again and saw that not only was Matthew Clay an executor, he had bought one section of Francis Wisdom's land from the estate. That confirmed I was standing on my sixth great-grandfather's land. I didn't know if this was the Wisdom house in front of me, but I knew I must be close. The couple walked me around more of the property before I had to leave. I wanted to cross the state line into North Carolina before nightfall, and I needed to keep in mind my deadline of Thanksgiving at Bill's in Austin, Texas.

I found the highway heading south and finally crossed the state line into North Carolina near Person/Caswell Counties where Francis Wisdom's son, my ancestor, Thomas, had died during the Revolution. I wasn't sure of the exact date or place, but in the county records I found his death. He died in Hillsborough, December 1780, well before the end of the Revolution. Thomas's wife, Martha Lewis Wisdom, and their young children lived just north in Caswell County, near the ravaging and pillaging by loyalist forces, which were at Martha's front door during her young motherhood and early years of widowhood. I couldn't imagine her in that predicament, as the raging Revolution suddenly became much more real than just having the Presidents Adams' houses near my childhood home in Massachusetts.

Sad that Thomas hadn't lived longer, that Martha had been widowed at such an difficult time in her life, and thinking that my ancestors actually owned slaves made me want to just to find Interstate 40 and begin driving west. I needed to clear my mind. I crossed the Smoky Mountains the next day and entered Tennessee. Tennessee! I still couldn't grasp that I came from Tennessee, after having grown up in a Boston suburb, where I never heard of anyone coming from this state. But here I was with ancestors and perhaps current cousins in Tennessee. Then I remembered one of my husband's partners, upon hearing about my travels, stopped by Jed's office and hummed the *Deliverance* theme song. I was much less amused by that kind of thing now.

The Tennessee State Archives in Nashville had information on military records, which confirmed my great-great-grandfather, Lucile Wisdom's father, Dew Moore Wisdom, fought in the Civil War as a Confederate cavalry colonel. I wasn't sure how to process this. This discovery meant I was not only descended from slave owners, but from a Confederate officer. Suddenly, I was facing an ancestral identity that I hadn't expected and was jealous of those who had a lifetime to process such information.

By the time I finished in Nashville, I had only a few hours left before sunset. I had learned my lesson in North Carolina after having a flat tire at sundown. I stopped at a small motel along the highway. Even though the interior was not up-to-date, it had a wonderful, peaceful feel. I went to bed early, and am still not sure whether I imagined an unseen hand shaking me awake early the next morning, or whether I dreamed someone was waking me for a historical battle nearby. As I drove out of the parking lot, I made a mental note that maybe I'd not stop there again.

Chapter 36

PURDY

After I shook off my rude awakening, I merged back onto Interstate 40. I figured I'd arrive in Jackson, Tennessee in time for a second cup of coffee. My great-grandmother was born in Jackson. Her father, Dew Moore Wisdom, was born close by in a small town called Purdy, although Purdy was no longer on any modern maps.

Jackson had multiple exits, lots of motels, and businesses close to the highway, but the center of town was farther south. I drove down Highland Avenue until I came to a centrally featured city hall, four courthouses, and multiple businesses. The eight square blocks were lined with lovely trees.

As I drove around the city square, I tried to imagine what kind of house Lucile Wisdom might have lived in—perhaps a Victorian? I laughed to myself, wondering why I thought she might have lived in something so grand. Her house was probably more like a log cabin. I stopped in front of the City Hall and climbed out of the car so I could take a closer look at the monuments scattered on its lawn. The tallest monument was one I had seen in other towns. A man in a military uniform stood high up on top of a stone pillar, honoring those who fought for the Confederacy. Another monument honored World War I and II veterans, while another honored David Crockett. I only knew him as Davy, but the man had been this county's United States Representative. When he lost his final election, his parting words—as quoted on the plaque—were, "You may all go to hell, and I will go to Texas." I became sad as I thought of his death soon after at the Alamo.

I strolled around the center of the town a little more, looking at the interesting architecture and the four handsome courthouses. Jackson even had a Federal Court. As I turned to get back in my car, I could see further down the road what looked like a neighborhood of Victorian homes. As I drove across the train tracks into the neighborhood to get a closer look, I saw an entire street ahead lined with lovely, large Victorian era homes, in a variety of architectural styles.

The first one was a beautiful, large, red brick house with gingerbread moldings and elaborate porches. As I passed that house, I noticed a small historical sign identifying the family who had once lived there—Wisdom. *Wisdom.* My head whipped back around to confirm what I thought I had seen. I couldn't believe it. I quickly turned the car around and pulled up in front of the magnificent home. The name Wisdom was even carved into the stone curb. I couldn't hold myself back. I strode up the front walk and stepped onto the porch. Up close, the front door was much larger than it looked from the street, and it had beautiful stained-glass panels over the door and down each side.

I rang the old-fashioned bell and heard an inside door open and then I watched the outer louvered door move. Standing in the opening was a perfectly pressed man in a short-sleeved cotton shirt and beige pants. He conveyed an air of confidence, poise, and manners. Then an announcer-style deep voice began, "Well…" and ended an octave higher with "Hi," all drawled so that each word had at least two syllables.

I apologized for interrupting his day, and I told him I was trying to locate the house where my ancestors might have lived, and I saw his historical sign. "I'm looking for a Wisdom," I said.

"Wwwelll…come…on…in," he said without hesitation.

His cadence was deliberate and even. His voice had multiple tones like Barbee's and mine, but his R's were hard like a New Yorker's.

"Hi, my name is Kemp...Kemp Reed." Each word came from the back of his throat, in a deep Southern accent, while his hand was extended for a warm welcome.

He took a step back and waved me inside as if I were a friend who shouldn't have rung the bell in the first place. The large foyer was long and darker than I had imagined. The house had a strong masculine feel in the Eastlake tradition. The ceilings were thirteen feet high, and all around the rooms were beautiful antiques displaying interesting pieces of silver and china. A wide stairway rose at the back of the hall, met the ceiling and then disappeared into the second floor. An ornate Victorian gas lamp was perched on the newel post at the bottom of the stairs. Kemp turned my attention to a picture on the left as we stepped inside—a handsome portrait framed in gold.

"This is Mr. John Lee Wisdom. He was the Wisdom who lived here," Kemp said with a bit of prideful ownership. "He built this house in 1880 for his bride, Kate Meriwether. She was about nineteen when he gave it to her." Kemp looked over at me and then back at the portrait. "Well, look at that. I think you do favor the Wisdoms."

"I haven't heard of John Lee Wisdom," I said. "My great-great-grandfather's name was Dew Moore Wisdom. His daughter, Lucile, was supposed to have been born in Jackson."

"Well, if your great-grandmother was Lucile Wisdom, then Mr. John Lee Wisdom was her uncle. Dew Moore Wisdom was John Lee's big brother."

I felt a joyful rush upon hearing that I was standing in the foyer of my great-grand uncle's house, a place that had probably been visited by my other Wisdom ancestors many times.

As Kemp escorted me into the formal parlor, a taller man entered from the back. Kemp called out to him, "Mickey, this here is Miss Margaret from Boston. She has come all the way to Jackson to find her ancestors. She's a Wisdom."

A statement like that still made me want to correct the speaker, but I was beginning to enjoy the truth of it.

"Well, it's very nice to meet you, Miss Margaret," he said, "Y'all came all the way from Boston? That is a long way just to visit Jackson," he said, as he nodded politely in my direction. "Kemp, let me get y'all some sweet tea."

Mickey's accent was softer than Kemp's. It was more like the Virginia accent I had heard in Chatham. Mickey grew up near Jackson. Kemp was raised farther north, just over the border in Kentucky. Mickey's last name was the same as a Tennessee county, and his mother's ancestors were known to have married into the Washingtons of Virginia. But Mickey, unlike Kemp, had no interest in family trees.

I moved about the living room and admired the attractive decor. Kemp designed and made the floor-length drapes to be copies of the period. The furniture were all antiques, but he lamented that not a thing in the house belonged to the Wisdoms except one china plate with a "W" on it. The living room was large enough for multiple chairs, a sofa, and a grand piano. Kemp sat down on the bench and began from memory a Scott Joplin style ragtime. The lively, bouncy tune gave the room a festive atmosphere, and I could imagine a century-old party with women in long dresses and handsome men enjoying themselves. He continued until Mickey came back with two tall amber glasses.

"It's a wonderful house," I exclaimed. "I've never seen such a beautiful Victorian."

"Mr. Wisdom wanted a special house for Miss Kate," Kemp began, "but it's funny that it has such a masculine feel to it. Miss Kate came from a prominent Meriwether family. Mr. Wisdom bought the plans and materials for the house and had them shipped to Jackson. The plans are now in the National Archives. No one knew how to build such a complicated house, so Mr. Wisdom became the contractor. He was the youngest surviving child of William Sargent Wisdom and Jane Anderson. He moved up to Jackson from Purdy after his father died in 1871. His mother, Jane Anderson, was from an early eastern Tennessee family, but she died when Mr. John was a baby."

"You mentioned Purdy," I said. "Where is Purdy actually? I read about it, but it's not on any current maps."

"Purdy is about an hour south of here, but it really doesn't exist," said Kemp. "Purdy is one of the saddest stories. A number of people, like John and Dew's father, William Sargent Wisdom, put their heart and soul into that town. It was the prettiest town between Memphis and Nashville. The early settlers of Purdy wanted to rival those towns. They built everything you'd want in a sophisticated town. There were schools, hotels, a theater, and stagecoaches coming through regularly. William Sargent Wisdom even built a university just before the war. You haven't been to Purdy then?"

"No, I just saw it mentioned in a book on McNairy County that New England Genealogical showed me."

"Well, maybe we should go down there tomorrow," Kemp said.

"Yes, I'd love that, if it's not too much trouble."

"Oh no, it's no bother at all."

Kemp was walking ahead of me into the dining room, which had a long mahogany table, a dozen chairs, and an enormous crystal chandelier sparkling like a hundred diamonds. He pointed out the one plate with a "W" hanging on the wall.

"You probably know about the close relationship between the Andersons and the Wisdoms," Kemp said.

"No, I really don't know much about them."

"Well, all the Wisdoms and Andersons are double cousins. William Sargent Wisdom married Jane Anderson, and Jane's brother married William Sargent Wisdom's sister, so all their children were double first cousins. Your great-great-grandfather, Dew Wisdom, was a double cousin to James Wisdom Anderson. James Wisdom Anderson's son was Monroe Dunaway Anderson."

A blank look went across my face. I had no idea who this Monroe Dunaway Anderson was or why he was important.

Seeing my blank look, Kemp said, "You know the Houston cancer center? It was named after him, M. D. Anderson."

I had no idea who M. D. Anderson was, but I made a mental note to find out who my new double cousin was.

"When John Lee Wisdom left Purdy and came up to Jackson, he partnered with his Anderson cousins and created a number of businesses. They started a bank, a railroad, an electric company, and a trolley company and helped other relatives with dry goods and hardware stores. Much fixing up was needed after the war. Mr. John Lee Wisdom became a very wealthy man, maybe even more so than his father, who was worth over a quarter of a million just before the Civil War."

Kemp invited me to see more of the Wisdom house, so we went into the next parlor, where the windows turned into doors for easy access to the wraparound porch. The fireplace in the second parlor was original and had hand-painted porcelain tiles of hunting scenes. Over the fireplace opening were the carved words, "Come, warm ye in Friendship."

By the time I was ready to leave, Kemp and Mickey had fed me pork, cornbread, collard greens, and fried green tomatoes for lunch. Their hospitality overwhelmed me. In the midafternoon, I left feeling warm and joyous. The South was wrapping me in a cozy cocoon. I stepped off the porch and began walking toward my car when I noticed the park across the street. There were the most beautiful weeping willows, rose bushes, and other ornamental flowers with a green lawn and central gazebo in honor of John Lee Wisdom's daughter-in-law, who was the last Wisdom to own the house. A Victorian-style wrought-iron fence surrounded the acre lot. In the corner was an official sign—"Encampment of General Grant, 1863—after Shiloh and before Vicksburg." This brought me back to the reality that the Civil War was all around us.

At the motel that night, I had difficulty keeping my excitement under control. I couldn't believe I had walked into a strange man's house today, and tomorrow he was taking me someplace I had never been and had no idea where it was. But I was thrilled with this adventure. The South was enveloping me. I wanted more…more of the people, the food, the scenery, everything. If the South had been a blanket, I wanted to wrap myself in it. I felt at home everywhere I went.

The next morning I arrived in front of the Wisdom house. Kemp was ready for our drive to Purdy. "Margaret, I found some papers last night with more Wisdom information. I'll give them to you when we get back. Come on, now, hop in." Kemp reached over the seat to unlatch the door of his new Grand Cherokee. "I also found directions to the other Wisdom Cemetery where William Sargent Wisdom's parents are buried. James and Susannah Wisdom came to West Tennessee when it was first opened for settlement. There wasn't a postage stamp of land to farm. Every acre was thickly covered with tall oak trees, and the animals were wild. The story is that James Wisdom died from felling one of those trees."

We drove south on Route 45 toward Mississippi. "Tell me more about the papers," I said.

"Well, John Lee Wisdom's son wrote out directions to his great-grand-parents' graves after he visited them in 1941. He also wrote notes about all his aunts and uncles, including your great-great-grandfather, and the other cousins he knew about. It's quite interesting, and it might be helpful if you want to know about more current relations."

We continued south on a divided highway, less traveled than I expect-ed. At the town of Finger, we turned onto a back road. If we had gone another fifteen minutes south on the highway, we would have arrived in Selmer, Tennessee, the current McNairy County seat and former work-place of Buford Pusser, the sheriff in the movie *Walking Tall.*

After we crossed the railroad tracks, we were back on a country road driving past a sawmill, a small farm, and sparsely settled houses. We went down a little hill and crossed a creek, and then Kemp pulled over on the side of the road and stopped. We were in what looked like the middle of nowhere. Two empty, unfenced pastures were on either side of the narrow country road before they disappeared into forest. An older house was off in the fields. A more modern house appeared up the road a bit and that was it.

"There it is," he said as he pointed across one of the fields of high grass. "Up there on the hill in that stand of trees. That's where the cemetery is."

"Really?" I countered incredulously while trying not to sound rude. "How do you know? That hill doesn't look connected to anything."

"Up on a hill like that is where many people buried their kin back then," he said.

When I left Jackson that morning with my latte in one hand and cell phone in the other, I never checked to see if I had proper footwear. I had not planned to walk through any woods or grass, let alone waist-high grass. My searching until that time was confined to libraries and historical societies. It was a good thing that I didn't know then what I learned later—the real dangers of high-grass walking were rattlesnakes, chiggers, and fire ants, to mention a few.

I climbed out of the car and proceeded to follow Kemp through the field of tall grass. The newer house up the street owned the land that we were walking on, and I wasn't sure trespassing was such a good idea. People in New England could be quite protective of their property. I wasn't sure how they protected land in Tennessee, but I tried not to think about it.

I followed Kemp as he confidently waded through the grass, and then climbed up the small hill as we pushed our way through some brush. Right in front of us were three grave markers in good condition. I knelt down to read the names—James Wisdom died March 13, 1828, 55 years; Susannah Wisdom died November 17, 1835; and Mary Anderson died October 3, 1832. These were three of my fourth great-grandparents.

We spent some time just being with the graves and taking pictures. Kemp was also a relative of Mary Anderson, which made us distant cousins. In the South that really didn't count much, as it seemed everyone was a distant cousin to someone, but I was thrilled to have him as a cousin. The South seemed to be a perfect place for someone like me who had been without relatives for so long—now I appeared to be related to everyone.

Before we drove on, we stopped at the modern ranch house up the street and introduced ourselves to the owner of the little cemetery. Brenda was very welcoming and happy to hear we were connected to the people buried on her land. She said one or two other visitors had come by over the years, but most people didn't know it existed, which was fine with her, considering the damage done to some of the rural cemeteries. I thanked her for letting us walk around her land and told her I would send her information on the souls buried there.

Kemp and I climbed back in his car. We were now heading to old Purdy. We drove farther along Route 45 again, and then exited at Bethel Springs, where we saw only empty streets. Then Kemp took a left onto the Bethel/Purdy Road. We drove a distance that seemed much too far, as we were already in the middle of isolated country. Just when I thought we must have missed our mark, an old weathered sign appeared in the brush— "Purdy"—with an arrow pointing to the left. The road went through more brush and then opened up to a lush green pasture about the size of a football field, spreading out lengthwise in front of us, encircled by a paved road. A little variety store called One Stop, with a single gas pump, was at the closer end of the field. We pulled up to see if someone could direct us to the cemetery. I walked past three men relaxing in chairs, and all six eyes kept looking in my direction. I greeted their stares with a "Hello." I had learned that manners were everything in the South, and quite frankly I was enjoying it. I received pleasant nods in return.

The store provided all the necessities. A deli case was next to the register. I could see some turkey and cheese, so I ordered the combination on wheat bread for two.

"Could you tell me where the cemetery is?" I asked.

"Yes, of course," the counter girl said in a very pleasant tone. "There are two of them. Which one do you want?"

"I'm looking for the one where the Wisdom family is buried."

"Oh, sure. Do you have family there?"

"Yes, yes, I do," I said more confidently.

"Who's your family?" she asked.

"The Wisdoms."

She picked up her head and took a look at me and then said, "You're a Wisdom?" Then after a longer pause, she said, "Well, of course, you are," as if I fit some preconceived perception of what a descendant from the family Wisdom looked like, although the last remaining Wisdom of Purdy had died there in 1871.

"It's just past the Hurst place on the left." She pointed in the direction of where we were going.

I paid her for the sandwiches and walked past the town meeting. Kemp backed out onto the pavement, which looked as if it had been a dirt road not long ago. The road divided before the store and then came back together at the other end, making a long oval around the green pasture, where just one house stood. We continued down the eastern side of the road, remarking not on what was there, but what was not.

Long gone were the large mansions and the beautiful brick county courthouse at the top of the ellipse. Gone was the hustle and bustle of the town, with people running to market or to the courthouse to hear a political stump speech by Adam Huntsman, when he ran against Davy Crockett. Gone was the Kincaid Hotel, where people lined up to hear one of the town founders, Benjamin Wright, share war stories with his old friend, Sam Houston, just before Sam went to Texas. And the university was no more. Everything was long ago silenced. Purdy had been a beautiful, elegant, sophisticated town, more important than Memphis. But what the Civil War didn't destroy, a fire finally did.

We found the Hurst house. It was the only house still standing from that early era—long and narrow with a two-story deck, now missing the upper porch. Kemp gave me a brief history about the complexities of its nineteenth century owner, Fielding Hurst, who was both respected and despised in the town. Down the road on the left there was nothing more than a dirt driveway. We drove down it. At the end of the road, the land opened up into acreage with tall, narrow evergreens and was dotted with a couple hundred broken cemetery markers. This had been an elegant cemetery at one time. Kemp and I climbed out of the car. The devastation was heart breaking. Not one tombstone was intact. The wind blew a song through the upper branches of the tall trees as if to mourn the damage at their roots. The Wisdom family plot was right at the front. A small section of Victorian iron fence attempted to recreate the old boundary around the Wisdom graves, but now it seemed sadly disconnected from everything.

William Sargent Wisdom and Jane Anderson Wisdom, my third great-grandparents, had been honored with separate tall, marble obelisks, which were now in pieces lying on the ground. I ran my finger over the raised letters of the name Wisdom on an exposed piece, and then read what I could decipher of an engraved message, "William S. Wisdom born in 1796 in Randolph Co., North Carolina, died in 1871." A touching sentiment became sad with the words, "He will never be forgotten." Yet he and most everyone here had been long forgotten.

Before I left Boston two weeks earlier, Chris Child at the genealogical society showed me the book *The Early Settlers of McNairy County*. Purdy was the county seat then, so the book was about the people who built Purdy, and many of them were buried in this cemetery. The write-up on William Sargent Wisdom's death was one of the longest.

"He was a man who achieved success in life, was ever the friend of the poor and deserving and the staunch defender of the widow and orphan. Strong men wept, and old men sobbed aloud and all felt that a friend of the poor, of the widow, and orphan had gone, and there was no one left to fill his place. His countenance was intelligent, and his expression mild, cheerful, and benevolent, indicative of contentment and happiness…his manners were courtly, amiable, unaffected…his conversation was entertaining and instructive, abounding in humor and playful wit."

I stood quietly, thinking of this man from whom I was descended and how proud anyone would be to have him as a relation. He had built a town, which stood the promise of an enterprising people, but was now home to the destroyed monuments of its founders. I knew it wasn't the fault of the small group who still called Purdy home. A few deranged people could do this kind of damage, which would take another lifetime to fix.

My sullen sadness was suddenly shattered by the racing motor of a large pickup truck flying down the little dirt road right toward us. It came to an abrupt stop next to Kemp. A very large man was the driver.

"What are you all doing here?" he demanded as he leaned out his truck window.

I looked at Kemp to answer him. I didn't think this was a good time to broadcast my northern accent.

"We were looking at the Wisdom graves," Kemp answered. "Margaret here is a Wisdom."

Mr. Hockaday's large shoulders relaxed and he introduced himself. He took his hand off the passenger seat, opened his door, and stepped out to greet us. He apologized for his aggressive entrance, but he told us how people came into the cemetery and destroyed the monuments, and he hadn't been able to stop it.

His family had been in Purdy since the beginning, and he talked about the Wisdoms as if they were still living down the road. "You know, Mr. Wisdom was probably the wealthiest man in McNairy County," he said, "actually, all Tennessee. But he was known best for his goodwill to the town." He continued, "The Wisdom house was always full of children, both black and white."

I looked at him with that hairy eyeball you use when you heard something potentially upsetting.

He read me correctly and added that these children belonged to the people who worked for Mr. Wisdom. "The Wisdoms didn't own slaves," he said.

I wasn't sure how to interpret that—black people worked for the Wisdoms, but they weren't slaves? I had never heard of that. He told me how the Civil War was very hard on Mr. Wisdom. He was a supporter of the South, but he worked hard to keep the opposing factions in the small town at peace.

"The Union took over the Wisdom house and removed everything that was not tied down and physically abused Mr. Wisdom. The house was used as Union officers' quarters and a hospital during the war, where the care was reported to be good. Some of the healed Union soldiers actually corresponded with Mr. Wisdom for years after the war, one of them right up until the time Mr. Wisdom died. William Wisdom was well loved," Mr. Hockaday said. After looking at more graves, trying to piece together what we could, we finally said our goodbyes to Mr. Hockaday and drove on out of town.

Chapter 37

Dew Moore Wisdom

$\mathcal{W}$hen we arrived back at the Wisdom house, Kemp gave me the family papers he had found describing my Wisdom relations. He had given me more than I ever could have discovered by locking myself in the back of a library. We vowed to keep in touch, and he said a room in the Wisdom house would always be ready for me when I came back. At the motel that evening, I opened up the pages of handwritten notes by John Wisdom, Jr. He had written short biographies on some of his relatives. William Sargent Wisdom, his grandfather, was described as I had already heard—a wealthy, successful merchant, and benevolent banker. "As wealthy as Wisdom" was a common saying around West Tennessee, according to the write-up.

There were also summaries on each of William Sargent Wisdom's children. The first and oldest living child was my great-great-grandfather, Dew Moore Wisdom: "He was a graduate of Cumberland College in Lebanon, Tennessee, and practiced law until the outbreak of the Civil War. After the war, he became editor and owner of the *Jackson Whig and Tribune*. After some years, he moved to Ft. Smith, Arkansas, where he was appointed by President Cleveland to be U.S. Indian Agent. He was in charge of the five Civilized Tribes: Creeks, Chickasaw, Seminoles, Cherokees, and Choctaws. He was greatly beloved by the Indians."

The other five surviving children of William Wisdom appeared to have lived successful lives, too. They and/or their spouses or children went into banking, shipping, diplomatic service, law, investments, and journalism in places like St. Louis, Louisville, and New York City. The story of Dew's sister, Loraine Wisdom, caught my attention. The description of her great-grandson read, "married, lives in California and is a television actor named James Franciscus." I was a great fan of James Franciscus. I loved his show *Mr. Novak* in the 1960s. He was a handsome man. I could picture myself sitting in the little living room in East Braintree watching him and never realizing the man on my television set was my third cousin.

As I sat on the edge of the hotel bed, I folded up the pages of the document and put them aside. I needed a moment to think. Everything about the South and Tennessee was so different from what I had expected. The North-South issues were much more complicated than I had been led to believe growing up in the North. I wanted to learn more.

I went over to the Jackson-Madison County Library to see if there were copies of Dew Moore Wisdom's newspaper. Upstairs in the Tennessee Room, I found film reels of local newspapers, and surprisingly, an editorial written by my great-great-grandfather.

In August 1871, six years after the end of the Civil War, Colonel Dew Moore Wisdom wrote an editorial entitled "Let Us Have Peace" (Jackson Whig and Tribune). The article was long and the writing formal. I had to read it a second time to understand its subtleties. It was not what I had expected from the wounded Confederate officer. Instead of advocating for the continuation of a divided country, my great-great-grandfather wanted the country to come together. He wanted both the North and South to cease their factional interests and put "this great country" together. He held no bitterness from his experiences in the war. He only wanted the country's pain to stop and be united again. This sentiment was far from how I thought people felt.

I finished at the library and said goodbye to Jackson. Thoughts of the abandoned town of Purdy and the developed town of Jackson created more questions than answers. I crossed the Mississippi River at Memphis and was amazed at its width. I was now truly in the West. Just before the Arkansas and Oklahoma border, I took the Fort Smith exit. This was my grandmother Mema Eleanor's birthplace. Garrison Avenue, the main street, was much wider than I expected—at least six lanes, even though it had been laid out in the early 1800s. Fort Smith had been developed as a supply town for people on their way to California. Mema's grandfather, a Swiss immigrant, opened a department store around 1850, which must have played a part in that. The town later acquired some notoriety as the judicial outpost of "Hanging Judge Parker."

At the local library, I received directions to where the Eberles were buried. The grave of my grandmother's grandfather, Johann Joseph Eberle was a marble marker. Over the top was carved what looked like a drape of fabric. Across the front, in large letters was carved, "From Walenstadt, Switzerland." He wanted to make sure his descendants would know from where we came.

I crossed into Oklahoma and headed to Muskogee, my father's birthplace and the capitol of the Creek Nation where Colonel Dew Moore Wisdom had his headquarters as the U.S. Indian Agent. I didn't know what it meant to be an Indian agent. My understanding was that a white man in an Indian Nation was trouble for the tribe and particularly if he were an employee of the federal government. I didn't think I could find the details of his job, but maybe an archived obituary might summarize his life.

The Muskogee newspaper published a glowing article about him upon his death. I also found a copy of *The Cherokee Advocate*, a newspaper published by the Cherokee Nation, "Official Journal of the Nation." *The Cherokee Advocate* was printed on two sides—one side in Cherokee and the other side in English. I was pleasantly surprised that there on Saturday, November 11, 1905, was an obituary on Col. D. M. Wisdom written in both English and Cherokee:

> The people of Indian Territory will no doubt learn with many regrets the death of Col. D. M. Wisdom at his home in Muskogee last Saturday night. Col. Wisdom was well and favorably known to the people of Indian Territory, having served as secretary to the Indian Agent, then as Indian Agent. Col. Wisdom, like all the old time white residents in Indian Territory was a warm supporter of separate statehood. The people of Indian Territory will long remember him as a great and good man, a true friend.

I had no idea Oklahoma wanted to be two separate states—one for the settlers in the West and the eastern half for the Native Americans. So many times on this trip, I learned something that seemed contradictory to what I had learned historically.

My southern trip had not given me the answers I expected. It just continued to open up more areas for me to investigate. As I drove back toward the interstate, I realized my trip was about to end, but in many ways it was only beginning. More trips were certainly in my future. My curiosity was not cured by two months on the road; it only made me anxious to learn more.

My siblings were expecting me to be in town for supper, so I hoped a state trooper wasn't watching as I sped down Interstate 40 past the Lotawatah Road exit and past the town of Okemah. I left behind the rolling hills and lovely grazing lands of eastern Oklahoma and entered the western flat lands, which unfurled in front of me like a giant flag. As I approached Oklahoma City, the 180-degree sky burned with the most beautiful orange, red, and yellow of an Oklahoma sunset.

Six months ago, I could not have placed Oklahoma City on a map, and now I was staring down at a place I had sung about, with geese scurrying and open surreys in the *Oklahoma* musical score. I was here and loving what people from Boston would call the middle of nowhere. But, of course, when you come from Boston, the country ends at the Hudson River.

I arrived in Oklahoma City just in time to participate in the family phone tree, which was called to action. In response, all in-town relatives began congregating at the Hideaway Pizza on Western Avenue. Catching up was, as usual, fun and full of conversation about what had happened here or there, to him or to her. Over the next day and a half, we all began migrating down to Austin to do some more laughing, connecting, eating, and football watching at my brother Bill's on Thanksgiving.

That warm and peaceful existence with my siblings enveloped me. The kindness and love shown for each other was inspiring. In addition to siblings, there were children and then grandchildren, making my life fuller than ever before. Between my maternal and paternal biological families, my life was extraordinarily full of love and support. My adoptive father had been dead for thirty-seven years; my adoptive mother had been dead for twenty-two years. I was so fortunate to have another chance at a family. My new families wove their lives in and around mine, and I wove my life around theirs, just as it should be.

Great-great-grandfather Col. Dew Moore Wisdom with his daughter
Lucile Wisdom Eberle, and granddaughter Mary Lucile. Circa 1893

Great-grandfather Charles H. Eberle, circa 1885, husband of Lucile Wisdom

The John Lee Wisdom house, built 1880, Jackson, Tennessee

Third great-grandfather, William Sargent Wisdom, 1796-1871

Fourth great-grandfather James Wisdom, original settler of McNairy
Co. Tennessee. Born in Virginia 1773, died 1828, McNairy Co., TN

Walenstadt, Switzerland

Receiving Eberle Family History from historian Paul Gubser
and cousin Albert Eberle, Walenstadt, Switzerland 2010.

With Thum cousin in front of family tree, Offerdingen, Germany, 2010

In Siracusa, Sicily taking a gelato break at Italian
Eberle Reunion, 2013, Catania, Sicily

Stueve Christmas, 2013

Gillentine Cousins in Nashville, Tennessee—Karen, Susan & Me

Chapter 38

LIFE CONTINUES TO BLOSSOM

A few years later, our daughter Lauren moved to California with her husband to have an adventure. Before long, she was pregnant with our first grandchild. I flew out to support her before the arrival. The baby took its time arriving, so I kept Lauren busy with shopping and organizing the nursery. When she began her labor, my anxiety level was out of control. My sanity was only saved by scrubbing anything that could tolerate it, although this truly was not my manner of coping at home. As time went by and no news came of a progressing labor, I drove over to the hospital, because I couldn't stand the suspense. The delivery nurse told me Lauren's labor had stopped. She shared that Lauren may need a C-section. I took my worries into the waiting room.

I found a corner and sat quietly, taking in deep breaths, while praying to whomever I thought might be listening. St. Polycarp had always been my go-to saint. Then, for some reason, thoughts of my maternal ancestors began infiltrating my mind.

First was my grandmother Mema Eleanor. She had delivered two babies successfully. Then I thought of her mother, Lucile Wisdom Eberle, who had at least five children. Then, my mind went further and further back into the lives of other ancestral mothers—Lucile Wisdom Eberle's mother, Anna Terry Wisdom, had borne five children, one during the Civil War. Anna Terry Wisdom was orphaned at thirteen years old, but not before her mother, Mary Gooch Terry, delivered six children. I thought of Dew Wisdom's mother, Jane Anderson, who had a baby every two years for twenty years and never lost one in childbirth. Dew's grandmother, Susannah Sargent Wisdom, had eleven children and at least five were delivered on the frontier of the Cumberland Plateau. I thought of Martha Lewis Wisdom, who had nine children, before and during the Revolution, raising them while the war raged on around her. Each time a grandmother came into my mind, I begged her and each one of these ancestors to think of my daughter, "their daughter" Lauren, as she was doing what they had all done successfully.

These mothers were the experts. I prayed they would be with my Lauren and help her bring her child into this world. Within an hour, Nora Elizabeth was born, a beautiful, healthy addition to our family. And with her birth, we reveled in the hope of more children to come.

Epilogue

My birth mother, Ann, and I continue to enjoy a normal mother-daughter relationship, sharing thoughts and activities. I feel very grateful to have found her and her family, particularly after losing my adoptive mother and father at such a young age. She enjoys the grandchildren and four great-grandchildren I brought into her life.

My siblings and I continue as if we had a lifelong connection. I visit Oklahoma City regularly. In addition to the siblings, I enjoy delightful nieces and nephews, grandnieces and grandnephews, and new friends. When we get together, the fun, humor, caring, and love is more than can be described.

My only regret is that our father, Charles Stueve, who died April 1, 2016, at the age of ninety-one could not still be with us. I enjoyed ten years of genealogical, historical and all around general chitchat with him. I am immensely grateful for those ten years.

I travel through the South whenever I can. I love it. I need it. I don't know why, but as soon as I enter Virginia, I feel at home. I still love New England, but the South resonates with me.

Kemp and Mickey in Jackson, Tennessee have given me an open invitation to stay at the Wisdom House whenever I come to town. I have already accepted it a number of times.

The good people of Purdy, Tennessee recently built a community center where the old courthouse had been, and they conduct square dances with a five-piece string band the first Saturday of each month where there is standing-room only. More houses have been built on the green, and now a house is being built right next to the Wisdom Cemetery. The owner assures me she watches over the cemetery to make sure no more damage is done, and she has the ammunition to back up her resolve.

I had the Wisdom grave markers repaired and they now stand tall again. A group of citizens now regularly mows the grass and a historian, Bobby Barnes, has uncovered hidden graves and repaired others.

In Nashville there are two cousins who feel more like sisters. Their brother, who I met first in Boston, introduced me to them. I visit them regularly. I have also kept in touch with the lovely Chatham, Virginia, family who took me in at the bed and breakfast.

In Arkansas is a Wisdom cousin, who lives up to his last name. His parents, Clara and James Wisdom, live in Sallisaw, Oklahoma. I have been treated to fresh venison at their table. James is a retired country preacher whose congregation was up in the Ozarks. He tells me he says prayers for me all the time, and I appreciate every one of them.

Once a year, the Gooch cousins meet in McNairy County in March. The first time, a couple of us cousins went over to the northern Mississippi town of Eastport and found the long forgotten grave of my fourth great-grandmother, Mary Gooch Terry.

Sometimes my driving route to Oklahoma goes through West Virginia into Kentucky so I can visit the area around Lexington and Georgetown where my Buford line settled after the Revolution. The Bufords left lovely country estates and were known as some of the original members of the horseracing industry. My first cousin, many times removed, Col. Abraham Buford of the Revolutionary era, is buried there with his wife Martha McDowell. Their graves were falling apart, so I had them repaired.

My research has taken me to so many interesting places where I have met wonderful people and had exceptional experiences. I continue to look forward to more trips and visits, which will keep me from sitting in front of my TV watching reruns of *CSI* shows.

—

*T*he retrieval of my sealed information has given me the opportunity to accept or reject a world that was taken from me through my adoption. Keeping those records locked, as they are in all but a handful of states, is cruel. Although many recent adoptions are following the kinder "open adoption" style, there are still thousands of adoptees who are coming to the end of their lives and may die before ever knowing who put them on this earth. That is morally indefensible. No one should be the purchased child for someone else's need and then have their identities taken from them. Adoptees should not be treated as someone's personal property. It is time for all adoptees to have access to their origins.

Acknowledgements

The first person I want to thank is Sister Lena Deevy, who as a complete stranger, heard about my story and would not let me go until I promised to write a book.

Next, there is Gotham Writers Workshop and particularly David Seigerman, who took me as a novice and saw some potential. He continued to encourage me towards a publishable project.

A special thank you to fellow writer, John D. Harris, who from the first pass, saw what I was trying to do and never thought to discourage me.

My undying gratitude goes to my copy editors, Jed Hendrick and Lauren Sutton, along with the team at Create Space. And to Jessi Rita Hoffman who helped me pare the book down from a 600-word document.

My sincere thanks goes to a group of the most wonderful women, to whom I will forever be grateful. When I asked if they would be interested in giving me feedback, they gave generously of their time and much appreciated opinions. I will never be able to thank them enough: Paula Allen, Anne Beneville, Lois Boggs, Gina Bruno-Dunn, Joni Claflin, Karen Dismukes, Lyn Hubina, Holly Janney, Kristin Liles, Marilyn McCarthy, Karen Picknell, Magda Rangel-Hendrick and Susie West-Morris.

About the Author

Margaret Meaney Hendrick, MA, LMHC is a lifelong adoptee, and a Licensed Mental Health Counselor in Massachusetts.

Margaret was a stay-at-home mom for many years until she decided to pursue a graduate degree in Counseling Psychology. During her years at home, she volunteered in a number of organizations, coached both girls' and boys' sports, was president of her local League of Women Voters, was elected to her town's School Committee twice and was a citizen reviewer on Foster Care Review teams.

Margaret holds a bachelor's degree in psychology from Salem State College, *summa cum laude,* and a master's degree in Clinical Mental Health from Lesley College in Cambridge, Massachusetts. She retired after working as a therapist in the Boston Public School system. Her private counsel is often sought on the topic of adoption, and after years of answering questions about the life of an adoptee, she decided to chronicle her own journey.

Margaret and her husband of forty-four years reside in the South End of Boston and Newport, Rhode Island. They have three children, Matt, Mike and Lauren and four delightful grandchildren, Nora, Samuel, Molly and Charlotte. She enjoys researching history and genealogy, riding horses, and playing tennis.

Made in the USA
Middletown, DE
10 February 2017